The Byways
of
BRITAIN

Byways of
BRITAIN

100 out-of-the-way places to explore

Edited by Brian Spencer

MPC

Published by
Moorland Publishing Co Ltd,
Moor Farm Road West,
Ashbourne, Derbyshire,
DE6 1HD England

1st edition 1986
2nd revised paperback edition 1990

British Library Cataloguing in Publication Data
The Byways of Britain.
  1. Great Britain — Description and travel —
  1971 — Guide-books.
  I. Spencer, Brian, 1931-
  914.1'04858 DA650

ISBN 0 86190 444 3

Black and white photographs have been provided by:
Anne-Louise Barton: pp 134, 135, 137, 139, 141, 144, 145; R.H. Bird: pp 69 (right), 73, 177, 190-1, 193, 213, 237; British
Tourist Authority: pp 122-3, 124, 125, 127, 187; C. Macdonald: pp 174-5, 178, 185, 188, 189; H.M. Parker: pp 18-19, 30-1,
40, 41, 42, 43, 60, 61; L. Porter: pp 52, 53, 54, 55 (top), 57 (top), 64, 76-7, 78, 79, 80, 81, 82-3, 84, 86, 87, 89, 90, 91, 92, 93,
96, 97, 180, 181; A. Proctor: pp 110, 113 (right), 116, 118, 120, 121, 126, 128, 129, 154, 155, 157; J. Rawson: pp 233, 235; F.
Rodgers: pp 119, 150-1, 156, 160, 161, 168, 169, 170, 171, 172-3, 182, 218-9; J.A. Robey: pp 9, 85, 88, 94, 95, 98-9, 108-9,
130-1, 146, 147, 148, 149; R. Sale: pp 106-7, 109 (right), 111, 112-13, 163, 166; R. Scholes: pp 39, 101, 103, 105; Scottish
Tourist Board: pp 196-7, 200, 201, 204, 205, 206, 207, 209; B. Spencer: pp 10, 11, 13 (top), 14, 17, 19, 20, 23, 24, 25, 27, 37,
44, 45, 46, 47, 50, 55 (bottom), 56-7, 58-9, 63, 67, 71, 72, 74, 75, 132, 133, 136, 138, 140, 142, 220, 223, 225, 227, 228, 239;
G.N. Wright: pp 12-13, 15, 21, 22, 26, 28, 29, 32, 33, 34, 35, 36, 38, 48-9, 51, 65, 68-9, 70, 114-5, 117, 143, 152, 153, 158-9,
162, 164, 167, 195, 198-9, 202, 203, 210, 211, 214, 215, 216, 217, 221, 229, 230, 231; Youth Hostels Association: pp 16.

Colour illustrations have been provided by: L. Porter: Rievaulx, Bole Hill, Upper Dove, Newborough Warren; J.A. Robey:
Arkengarthdale, New Forest, Freshwater Bay; R. Scholes: Ennerdale, Duddon Valley, Hadrian's Wall, Swaledale, Long
Mynd, Berwyns, Eyemouth, Cuillins.

Printed in the UK by
Butler & Tanner Ltd,
Frome, Somerset

Contents

Introduction

Walking and generally exploring our beautiful countryside has never been as popular as it is today. The honeypots of such scenically attractive places like Tarn Hows in the Lake District, Dovedale in Derbyshire, or Symonds Yat above the Wye Valley, all bring their admirers, often in their thousands, on sunny weekends. It is this very beauty which might one day be their downfall for all of them, and many, many others, are in danger of being spoilt by being over-used. Too many visitors to a place of special interest or beauty can by their volume quite unintentionally destroy the fragile environment of that beauty spot. Footpaths are widened all too easily with over-use, and attractive flowers are often trampled under foot by the most caring and well-meaning visitors.

The popular places of our countryside are all well documented, but there are countless others equally attractive, and virtually unknown. By gathering local knowledge from people who have explored these places, we can find our way into the lesser known but worthwhile parts of our countryside, and by switching our eyes and feet to these pleasant acres we can learn more about them.

This guide is about some of the lesser-known corners where we can walk, content in the knowledge that we are only in the company of a mere handful of others who prefer the quieter places. In the main, the places described in this book are unknown to the majority. Quite often, as well as describing completely new areas, an indication of where to find quieter walks, or little known corners near some of the more popular beauty spots is given. It is not unusual, say, in the Peak District, to find the Stepping Stones in the lower reaches of Dove Dale looking like Blackpool on a busy bank holiday. At the same time, only a scant half-mile downstream below Thorpe, there may only be a handful of walkers. The area around Coldwall Bridge near Thorpe is at least as attractive as the more popular Stepping Stones upstream, and long may it be so! The list of similar cases must be endless, and so the purpose of this book is to guide the questing walker towards places like Coldwall Bridge, and others such as the range of low hills behind Arnside, where there is a veritable natural rock garden, known only to the few.

Some of the areas described in the guide may be fairly well known, but others are in the remotest corners of the British Isles and therefore a visit to them needs careful planning. For example, for those who want to follow some of the walks around say, Loch Hourn in the chapter devoted to the Scottish Highlands, a drive along a road almost devoid of habitation and twenty miles from the nearest shop must be taken. Having reached Loch Hourn, accommodation is limited to a farm and a small but dramatically situated campsite. So a certain amount of planning is essential, but the rewards are great. On the other hand, a visit to the New Forest would pose no similar problems, for there are hotels, guest-houses and campsites to suit all tastes and pockets. No difficulties should be encountered except in the busier times, and anyone using this guide can easily get away from the more popular parts of the New Forest.

The book is divided into regions which are further subdivided into areas. Each area is described, and then either a series of walks, or specific places where good, little known footpaths and open country can be enjoyed to the full are recommended. Lists of interesting features and places to visit nearby complete the information on where to walk and discover comparatively unknown places.

It should be noted that this book is in no sense a comprehensive guide to the whole of Britain, and that many regions, and areas within regions, have not been covered. If a favourite region, or byway, has not been included, this is due to lack of space.

The guide is intended to be used purely as an indication of where to go to find the best and quietest walking along our 'Byways of Britain', and it must be used together with an Ordnance Survey Map of the area, either the 1:50,000 Landranger series, or the 1:25,000 Outdoor Leisure

Map, if it is available. Use the maps as you would use the help of a knowledgeable friend, and learn what they have to offer. Cast your eyes beyond the immediate footpath or village to which you have been led by reading 'Byways of Britain' and you are most certain to find something worth visiting.

To meet any potential critics head on, try to keep the special places mentioned in these pages as quiet and remote as they were before you visited them. Observe the Country Code at all times and remember a good walker leaves only footprints and takes only photographs.

Brian Spencer

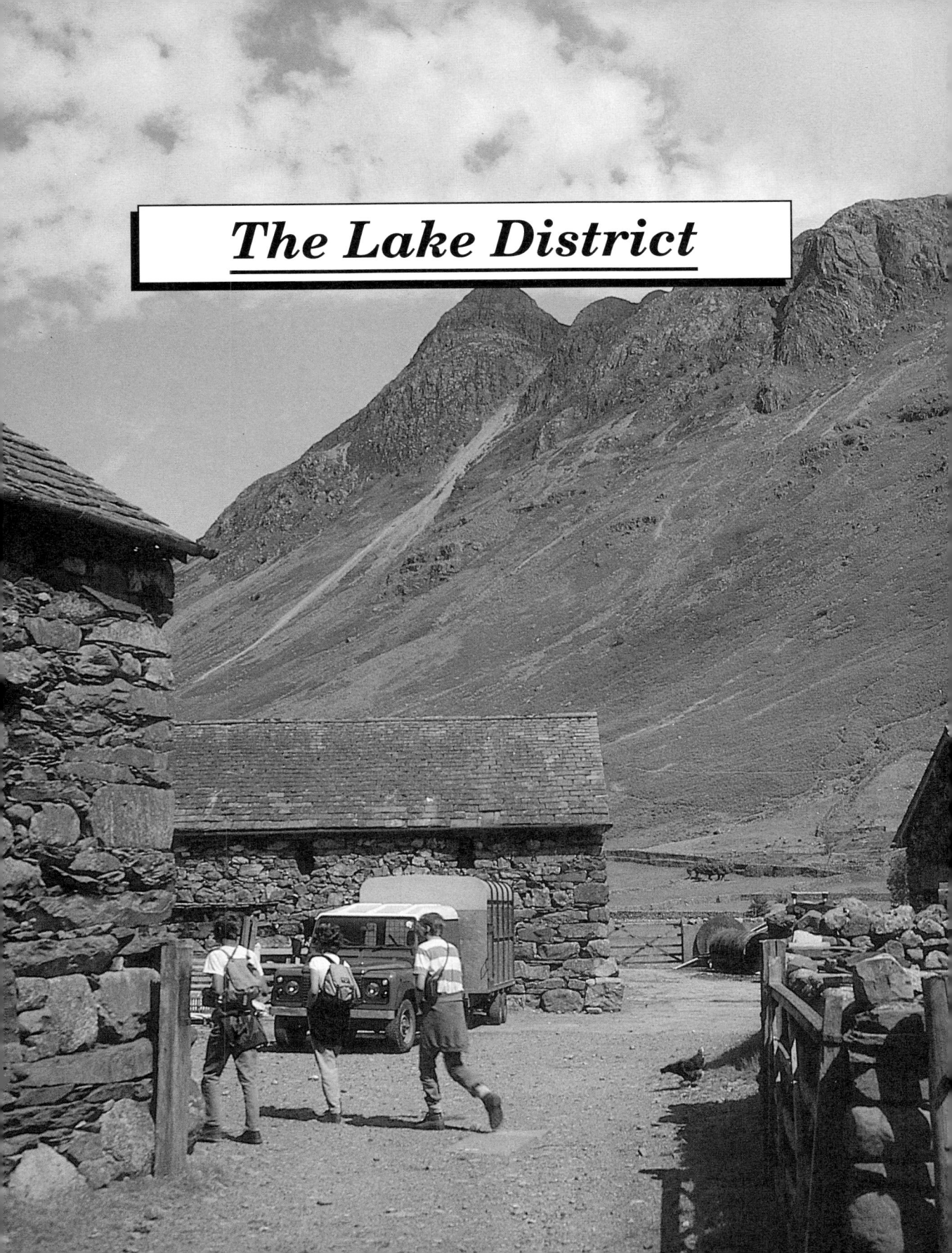

The Lake District

CALDBECK

Cumbria

OS Map: 1:50,000 Sheet Nos 85 and 90

Location

Caldbeck village is on the B5299 from Carlisle to Cockermouth via Dalston, and is about 12 miles south-west of Carlisle. If approaching from Penrith take the B5305 (Wigton road) to where it crosses the B5299 and turn left for Caldbeck.

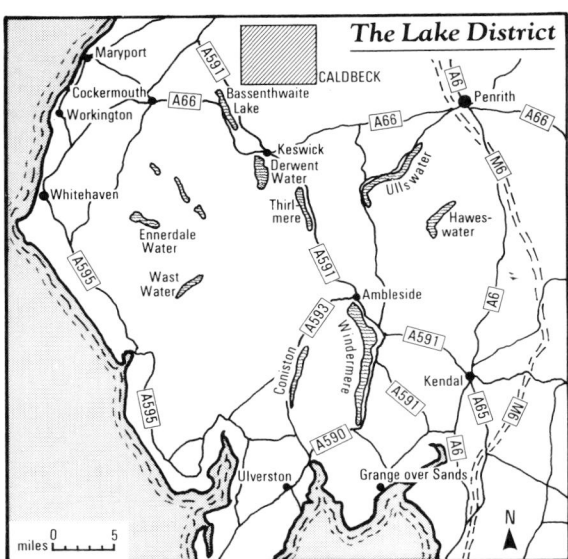

The locals call this country the Back O'Skidda. The fells north of Skiddaw are amongst the most remote and little-known of the whole of the Lake District, but at one time they echoed with the sound of industry when a whole variety of minerals were mined. Now, with the exception of small scale barytes mining, industrial activity has gone and the fells are left to shepherds and walkers who prefer to escape from the more popular areas of the south. Sheep are now the only cash crop of these fells.

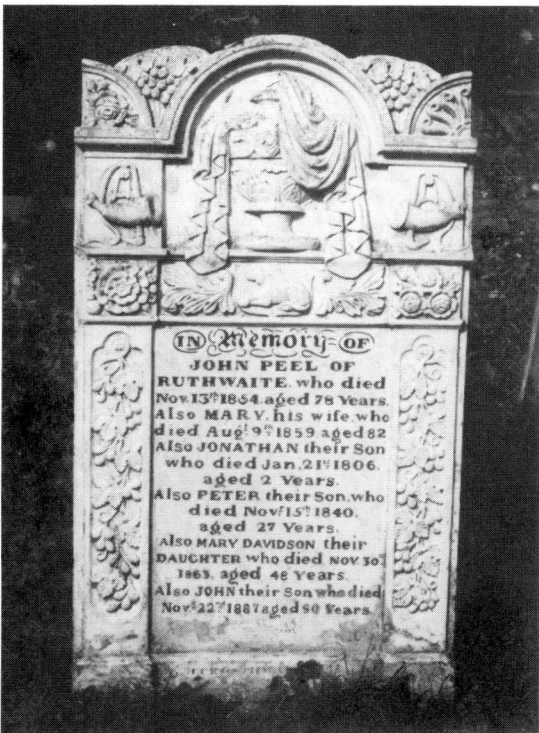

John Peel's grave, Caldbeck

John Peel hunted in this area and his latter-day successors still pursue foxes on foot in this traditional tough sport on the northern fells. John Peel was born in Caldbeck, and although he spent most of his life in nearby Ruthwaite he was buried in Caldbeck churchyard. Peel's fame was immortalised by the famous ballad 'D'ye ken John Peel', written in 1832 by his lifelong friend and fellow huntsman John Woodcock Graves.

Geologists who do not know the area should make a point of visiting Carrock Fell above Mosedale to the south of Caldbeck. The rocks that make up the fell are igneous and volcanic in origin, and so are unique in Lakeland geology. There is even an outcrop of gabbro, a curiously rough, but very hard rock mostly found in the Cuillin Hills of Skye; and the rare metal, tungsten, used in hard steel alloys, was once mined beneath Carrock Fell.

To the south, High Pike and the Caldbeck Fells dominate Caldbeck village. Mostly grass-covered, but with heather encroaching on the higher ground, these fells rarely see more than the occasional walker from one week to the next. Compare their quiet sanctuaries with the treadmills of the more popular fells to the south and it can be seen that there is more to the Lake District than simply following the crowds.

The triangle of high land with Skiddaw and Blencathra as its base and High Pike the apex is a region of contrasts in popularity. The path up Skiddaw from Keswick can look like Blackpool promenade in the holiday season; Blencathra is not quite so crowded. To the north of these hills,

St Kentigern's Church, Caldbeck

however, are miles and miles of open ground offering enjoyment for all.

Attractive waterfalls in remote valleys complete the picture of these least known fells in the Lake District.

PLACES OF INTEREST

Carrock Fell Geological formations.
Roughton Gill Above Fell Side. Waterfalls. Old lead mines.
Caldbeck Church Typical Lakeland church. John Peel's grave.

WALKS IN THE AREA

Important Note: Do not enter any of the mines in the area — all have become dangerous with age.
High Pike From Nether Row (1 ¼ miles south of Caldbeck), follow the mine track to Potts Gill Mine. High Pike is due south across an open fellside. Return by a track which crosses the south-eastern slopes of the hill. Turn right at the mine road and then left by a footpath at How Beck. This path will lead back to Nether Row.
Roughton Gill (shown as Dale Beck on some OS maps). Take the Fell Side road as far as the village. Turn left and follow the track up Roughton Gill. Return by way of Potts Gill Mine and Little Fell Side Farm.
Carrock Fell Climb the fell from the hamlet of Mosedale (there is a faint path from the Carrock Mine road as far as a sheep fold, beyond which a route may be made by zigzagging uphill). Continue along the summit ridge to the north-west and join a track — indistinct at first— to the right and into Carrock Beck. Follow this until it reaches the mine road from Driggith Mine. Turn right and walk downhill to the Caldbeck – Mosedale Road. Right turn and Mosedale is a further two miles.

BASSENTHWAITE

CUMBRIA

OS Map: 1 inch Tourist Map of the Lake District

Location

M6 exit 40 (Penrith). A66 west to Keswick then A591 (Bothel – Carlisle road). Bassenthwaite village is ½ mile north of the A591, 7½ miles north-west of Keswick.

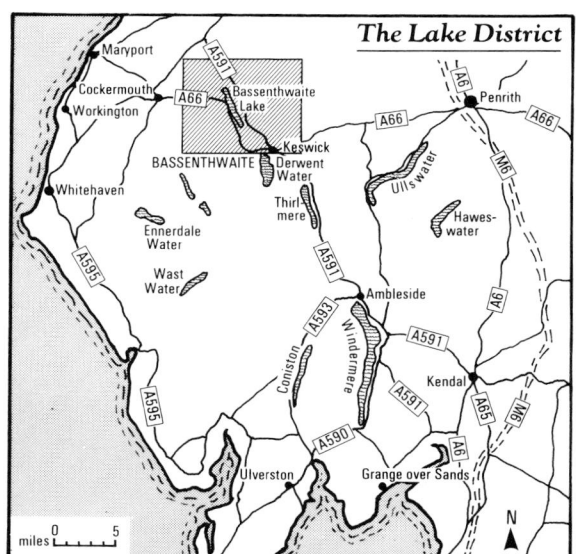

The Lake District

If you hear a local refer to 'Bass', he is not necessarily talking about beer, but using the colloquial term for Bassenthwaite. This unspoilt village, with its snug cottages built from Lakeland stone, manages to keep off the tourist route even though it is only a few miles from hectic Keswick. The fact that the main A591 misses it by at least half a mile helps, and also the narrow intermediate roads in the area deter anyone looking for easy motoring.

Reached by footpaths across pasture to the south-west, Bassenthwaite lake has no ferry boats or hire craft, or anything to make it a popular tourist attraction. As a result, the lake has become the preserve of those who count themselves privileged to have made its acquaintance on foot. Many hours can be spent wandering the quiet paths along its northern shore.

Above the west bank of the lake, Lord's Seat rises steeply, and beyond, the slopes of Lorton Fells are now covered by plantations of pine trees. As if to make amends for these regimented forests, the Whinlatter Pass Visitor Centre, run by the Forestry Commission, has audio visual displays of man's impact through the ages on the fells and forests in the area. A trail from the centre leads to magnificent views of Bassenthwaite Lake and Derwentwater.

Between the Whinlatter Pass and Bassenthwaite Lake, the Swan Hotel near Thornthwaite is home of a quaint custom where each year, or whenever it is considered necessary, two rocks opposite the pub are whitewashed. Known as the 'bishop' and his 'clerk' the rocks have become quite a landmark, especially the bishop. The job of whitewashing the clerk is easy, for he is in the middle of a field. However, the bishop is a different kettle of fish; he stands in his pulpit, at the top of a steep scree slope beneath the summit of Barf. Carrying a bucket of

Bassenthwaite Lake

whitewash up this steep and slippery slope is not easy and one cannot help wondering how much actually reaches him in the process!

With the exception of Binsey, a conical outlier to the north-west of the main fells, all the hills accessible from Bassenthwaite are to the east and are mainly outliers of Skiddaw. The best is Ullock Pike, a heather clad beauty which rises as the knobbly spur of its big brother below Broad End. Dash Beck leads round to the north of Skiddaw and is followed as part of the circuit of the hill from Bassenthwaite. This is a lonely walk, but is enlivened by Whitewater Dash, a beautiful waterfall at the head of the Dash Beck valley.

PLACES OF INTEREST

Lorton Hall, Cockermouth Fifteenth-century pele tower with seventeenth-century additions. Open only by prior arrangement. Tel: Lorton 252.

Whinlatter Pass Visitor Centre Keswick – Lorton road. Audio-visual displays. Forest trail.

Lingholme Portinscale (Derwentwater). Formal woodlands.

Keswick Shops, museums, guided walks.

Wordworth's House Cockermouth (National Trust). Birthplace of the poet.

Maryport Maritime Museum The story of this purpose-built town and its port.

WALKS IN THE AREA

Ullock Pike Climb the ridge south from Barkbeth and on to Skiddaw. Return north by way of the Skiddaw House track and Dash Beck.

Bassenthwaite Lake Linking paths along the lakeside can be reached from several places along the A591 between the Castle Inn and Mire House.

Whitewater Dash Follow the Skiddaw House track from Bassenthwaite.

Bassenthwaite's Meadows For a pleasant evening stroll, a series of lanes and paths which radiate from the village can be linked by quiet roads to make the circuit of Bassenthwaite.

View near Bassenthwaite village

LOWESWATER

Cumbria

OS Map: 1:25,000 Outdoor Leisure Map,
The English Lakes NW sheet.

Location

From Cockermouth, take the B5292 to Low
Lorton, and then the B5289 to Loweswater
village. From Keswick, take either the Newlands
Pass road or Honister Pass to Buttermere and the
B5289 as far as Brackenthwaite. Turn left for
Loweswater.

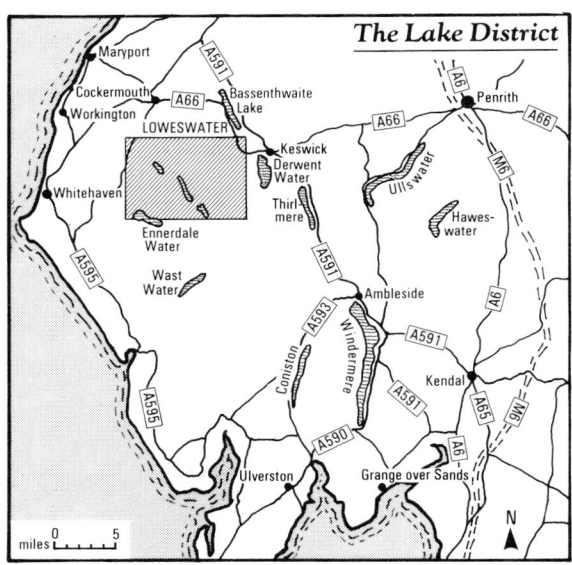

Loweswater Lake, not half so well known but in its
own way just as attractive as its famous neighbours
Crummock Water and Buttermere, is the Lake
District in miniature. To the south are five fells,
the highest a mere 1,878ft, but all with the rugged
grandeur expected of Lakeland. Even Loweswater,
itself barely a mile long, manages to convey the
magical effects of light on water so evocative of
this region.

Between the five fells, secluded valleys radiate
like a spanned hand south of the lake. All are
accessible either by path or open country. Whilst
the northern dales climb to cols adjacent to peaks
like Blake Fell or Gavel Fell, paths through
Whiteoak Beck Valley and Mosedale cross low
cols. Routes over these have been used by local
shepherds for centuries as a means of access to
high grazing.

Melbreak Foxhounds take their name from a
fell which rises steeply above Loweswater village.
This is one of the oldest hunts in the Lake District,
and confines itself to the fells east and west of the
Buttermere Valley.

As with most of the other Lakeland lakes and
tarns, those in this area were formed by glacial
action which carved out deep holes or created
natural dams in valley bottoms. Nearby Mockerkin
Tarn, by the side of the A5086 Cockermouth to
Whitehaven road, is of glacial origin, but it is
unique, as it owes its existence to the fact that the
surrounding land was built up, not worn away as is
the usual case. At the end of the last ice age when
ice covering the land was melting, pockets remained
trapped amidst built-up debris. Eventually these
pockets of ice melted, leaving holes known as
'Kettleholes' which quickly filled with water.
Mockerkin Tarn is a typical example. Due to their

design they rarely have natural outlets and so
eventually fill with vegetation to become bogs.
Eventually this will happen to Mockerkin.

PLACES OF INTEREST
Mockerkin Tarn By the side of the A5086, 4½
miles north-west of Loweswater village. Interpretive
Centre close by.
Whinlatter Pass Visitor Centre
Buttermere and Crummock Water (National
Trust)
Scale Force Above Buttermere village.

Buttermere village

Crummock Water

WALKS IN THE AREA

Mosedale Follow the path south from Loweswater village until it reaches the Ennerdale – Crummock Water track. Turn left and walk downhill past Scale Force to Crummock Water. Left along the lake shore back to Loweswater.

Loweswater Woods A track from Loweswater village crosses Dub Beck at Maggie's Bridge and reaches Loweswater Lake below Watergate Farm. Follow a path through Holme Woods as far as Hudson Place. Turn right and join the road by Grange Farm on the far side of the lake. Follow the road back to the village or climb Darling Fell on the way.

Crummock Water It is possible to walk round this lake mostly by footpath, and also avoid most of the lakeside stretch of the road by using the paths below Low Bank into Rannerdale.

Gavel Fell An easy climb first by path from High Nook Farm into Whiteoak Beck Valley and then right at its head for the ascent of Gavel Fell itself.

ENNERDALE

Cumbria

OS Map: 1:25,000 Outdoor Leisure Map,
The English Lakes NW Sheet.

Location

A591 from junction 36 on the M6, then A590
(Barrow in Furness road) to Greenodd, A5092 to
Broughton in Furness, A595 (Whitehaven road)
to Egremont. A5086 north to Cleator, then the
side road to Ennerdale. Or from the north to
Cockermouth and the A5086 and turn left for
Kirkland and Ennerdale about five miles south-
west of Cockermouth.

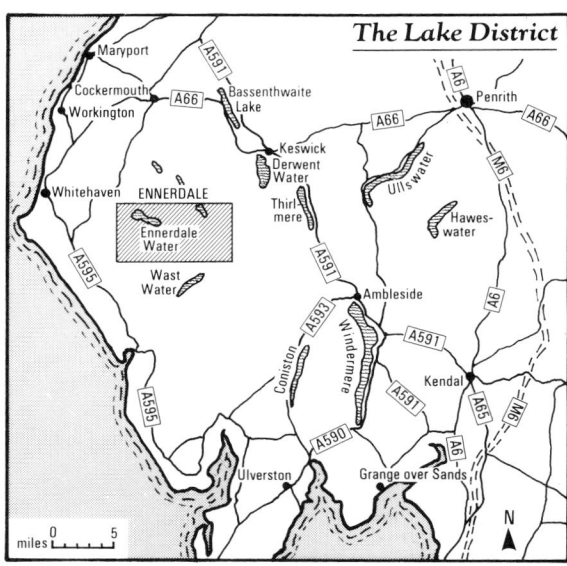

The problem with Ennerdale is its distance from
any other part of the Lakes. No matter how you
approach this far western dale, it means a long and
often tiring drive, but once reached all tiredness
from the journey is soon forgotten. It is this
comparative inaccessibility which helps to make
the valley more attractive, and as a result Ennerdale
is considered the special preserve of those climbers
and anglers who have made the discovery. This
does not mean that it is unknown territory for
walkers— but as a Lakeland valley it deserves to be
better known by the walking fraternity.

One of the major advantages of Ennerdale is
that cars, other than essential vehicles, or those
owned by the few residents, are banned beyond
Bowness Knott car park. However, the car park is
well situated making the lower tracks of this dale
accessible to everyone.

The surface of the road and its gradient make it
suitable for wheelchairs to be taken well beyond
Ennerdale Youth Hostel, and so allows even the
most incapacitated to enjoy remote mountain
scenery at close hand.

Well-established pine forests fill most of the
lower slopes of Ennerdale, but the valley sides are
so steep that views of the high crags, such as Pillar

*Black Sail Youth Hostel —
a converted shepherd's bothy
— makes an ideal base for
exploring this remote valley*

Rock, can be seen close at hand either along fire breaks or through deep cut side valleys. Pillar and its famous rock were first climbed in late Victorian times and since then more and more difficult routes have been explored by subsequent generations.

It is quite probable that Ennerdale was first settled by a Viking family. Certainly there are local links with our Scandianavian forebears; these links show most clearly in the name of the main river, Liza or 'lysa' which is an old norse word meaning 'bright water'. It is thought that the Viking settlement was in the field below Gillerthwaite Farm.

Ennerdale Water has some excellent angling and is the home of that strange but palatable fish the char, which lives at the bottom of our deepest lakes, preferring the colder water of those depths. Fishing for them is very specialised as the bait and its hook must remain deep despite being dragged along by a rowing boat.

PLACES OF INTEREST

Smithy Beck Nature Trail From Bowness car park. Leaflets and information plaques available.
Nine Becks Walk Waymarked trail through the forest south of Gillerthwaite Farm. Starts and finishes at the car park.
Whitehaven Museum Local archaeology, industrial and marine history.
Egremont Ruins of Norman keep with twelfth-century additions.

WALKS IN THE AREA

Ennerdale From Bowness car park, walk up the dale to Black Sail Youth Hostel. Side tracks can be explored at will, but the return is by the same route.
The Lake Cross the Liza below Gillerthwaite Farm where it is possible to walk all the way round Ennerdale Water.
Nine Becks Walk Follow this waymarked path from the car park and across the lower slopes of Lingmell.
Red Pike and High Crag ridgewalk Steep climbing. **Boots are strongly recommended. Unsuitable walk in bad weather.** Climb Red Pike by the footpath at the side of Gillerthwaite Beck, a hundred yards or so east of the youth hostel. This track climbs steeply to the summit of Red Pike. Turn right along the ridge, crossing High Crag and then steeply downhill to Scarth Gap. Turn right and walk downhill to the valley where another right turn leads back to the car park.

Upper Ennerdale from the High Stile ridge

WASDALE

Cumbria

OS Map: 1:25,000 Outdoor Leisure Map,
The English Lakes SW Sheet

Location

From Ambleside and central Lake District, take
the Wrynose and Hard Knott Pass road to Esk
Dale Green. Turn right for Santon Bridge and right
again for Wasdale. South from Cockermouth by
the A5086 to Egremont. A595 to Gosforth and
left for the valley road. Or, from the south via the
M1 and Junction 35. A6 to Levens. A590 to
Greenodd. A5092 to Duddon Bridge. A595 to
Holmbrook. Turn right for Santon Bridge and
Wasdale.

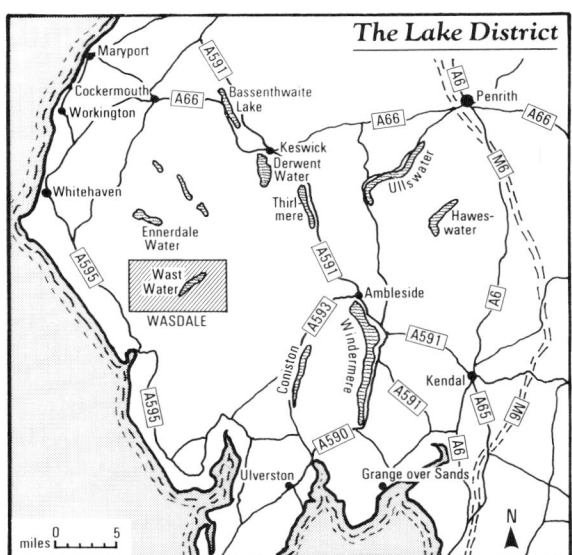

The lower reaches of Wasdale tend to be ignored
by walkers and climbers usually more intent on
reaching their mecca beyond Wasdale Head.
Certainly the majestic giants which range round
the upper dale — England's highest point on
Scafell Pike, Great Gable and Kirk Fell — all make
this the most spectacular mountain scenery in
England. However, if those walkers and climbers
lowered their sights just a little they would find
miles of almost untrodden fells closer to hand.

Not only are there 'unknown' fells on either
side of lower Wasdale, but valley and moorland
walking is available to entertain either the less
ambitious, or fill the odd hour or two when
weather or time prevents the walker going on high.
Side valleys wander off beneath lofty summits and
many lead to quiet tarns, smaller of course than
their big brothers the central lakes, but retaining in
essence the true spirit of the Lake District.

This is an area where not long ago it was the
custom around Wasdale to drive cattle through
the smoke of Beltane fires on May Day. This Celtic
festival was meant to rid the beasts of evil
influences lingering from winter darkness. Another
custom, also now abandoned, was that of leaving a
new born child's finger nails and hair uncut or not
washing its arms before it was six months old.
This, the local people believed, would prevent it
from becoming a thief. It was not recorded if the
outlaw, Prentibjorn, was treated this way, but he
was a wrongdoer and ended his life on a gallows by
Sty Head Tarn beyond the head of Wasdale.

Further downstream, Gosforth shows its links

The 'Mountain Goat' bus at Wasdale Head

with the ancient past with a Viking cross in its churchyard. This slender memorial is some 15ft tall and is delicately carved with a combination of Christian and Nordic designs. Stone circles outside the village speak of an even older population.

By complete contrast, the controversial nuclear power station at Sellafield on the nearby Cumbrian coast brings us into the twentieth century with a jolt. Its chimneys and cooling towers, while their appearance is a shock to the senses, do not completely dominate the scene and can be mostly ignored amidst the natural beauty of the inland heights.

PLACES OF INTEREST
Gosforth Viking Cross
Hard Knott Roman Fort
Sellafield Nuclear Power Station
Ravenglass and Eskdale Railway
Wast Water Lake

WALKS IN THE AREA
Greendale and its tarn From Greendale Farm on the Gosforth road (¼ mile west of Wast Water Lake), follow the track up Greendale as far as the tarn, which is an ideal place for a picnic. Return by the same route.

Burn Moor Tarn There are several ways of approaching this moorland tarn. The best one is from Brackenclose at the head of Wast Water and could be combined with a return journey down Miterdale into Eskdale. The Mountain Goat Bus Company have a connecting bus route between Wasdale Head and Eskdale.

Wast Water to Gosforth Footpaths and quiet back roads can, with easy map reading, be used to link the lake to this ancient village.

Bleng Dale From Cinderdale Bridge upstream from Old Strands in Nether Wasdale, there is a footpath which leads north through rough pasture to the Wasdale – Gosforth road. Turn left at the road and after 100yds turn right on an old track which climbs gently round the side of Gray Crags. Follow this across open moorland for about 1½ miles to the River Bleng. Continue as far as the dale head, but no further, especially in mist or poor visibility. Return by the same route.

Wast Water

ESKDALE

Cumbria

OS Map: 1:25,000 Outdoor Leisure Map,
The English Lakes SW Sheet

Location

M6 Junction 36. A591 to Levens Bridge. A590 to
Greenodd. A5092 to Broughton in Furness.
A595 via Bootle and turn right for Eskdale about
1¼ miles before Ravenglass. From Ambleside
and Central Lake District, over Wrynose and
Hard Knott Passes to Boot in Eskdale. Or from
Cockermouth and the north; A5086 to Egremont
and A595 to Ravenglass.

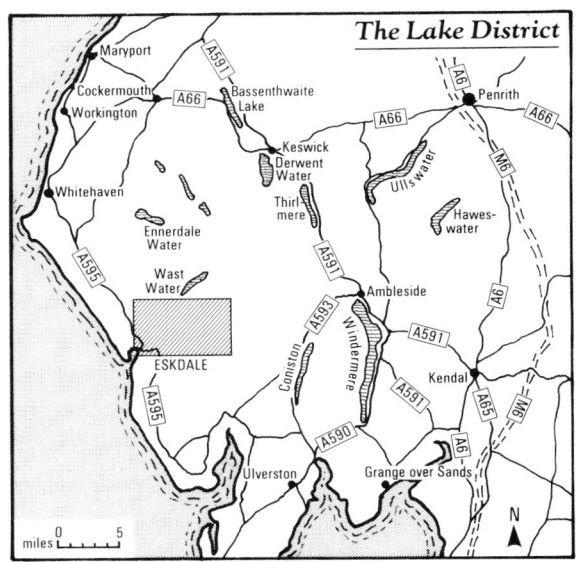

*Upper Eskdale
from Harter Fell* ▷

*A diesel locomotive, which
supplements the Ravenglass
and Eskdale Railway's
steam trains.*

The name Eskdale, to most visitors of the Lake
District, is firmly linked with the Ravenglass and
Eskdale Railway, probably the most scenic of all
English railway journeys. The fact that trains run
on narrow gauge tracks pulled by steam engines is
almost gilding the lily. 'Ratty' as the line is
affectionately called, was built in 1875 on standard
gauge track to carry iron ore from mines near Boot
in the upper dale to the main line at Ravenglass.
Never a commercial success, it closed in 1913 and
two years later was taken over by Mr W.J. Basset-
Lowke, a famous model maker, who converted

the track to fifteen-inch gauge. As a builder of
model steam locomotives, he was delighted to
have a track in such beautiful surroundings. After
many financial ups and downs, the line was finally
bought by the Ravenglass and Eskdale Railway
Preservation Society in 1961.

With such an obvious attraction as this wonderful railway, one would expect Eskdale to be the
best-known walking area in the Lake District.
Certainly it is known to a few, but whilst the train
might be carrying a hundred or so passengers on its
journey along the valley, it is rare to find many

who use it as a convenient means of access to or from a walk. This is a great pity, as stations up and down the line link with footpaths to easy fells and side valleys, many with waterfalls making ideal spots for summer picnics.

Eskdale was well known to the Romans who built a major fort at Hardknott to command the upper valley. They called it *Mediobogdum* and left a fort so well constructed that its remains, with the help of a little reconstruction, can be easily understood today. There was a parade ground close by the fort. It is not certain whether this was to impress the local natives or boast of conquests, but it is known that the local tribes gave the invaders quite a hard time. It needs little imagination to picture their guerilla strikes from hidden recesses in the surrounding fells.

PLACES OF INTEREST
Ravenglass and Eskdale Railway
Hardknott Roman Fort
Muncaster Mill   (1 mile north-east of Ravenglass).
Muncaster Castle   Built on the site of a Roman tower.
Millom Folk Museum   Local life and agriculture.
Stanley Force   Waterfall near Dalegarth Station.

WALKS IN THE AREA
Muncaster Fell   From Eskdale Green station climb the fell by way of Rabbit How and follow the track across Muncaster Fell to Muncaster Castle and Ravenglass.
Stanley Force   The short walk to this waterfall starts from Dalegarth Station.
Blea Tarn   From Dalegarth Station walk towards Boot village and climb Boot Bank. Turn left below Brown Band and then across Bleatarn Hill to Blea Tarn. Turn left at the tarn and walk downhill to Beckfoot station.
Muncaster Castle   From Ravenglass follow the estuary of the Esk upstream to Walls Bridge, turn left and pass the site of the Roman fort of *Glanaventa*. Keeping a narrow belt of trees on your left, walk to Newton and enter Muncaster Castle's deer park. Climb the small hill in front and drop down through Dovecot Wood to the castle. Continue as far as the A595 and turn left, leaving the road where it turns sharply to the left. Walk north through woodland almost as far as the Ravenglass and Eskdale line. Turn left above Mill Wood, and then down to Ravenglass, joining the road by Grove Plantation.

THE DUDDON VALLEY

Cumbria

OS Map: 1:25,000 Outdoor Leisure Map,
The English Lakes SW Sheet

Location

M6 Junction 36. A591 to Levens Bridge, A590 to
Greenodd then A5092 to Duddon Bridge; turn
left into the valley. From Ambleside and Central
Lake District, A593 via Broughton to Duddon
Bridge, or, by way of Little Langdale and the
Wrynose Pass road, turning left at Cockley Beck
from Cockermouth and the north. A5086 to
Egremont, then A595 to Duddon Bridge.

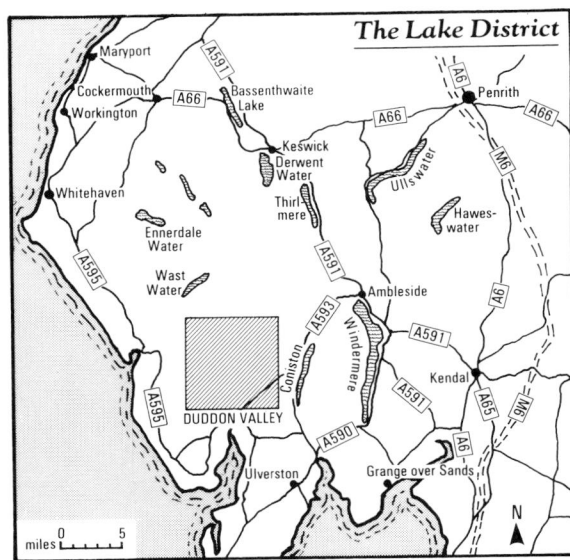

West of the Three Shires Stone on Wrynose Pass a
tiny mountain stream, together with its more
exuberant brothers, drains south from Pike
O'Blisco to form the Eller Dub. This is the wild
beginning of one of the finest Lakeland valleys,
which in its upper reaches gives no hint of the
beauties of the lower dale.

The Duddon Valley must be one of the least-
appreciated valleys of the Lake District, as it is
often only used as an escape road by motorists
who, having 'stormed' Wrynose in a queue of
slow moving traffic, turn left at Cockley Beck
Bridge and drive quickly down the Duddon in
search of teas and gift shops.

The amenities of Windermere and Ambleside
soak up the major portion of visitors, and leave
comparatively remote dales, such as the Duddon,
for those with their senses trained to appreciate
these wonders.

The Duddon cuts its way south from Pike
O'Blisco, the southerly outlier of the Bowfell
massif; to the west is the graceful symmetry of
Harter Fell and the wild expanse of the Ulpha
Fells. To the east, the venerable giants of Dow
Crag and Coniston Old Man top an area of
jumbled crags and remote combes. There are no
large lakes, but dozens of tarns, the longest being
the partly man-made Seathwaite Tarn. Of all the
tarns around the Duddon, perhaps tiny Stickle
Tarn is the best. High up on the Dunnerdale Fells
and protected by the crags of Stickle Pike, it can
only be reached by a difficult scramble from the
back road between Hall Dunnerdale and Broughton.

The valley bottom is the Duddon's best feature;
crags force the road to meander in a manner
designed to delay those in a hurry, but to please

River Duddon at Cockley Beck

Whistling Green Bridge, Duddon Valley

those with time to spare. The true valley bottom is given over to grazing and hayfields, and what little is left has been kept as semi-natural woodland. In spring and summer a pageant of wild flowers bloom in their season, including wood anemones, violets, primroses and bluebells as well as rarer flowers.

Ulpha village, the capital of Duddon, has a typical dale chapel where, during redecoration in 1934, a set of wall paintings was discovered. The old hall is a sixteenth-century pele tower built to defend its inhabitants from the Scots in the wild days of border warfare.

PLACES OF INTEREST

Hardknott Roman Fort Below Hardknott Pass.
Millom Folk Museum (of Local Life and Agriculture). Replica of a miner's cottage.
Coniston Lake
Swinside Stone Circle.
Devoke Water

WALKS IN THE AREA

Ulpha Fell and Devoke Water Open fell with access paths.
Ulpha and the River Duddon A series of valley-bottom paths and minor roads which can be linked to form a continuous walk.
Dunnerdale Fells Lower level, but rough walking with access paths from Ulpha and Broughton Mills (Lickle Valley).
Harter Fell A steep path climbs directly to the summit from Hinning House car park.
There are also a series of woodland walks which radiate from the car park.
Seathwaite Tarn From Hinning House car park walk along the road towards Hinning House (NE) for about 150 yd. Turn right on a path south and gradually contour around the flank of Loft Rigg Howe into Tarn Beck Valley. Seathwaite Tarn is to the east. Follow the path to the head of the tarn and turn right to join a path back down to the Duddon Valley. Do not go all the way to the valley bottom, but turn right at Tarn Beck to follow another path north and back to the road above the car park.

GRANGE OVER SANDS AND THE CARTMEL PENINSULA

Cumbria

OS Map: 1:50,000 Sheet No 96

Location

M6 Junction 35; A6 to Levens Bridge then A590 to Lindale and left for Grange. Or south from Windermere by the A592 to Newby Bridge and Haverthwaite. Turn left at the latter on the B5278 to Cark in Cartmel and the B5277 for Grange.

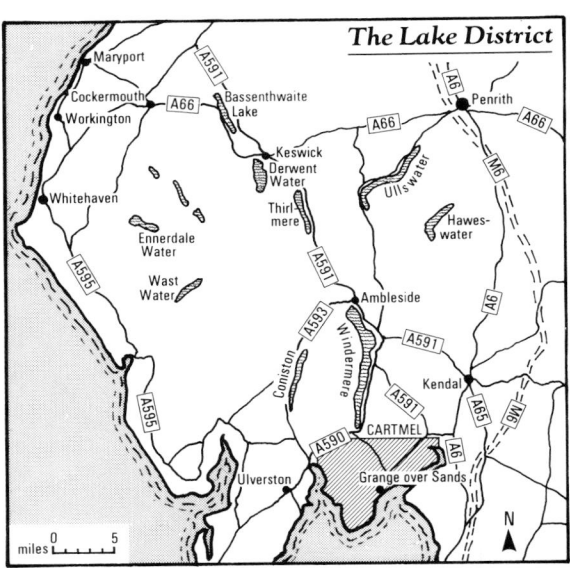

They call Grange Over Sands the Torquay of the north. It is not quite as warm and sunny as its southern counterpart, but it enjoys a much better climate than the more mountainous parts of Lakeland. Its location, south facing across the Kent estuary and sheltered by Eggerslack and Newton Fells to the north, helps to give Grange its favourable climate, as witness the lush vegetation growing even in gardens close to the shore. Rhododendrons and azaleas seem to do exceptionally well around here.

Grange really is 'over the sands'; in fact it has miles and miles of them every time the tide goes out! To the west of its peninsula are Cartmel Sands, left bare when the Levens estuary ebbs, to join those of the Kent. This is a dangerous area for the unwise, and many have been caught in the quicksands or between channels which flood at an alarming rate even close inshore.

The vast expanse of sand left by the ebbing tides

Milestone at Cartmel, showing the distances across the Morecombe Bay sands

have long been an attraction to travellers. At one time, before the Levens Bridge road was built, stagecoaches from Lancaster to the Barrow area avoided the long journey through Kendal by crossing Morecambe Bay at low tide between Hest Bank and Grange over Sands. There was also another but shorter crossing over the Cartmel Sands. These crossings were recognised as long ago as Tudor times and a guide was always available. Morecambe Bay crossings are still undertaken and a Society of Morecambe Bay Guides takes parties across at convenient times during the summer months. Details of the crossings are published by Morecambe Corporation or by the Morecambe Bay Guide (tel: Grange over Sands 2165). **On no account should anyone attempt the crossing without a guide. The route threads a complex way around quicksands and deeply cut channels which can change from tide to tide. The area is also prone to sudden changes of visibility and the tide comes in very fast.**

The Cartmel Peninsula begins as the dramatic little headland of Humphrey Head, but behind it is marshland, the haunt of seabirds. Next is Holker, where the sixteenth-century hall has a motor museum and a large gauge model railway, set in twenty-two acres of wooded grounds, with many beautiful rhododendrons and rare shrubs and trees not normally found so far north, growing in profusion. Cartmel had a priory founded, so they say, by Irish monks. Little remains since it was

The Gatehouse, all that remains of Cartmel Priory

dissolved on the orders of Henry VIII, but the gatehouse, which was once used as the local grammar school, is still recognisable. Races are occasionally held, under National Hunt Rules, at the Cartmel Racetrack.

Moving to higher ground, the fells west of Cartmel and north of Grange are criss-crossed by little-used paths and Newton Fell can be said to be a miniature of its big brother further inland. No more than 585ft at its highest point, it is steep sided, wild and has twin stonebuilt farms above High Newton to complete the Lakeland picture.

PLACES OF INTEREST
Holker Hall Cark-in-Cartmel. Stately home and gardens.
Cartmel Priory Ruins and gatehouse.
Lakeside and Haverthwaite Railway Steam railway from the southern end of Lake Windermere.

WALKS IN THE AREA
Cartmel Peninsula Follow the lane and coastal path from Cark as far as West Plain Farm. Return by the road to Flookburgh and Cark. Sea and marsh birds are a feature of this walk as well as the views of Morecambe Bay sands.
Eggerslack Fell Climb from Merlewood and turn left across the fell as far as Fell End. Walk down to the road back to Grange.
Newton Fell Start in Lindale and wander across this fell as far as you wish. There is a road from High Newton which could be used to gain height without any undue effort.
Cartmel Fell This fell, to the west of Cartmel village, has at least four quiet farm lanes, any of which can be used to gain access to the start of the paths which wander across its heights. To the south, Bigland Scar woods are made for pleasant strolling.

ARNSIDE

Cumbria

OS Map: 1:50,000 Sheet No 97

Location

From the north by the M6 to Junction 36 then
B6385 Milnthorpe and the B5282 to Arnside. Or
from the south by the M6 to Junction 35 and 35A
for the A6. Turn left for Yealand Conyers and
Arnside by the system of minor roads west of the
A6.

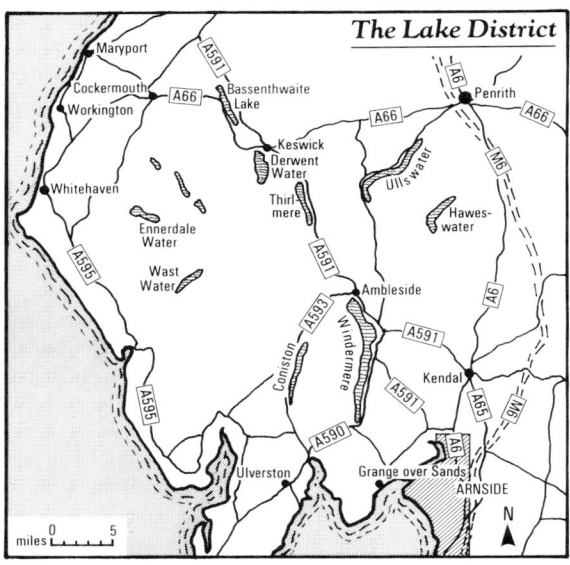

Arnside, like Grange, its neighbour across the
estuary of the Kent, enjoys a mild climate not
granted to other areas further north. You only
have to take a peep into local gardens in spring, and
see the abundance of early flowers, to realise how
favourable is the climate.

Limestone is evident in the low rocky crags
bounded by Arnside, Beetham and those two
curiously-named villages, Yealand Conyers and
Yealand Redmayne. South-west of the crags, the
sea is on the retreat, leaving a flat marshy plain and
an area of sea-washed turf once much in demand
for bowling greens.

Every crag has its range of paths, and most of
them wander through quiet woodland leading to
low summits where the panorama is of Morecambe
Bay and the giants of Lakeland.

Commercial fishing in Morecambe Bay is by
lorry, not boat! Miles of sand are uncovered at low
water and the traditional method of fishing for
both whitefish and the famous Morecambe Bay
shrimps is known as flook fishing. Traps erected
at low water wait for the tide to bring in the fish and
fishermen then go out at the next low tide in
specially adapted vehicles.

Probably the prettiest part of this area, but still
only visited by a few, is the Fairy Steps near
Beetham. This is a natural limestone staircase

Arnside Tower

Topiary Gardens, Levens Hall

leading to a ravine which in summer is filled with masses of ferns and other shade-loving plants—an ideal place to visit on a hot summer's day. Beetham has an ancient water-driven corn mill which was still commercially viable in the early 1950s. Now restored, the mill uses four pairs of millstones and regular demonstrations are given.

Leighton Hall, near Yealand Conyers, the eighteenth-century home of the Gillow family who were makers of good quality furniture, contains much of their craft, along with paintings and one of the largest dolls' houses in the world. Outdoors, the chief attractions are birds of prey, including eagles, which are free-flown every afternoon in summer, weather permitting.

Steam railway enthusiasts head for Warton Road in Carnforth. This is the Steam Town Railway Museum, the largest railway centre in the north-west where magnificent giants such as the *Flying Scotsman* and *Sir Nigel Gresley* are preserved. These and others are regularly run under steam, both in the museum or pulling special trains on the main line.

PLACES OF INTEREST

Levens Hall 5 miles south of Kendal on the A6. Elizabethan mansion containing fine panelling and plasterwork; topiary garden first laid out in 1692; collection of steam-operated machinery.
Heron Corn Mill Beetham. Restored watermill.
Yealand Hall Eighteenth-century home of the Gillow family.
Steamtown Railway Museum Carnforth.

WALKS IN THE AREA

Arnside Knott Climb this vantage point from the south-western end of the town. At the summit, walk on downhill to Far Arnside where a right turn joins a coastal path around Arnside Park back to the town.
Beetham and the Fairy Steps This lovely little dell is signposted from Beetham towards Underlaid Wood.
Warton Crag Climb from Warton village and return by the Silverdale road.
Yealand Conyers to Haweswater A path leaves the highest point of Yealand Conyers village and climbs through Cringleborrow Wood as far as the road at Yealand Storrs. Turn left along the road and at the fork take a rough track in the middle of the junction. This leads directly to Haweswater. Turn left at the tarn on a path which joins the Yealand road north-east of Silverdale station. Turn right along the road, then in about 50yd turn left on a path across Grisedale marsh. Follow this path to Grisedale Farm and on to Leighton Hall. Walk through the park back to Yealand Conyers.

SHAP

Cumbria

OS Map: 1:25,000 Outdoor Leisure Map,
The English Lakes NE Sheet

Location

M6 to Junction 39 (Shap). B6261 west to the A6
and turn right for Shap village.

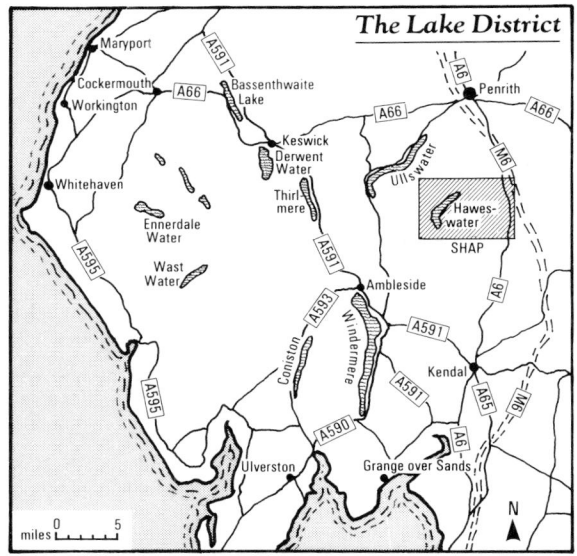

There are times when even the grandeur of Central
Lakeland begins to pall. It is a rare occasion,
admittedly, but it does happen. Maybe the roads
are too crowded, or perhaps after a long spell of
hot weather, the high fells start to become a little
overpowering. It is on these occasions that one
longs for somewhere quiet. Before the M6 was
built, Shap village was a place to drive through;
traffic problems were common and very unpleasant.
However, the M6 has changed all that and Shap
village has now reverted to being a sleepy double
row of stone cottages and old coaching inns.

Shap is built on ancient ground; there was once
a stone circle nearby. It was ruined when they built
the railway, but the processional way can still be
recognised from massive stones which lie in fields
west of the village. In comparatively recent times
(only 700 years ago as against the stones' two or
three thousand years), Premonstratensian canons
built a monastery in a quiet spot by the side of the
River Lowther, which stood four square until its
dissolution under the officers of Henry VIII.

Although there are plenty of field and moorland
tracks around Shap, walking has not the same
mountaineering quality of the high routes in
Central Lakeland; what it has is miles of tracks
where the walker can wander in complete freedom.
This is where moorland birdsong comes into its
own, and where the huge panorama of fell and sky
become as one. If you want somewhere quiet and
relaxed then try Shap; the walking might be far
better than expected and certainly it is a good area
for lazy days.

Shap Abbey

Long Sleddale

PLACES OF INTEREST

Shap Abbey   In the Lowther valley west of the village.

Lowther Wildlife Country Park   European animals and birds roam freely or in special enclosures.

Brougham Castle   1½ miles east of Penrith. Interesting ruins of the castle built in 1176.

Penrith Castle   Town centre. Once the home of Richard III.

Dalemain House   On Penrith – Ullswater road. Imposing building set in parkland.

WALKS IN THE AREA

Keld and Shap Abbey   Take the field path south-west from Shap and as far as Keld. Turn right and follow another path to Shap Abbey. Return to Shap village by the lane from the abbey.

The Lowther Valley   Follow the abbey lane almost as far as the River Lowther. Turn right and follow a field path north-west to Rosgill. Turn right and walk south-east by another field path back to Shap.

Sleddale and Swindale   Walk to Keld and turn left for Thornship. Turn right to cross the River Lowther and join a farm track to Steps Hall. Turn right at the farm and follow the moorland track above the reservoir to Sleddale Hall. Turn sharp right and climb across the moors by way of Gambling Crag and Goathercrag Gill into Swindale. Do not cross the river, but turn sharp right to follow the gently contouring path up Trussgap Brow and Dog Hill. Gradually work your way round towards Keld and join a metalled track. Follow this until another track forks left to Keld.

Haweswater   A quiet road and paths can be used to complete the circuit of this manmade lake.

North-East England

DUNSTANBURGH AND CRASTER

Northumberland

OS Map: 1:50,000 Sheet Nos 75 and 81

Location

From the south take the A1 to Alnwick, then B1340 for about 3½ miles north-east to the Hacketwell crossroads. Craster is a further 3½ miles north-east along the signposted minor road.

If coming from the north, leave the A1 at Charlton Mires and turn left for the B6347. There are several cross-country minor roads, but the easiest route is via Embleton.

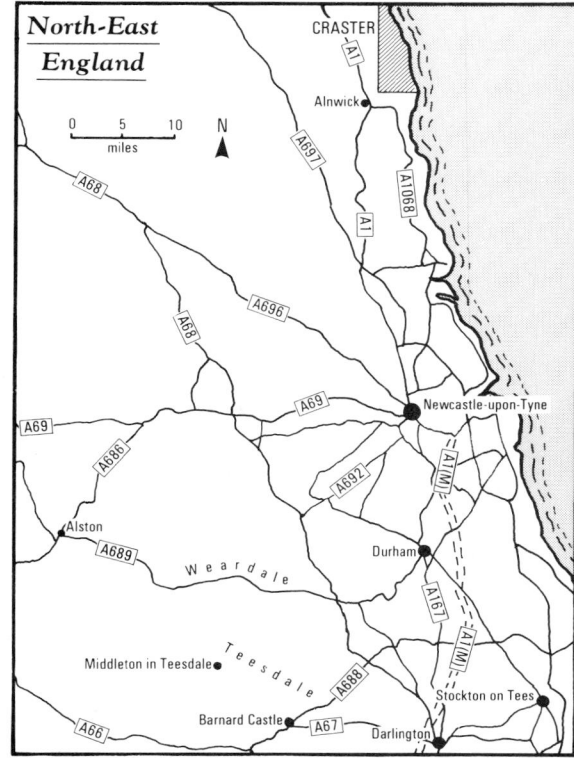

All the way down the north-east coast of England, gaunt ruined castles tell of the urgent need for defence against seaborne attack in the Middle Ages. Bamburgh and Dunstanburgh are just two of these castles, where even today their ancient strength offers mute defiance against possible aggressors.

The short stretch of coast between Dunstanburgh and the fishing village of Craster offers hours of interest, either by pottering amongst the rocky coves or by exploring the castle or village. Dunstanburgh Castle was built in the fourteenth century on much earlier foundations, but as the threat from seaborne attack faded, it was left to the relentless siege of the elements to produce the ruined bastion of today. It belonged to John of Gaunt, but it was perhaps the artist Turner whose paintings so captured the true romance of Dunstanburgh.

Craster's harbour is protected by an outcrop of the Whin Sill; crab and herring fishing are the main occupations of local fishermen, also the kippers made in local curing sheds are second to none. Smoked over a slow-burning fire of oak chips, they can be bought locally or eaten in the tiny village restaurant.

Local walking is at its best along the coast on either side of Craster, but the quiet pastoral land a mile or two inland makes a pleasant change.

Dunstanburgh Castle

Bamburgh Castle

PLACES OF INTEREST
Bamburgh Castle and **Dunstanburgh Castle**
Two of the ruined castles on the north-east coast.

WALKS IN THE AREA
Craster From Craster, walk along the coastal path to Dunstanburgh Castle. Either return the same way or continue along the coast to Newton Haven, if you can arrange transport back. Alternatively, walk inland from Dunstanburgh to Dunstan Steads. Turn left along the farm track to Dunstan Square, then left again towards the inland facing cliffs known as The Heughs. Turn right at their foot for the way back to Craster.

Howick Harbour This easy walk follows the coast as far as the natural harbour of Howick Haven. Return by walking along the road towards Howick Hall, turning right by the entrance. Follow the path on the right hand (facing) edge of the narrow belt of trees and turn right where the main path crosses back through the woods. Follow the right-hand path over the fields as far as the car park.

Embleton to Beadnall Walk down the lane to Dunstanburgh golf course and on to the coastal footpath which starts beyond the club house. Turn left along the coast past Newton Haven, Football Hole and walk around Beadnall Bay into Beadnall. Unless transport can be arranged, retrace your steps back round Beadnall Bay as far as Newton Links House and turn right for High Newton. A field path continues from the other side of the village to a point just above the small quarry on the B1339 outside Embleton.

WOOLER

Northumberland

OS Map: 1:50,000 Sheet No 75

Location
Wooler is on the A697 Morpeth – Edinburgh road about 31 miles north-west of Morpeth and 15 miles south-east of Coldstream and the Scottish border.

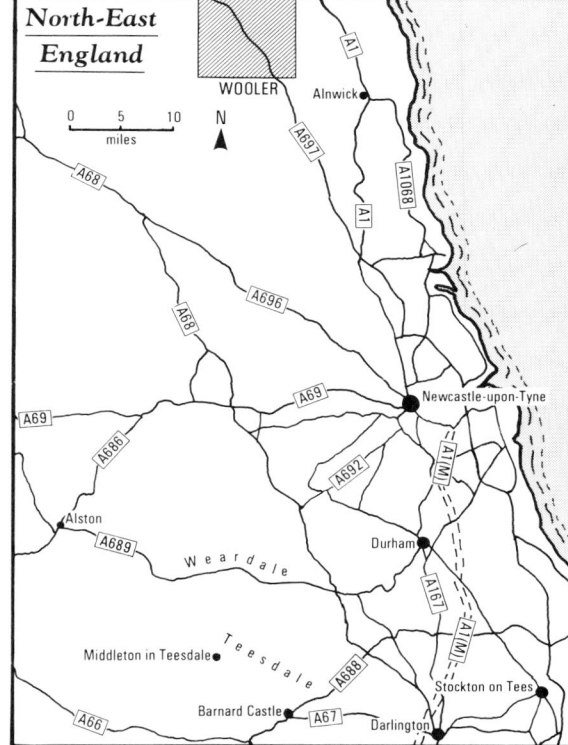

Sheep and dairy farming are the main occupations of Cheviot farmers and Wooler is the market for their produce. In the days of cattle droving, when animals walked to their eventual destinations, several fairs were held each year in Wooler, but with the exception of the Trinian Fair, on 27 September, all are now abandoned. Haulage firms have taken over from the colourful drovers of less than a century ago, but life goes on in this little town at very much the same pace. Its cluster of shops may have modern trappings, but they are on the sites of much older businesses; many have been owned by the same families for generations.

The country around Wooler is a contrast of gentle broad valleys with wild rugged heights. To the south-west rear the outliers of Cheviot Hill, granite mountains ancient long before the ice ages made their present contours. Side rivers drain steep-sided narrow valleys into the flat calm of the Till, which in turn feeds the Tweed, one of Scotland's major salmon rivers.

Man came early to this area to build his camps and forts on high vantage points in the Cheviot foothills. In more settled times, the long-deserted villages of Cefrin and Melmin speak of a growing civilisation. Strife was never far away, especially during the wild unruly times of the fifteenth to seventeenth centuries, and even later when the bloody border feuds were at their height. Cattle and lands changed hands constantly when might was right.

PLACES OF INTEREST
Chillingham Castle Home of the famous herd of wild cattle. Castle and Wildlife Park.
Cefrin (GR925305). Site of an ancient village.
Melmin (GR941339). Site of an ancient village.
Cheviot Hills

Harthope Valley

The Cheviot Hills from Ford Common

WALKS IN THE AREA

Cefrin (GR925305). Follow the track of the railway line from Wooler to the site of this ancient village. Return by the Yeavering-Coupland lane, turning left over the ford. Follow the road to the A697. Cross over and walk along a track to the north end of Ewart Park. Turn right at the road, then left after ½ mile along a farm track to Bridge End Farm and walk towards the River Till. Do not cross the river, but turn right to join a field path back to Wooler.

Wooler Common, Harthope Burn, Happy Valley and Wooler Water Walk out of Wooler on the Commonburn road. At Waud House (GR984278), turn left away from the road and follow the path (obscure in places) south-west across Wooler Common into Carey Burn. Climb up to the ruins of Broadstruther Farm and then aim south for the col between Broadhope Hill and Cold Law. Walk down into the Harthope Burn valley and turn left along the road. At Langlee cottage, turn right and climb Brands Hill to drop down to Middleton Old Town, onwards to the road and turn left, past North Middleton. Cross Happy Valley and take the second lane on the right to Earle Mill. Turn left along the side stream back to Wooler.

The Cheviot from Langleeford From a car parked carefully near Langleeford (GR949220) follow the valley up to the col and turn right to follow a faint track through the boggy wastes of Cheviot Hill. Return eastwards across point 2650 and Scald Hill, re-entering the Harthope Valley by one of the side burns below Langleeford.

Note This walk is dangerous in mist and bad weather. Also the bogs on the summit of Cheviot can be very deep, but in fine weather the views are stupendous!

BELLINGHAM

Northumberland

OS Map: 1:50,000 Sheet No 80

Location

Bellingham lies on the B6320 Otterburn to
Hexham road, about ten miles south-west of the
former. The best approach is by the A68. From
the north, turn right at the crossroads with the
B6320. Or, from the south by the A69 Newcastle
– Carlisle road to Hexham, and turn right on the
A6097 as far as Chollerford. The B6320 starts
from the junction on the far side of the North Tyne
river.

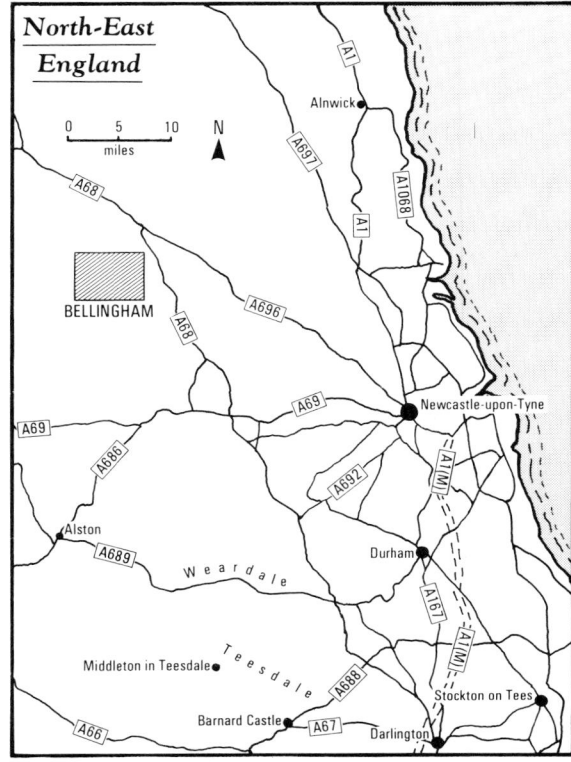

Bellingham (pronounced Bellinjam) once was an
important colliery town; it had its own railway
station and goods yard on a scenic line which
followed the North Tyne before it meandered on
through the Borders into Scotland. The coal was
worked out and eventually the line closed to leave
Bellingham in something of a backwater. Today its
importance lies in its position as the market for
sheep reared in their thousands on the surrounding
moors.

   Although the Pennine Way passes through
Bellingham, and is also an ideal centre to explore
miles and miles of untrodden moors, it tends to be
a little-known place. To the north lie Hareshaw
Common and Abbey Rigg, wild places, where the
silence is broken only by the fluting curlews.
South and west are the dense fastnesses of Walk
and Kielder Forests. Keilder Reservoir, Europe's
biggest manmade lake, is about twelve miles to the
north-west.

   The village is well worth an hour or two to
explore its neat little back streets. A curious
gravestone in the churchyard is said to depict a
traveller's pack. It marks the grave of a tinker who
was smuggled, hidden inside his pack, into a
remote farm one night, with the intention of
robbing the farmer. On seeing movement, the
farmer's daughter stabbed the pack with a sword
and killed its unknown occupant. Pride of place in
the village square is given to a Chinese cannon
brought back by the son of one of the local gentry
at the time of the Boxer Rebellion.

Kielder Water

A little to the north of the village is Hareshaw Burn, a pretty woodland dell which ends at a gritstone amphitheatre. Down it cascades Hareshaw Linn, one of Northumberland's most famous waterfalls. There is a nature trail through the woods leading up to the waterfall.

PLACES OF INTEREST
Hareshaw Linn
Bellingham Church and the 'Pack' grave, Chinese Cannon in the square
Kielder Reservoir and Nature Trails
Padon Monument (GR820922). Imposing cairn erected to the memory of Alexander Padon, a Scottish Covenanter.

WALKS IN THE AREA
Hareshaw Linn Simply follow the signposted path from the old railway goods yard as far as the waterfall. It will be necessary to retrace your steps as there is no official exit above the Linn, but the walk is worth doing twice over.
North Tyne, Redesmouth and Rede Bridge Walk downstream as far as a footbridge below the Redesmouth road. Do not cross the bridge but turn left up to the road and then right. Follow this road to Redesmouth village and left along the old railway track as far as Rede Bridge. Turn left and cross the bridge, then immediately left again on to a field path back to Bellingham.
Pennine Way to Abbey Rigg Follow the Pennine Way (signposted) north past the youth hostel and as far as Hareshaw House. Turn left down the farm track until a footpath turns left above the valley of Hareshaw Burn. Follow this to Hainingrigg and beyond it to join the B6320 to Bellingham.
Shitlington Common From Mantle Hill, about 1¾ miles north-west of Bellingham on the Kielder road turn left and follow the path by way of Brieredge Farm across Shitlington Common until it reaches the forest boundary. Turn right by way of Watch Crags and Watson's Walls to a junction of tracks above Whitchester. Turn right across Snabdaugh Moor and down to the Kielder road. There are two routes at this point. Either turn right and follow the road back to Bellingham, or, alternatively, turn left to cross Chirdon Burn and in a little under ½ mile turn right over the North Tyne. Join the old railway track and turn right to follow it all the way back to the village.

The Chinese Cannon at Bellingham, a relic of the Boxer Rebellion

HADRIAN'S WALL

Northumberland

OS Map: 1:50,000 Sheet No 87

Location
Approach Once Brewed by the B6318 Newcastle
– Carlisle road or via the A69.

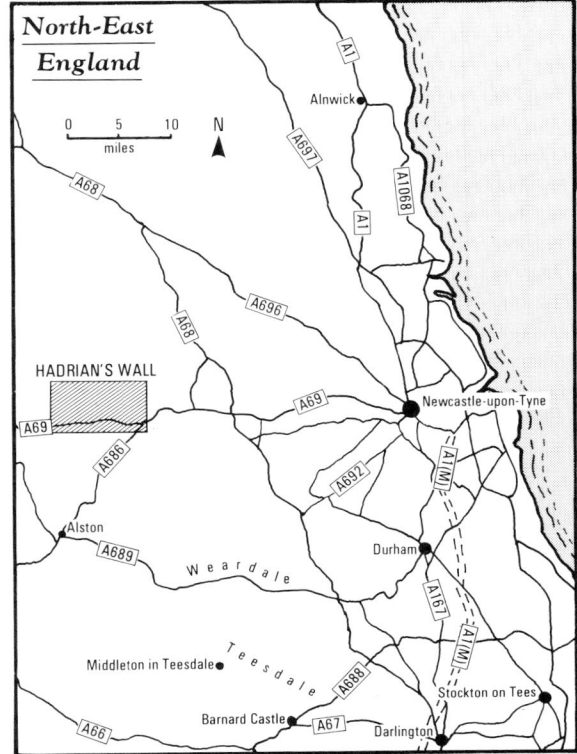

The B6318 parallels much of Hadrian's Wall and
most of its central section lies within the Vallum, a
defensive ditch built, it is thought, to trap the
enemy should they break through the Wall. The
modern road follows a route laid out by General
Wade, a brilliant military engineer, to aid rapid
troop deployment after the Jacobite rebellions of
1715 and 1745.

Emperor Hadrian's engineers must have viewed
the chosen route of the Wall with great satisfaction.
Not only is it the narrowest part of England and
well to the north of what was becoming settled
land, but also the central part of the Wall stands on
top of the north facing Whin Sill, an outcrop of a
vast extrusion of dolerite, stretching across Northern
England from High Cup by way of Cauldron

Hadrian's Wall

Snout, to the Farne Islands. It even has an outlier not far from Whitby to the south. It is, however, this northerly outcrop which had strategic importance and today makes Hadrian's Wall a thing of scenic beauty as well as historical importance.

Much of the Wall east and west of the central section was plundered for building material, but this portion was unwittingly protected by being the base for a band of Moss Troopers in the sixteenth century. These were bandits who terrorised the local farming population with their cattle-rustling activities.

Not only do we have tangible links with our ancient history cropping up in profusion all around the Wall, but the very nature of the countryside on either side of it, much of it little used, makes for exhilarating walking. High rolling moors, steep rocky escarpments and dense sombre forests all help to make an area where the walker can explore both the well-known and out-of-the-way Roman remains.

PLACES OF INTEREST
Hadrian's Wall Between Twice Brewed and Housesteads
Housesteads Roman Fort
Vindolanda excavations and museum
Temple of Mithras
Brocolita Fort
Thirlwall Castle
Crag, Broomlee and Greenlee Loughs

WALKS IN THE AREA
Once Brewed, Housesteads and Crag Lough Follow Hadrian's Wall eastwards from the Information Centre at Once Brewed to a point ½ mile east of Housesteads. Turn left along a cart track which first passes beneath and then runs about ¼ mile north of the Wall. Where the track turns sharply left towards the Wall, turn right to continue a parallel course until reaching the Twice Brewed – Melkbridge road. Turn left and return to the Information Centre.

Housesteads, Stanegate and Thorngrafton Common From Housesteads car park, walk towards the Wall and turn right along it for ½ mile. Turn right again to cross the Vallum by a footpath to the B6318 and Moss Kennels. Beyond the farm a path meanders south over the moor to Stanegate Roman road. Cross over and down the lane to Seldom Seen. Go through the yard and walk over Whinnetley Moss as far as a walled lane. Turn right and in just over two miles reach the road at Thorngrafton Common. Another right turn to a 'T' junction with Stanegate. Cross the Roman road and go by way of Grindledykes to the B6318. Turn right for Housesteads car park.

Vindolanda, Bardon Mill, Parkside, Once Brewed Start at Once Brewed car park and either take the bus or walk by road past Smith's Shield to Vindolanda and its Interpretation Centre. Walk through the fort to Chesterholm. Turn right and walk down the valley to Bardon Mill. Leave the village by the path which climbs up to Parkside. On to Hunterscrook, Layside and so to the Once Brewed road.

Hadrian's Wall, the Pennine Way, Greenlee Lough and Gibbs Hill Follow the Pennine Way from Once Brewed as far as Stonefolds Farm on the outskirts of Wark Forest. Turn left on a farm lane, following it to Gibbs Hill Farm. Turn right beneath Swallow Crags on the field path to Wealside. Left at the farm then to Longsyke and Cawburn Shield. Walk down the farm lane to a road and turn left, following it as far as the Wall. Turn left along the Wall to follow it (also the Pennine Way route) back to Once Brewed.

Roman mile castle at Housestead Crags

ALSTON

Cumbria

OS Map: 1:50,000 Sheet Nos 87 and 91

Location

From M6 Junction 40 (Penrith) take the A686 north-east across Hartside to Alston. Alternatively, south-west along the A686 from Haydon Bridge (on the A69 Newcastle – Carlisle road).

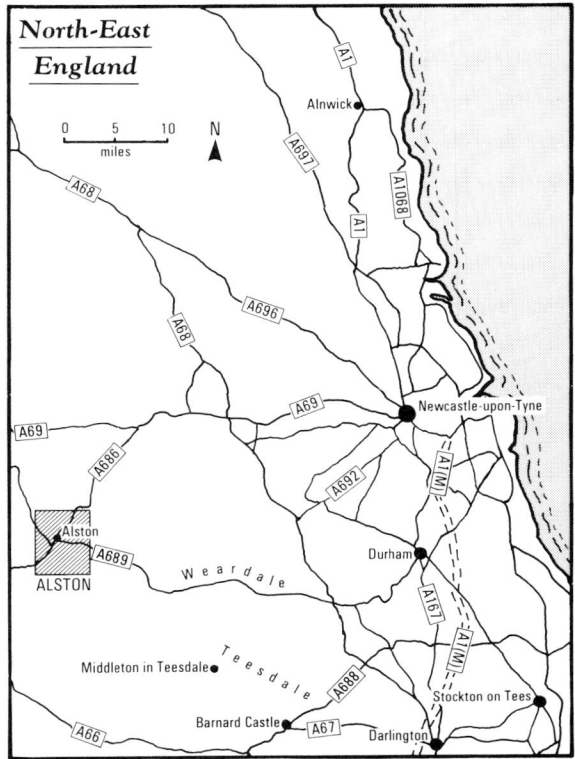

Winter radio bulletins frequently report Alston being cut off by snow. This is not surprising when one realises that roads linking the town to the outside world mostly cross the 1,000ft contour line. The A686 to Penrith across Hartside has the doubtful record of being closed by snow more than any other road in England.

Once the centre of lead mining in the area, Alston's character survives, a quaint place retaining the atmosphere of market town, despite the disappearance of its industry and latterly its railway link. Before the cutback of small branch lines, the railway was often the only link Alston had with the outside world in winter. Diesel trains with delightful regional names like 'Coffee Johnny' or 'Bobby Shaftoe' ran between Alston and the main line at Haltwhistle. Economic policy decreed that this link should be cut, but at least the line is kept open from Alston as far as Lambley by the South Tyne Railway Society.

The Pennine Way passes Alston on its way north alongside the South Tyne. This section of the Way is a pleasant riverside and moorland link between Hadrian's Wall and Cross Fell. It offers a gentle contrast between an historical walk in the north and a tough mountain climb southwards.

Apart from walkers from industrial Teesside, and maybe the Pennine Wayfarers who in any case only see the valley, few walkers have discovered the delights of this remote area. The valley bottom offers short riverside walks with vistas of the tree-lined infant South Tyne. Away from the river, it is possible to walk in the footsteps of Roman legions along the Maiden Way, for this was once a main artery south from Hadrian's Wall.

Moorland walking around Alston has an archaeological flavour; many of the tracks were created to take miners to their work in the lead mines high on the fell sides. Lead mining as an economic industry died by the mid-nineteenth century, but

tangible relics dot the wild remote moors. Shafts, which were built with great skill to exploit the subterranean riches, are now neglected and as a result are no longer safe despite their apparent attraction for the more adventurous.

Alston Market Place

The Nent Valley, near Alston

PLACES OF INTEREST

South Tyne Railway   Preserved section as far as Lambley. Steam trains.

Whitley Castle   Roman Fort (GR695488)

Garrigill Waterfall   (GR759405) Access via B6277 south-east from Alston.

Alston Village   Market Cross, old houses.

Long Meg and her daughters   Stone circle (GR571372)

Appleby Castle   Rare Breeds Survival Trust.

High Cup Valley   Glacial valley, access from Dufton.

WALKS IN THE AREA

Garrigill's Waterfall   From Garrigill village, close by the George & Dragon on the village green, walk uphill on the opposite side of the river near Loaning Head Farm. Turn right to follow a field path and pass by Pasture Houses and Ashgillside farms until the waterfall is reached close to the road. Cross the stream beneath the fall and walk downhill and across the main river. Turn right on a fieldpath back to Garrigill.

The Pennine Way between Garrigill and Alston   Follow the Pennine Way signs downstream from Garrigill, but return by way of a minor road to Leadgate. Turn left by a field path to Low Ameshaugh, then walk 200 yd along the farm lane to the next building on the left. Turn left again and walk down to Black Burn. Cross over and follow the main river as far as the Pennine Way footbridge. Turn left over the bridge and then right for a path along the top side of Crag Woods as far as Dodbury. Follow the lane back to Garrigill.

Ayle Burn   A mile north of Alston on the A686, a path crosses the valley of Ayle Burn. Follow it to the hamlet of Ayle and then left downhill to Randalholme Farm. Turn left along the road back to Alston.

UPPER WEARDALE

Durham

OS Map: 1:50,000 Sheet Nos 87 and 91

Location

A686 to Alston either via M6 Junction 40 or Haltwhistle by the A69 and then the A689 into Weardale; or A1 (M) to Bradbury and then the A689 via Bishops Auckland; or A690 south-west from Durham to Crook and join the A689.

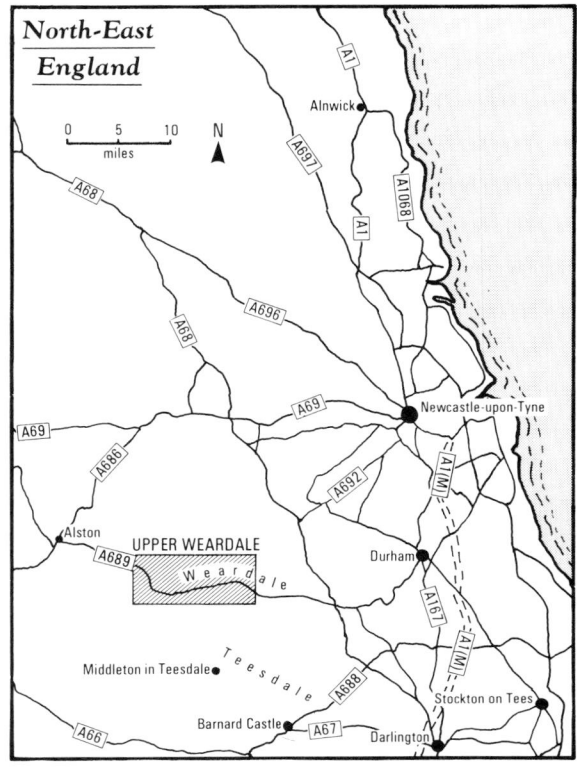

An area of industrial dereliction — the remains of uneconomic lead mining activity in Upper Weardale — is rapidly being converted into an exciting tourist attraction. A complex network of footpaths, which once took the miners from their hamlets and smallholdings, criss-crosses the valley sides and moors. So now a valley which was once shunned by all self-respecting walkers is coming into its own again. It has ample scope, offering miles of uninterrupted walking for all who are prepared to explore this region.

At Killhope, the ruins of a hamlet and its extensive lead processing machinery, including a massive waterwheel, have been renovated to make

The Killhope Wheel

an interesting open air exhibition demonstrating the tough existence of lead miners, a little over a century ago.

Footpaths form a haphazard pattern across the field system around Cowshill, linking smallholdings which once were the homes of the local mining population. In the eighteenth century, large families were brought up on the produce of one cow, a couple of pigs and a handful of sheep on the communal grazing of local moors. The men worked a five-day week in the mines, returning to their smallholdings at weekends. Until foreign competition undercut the local lead industry, this part industrial, part agricultural community had a comparatively prosperous existence.

Moving back in time, border raiders, known as Moss Troopers, once attacked Rookhope Dale (one of Weardale's side valleys), and tried to steal a number of cattle. Incensed by this loss, forty or so locals chased a hundred Moss Troopers across Nookton Edge at the head of the dale. After a fierce skirmish the locals regained their animals and sent the surviving raiders back beyond the Tyne.

Restored lead mine at Killhope

PLACES OF INTEREST
Killhope Wheel Visitor Centre B6293, 2½ miles east of Nenthead. Exhibition showing the life of the lead mining community, and processing plant.
Derwent Reservoir B6306. 7 miles north-west of Consett. Fishing, sailing, nature reserve, Pow Hill Country Park.
Blanchland B6306, 4 miles east of Edmundbyers. Site of thirteenth-century abbey.
North of England Open Air Museum, Beamish Off A693 near Chester le Street. Working examples of tramcars, pit gear and steam trains. Victorian pub, etc.

WALKS IN THE AREA
Killhope Wheel Visitor Centre Tracks leading away from the car park can be used to link a valley walk towards Cowshill. Here a complex of field paths offer unlimited scope from either the odd hour or so, to a whole morning or afternoon's walking.
Puddingthorn Moor From Lanehead, about 1¼ miles north-west of Cowshill, follow the moor lane north on to Puddingthorn Moor. The lane ends at the moor edge, but a footpath continues across the moor, turning sharply to the right. Aim for the highest point of the B6295 (Cowshill – Allenheads road). Cross the road and follow a track east for about a quarter of a mile and then hard right downhill across Burtree Fell and back to Cowhills.
The back lanes of Upper Weardale This is a walk mostly suited to a rainy day as it keeps almost entirely to metalled roads. Take the top road south-east from Cowshill as far as Daddy Shield. Use field paths westwards to St John's Chapel and then either footpaths or the road over Hawkwell to Ireshopeburn and use field paths to reach Cowshill.

UPPER TEESDALE

Durham

OS Map: 1:50,000 Sheet No 92

Location

A66 as far as Barnard Castle and then the B6278 to Eggleston and turn left for the valley on the B6277. Or A868 (Penrith – Haydon Bridge road) as far as Alston and then turn right for the B6277 into Teesdale.

Nature has gone overboard in the eight or nine miles of dale between Middleton and the waterfall of Cauldron Snout. These are miles of pure delight — dramatic waterfalls, woodlands and plants so rare that patrols of vigilantes guard them in springtime.

The Pennine Way is for much of its length often a boring slog, but when the tired walker reaches Teesdale spirits begin to soar. Here, at all seasons of the year, there is something to delight the eye.

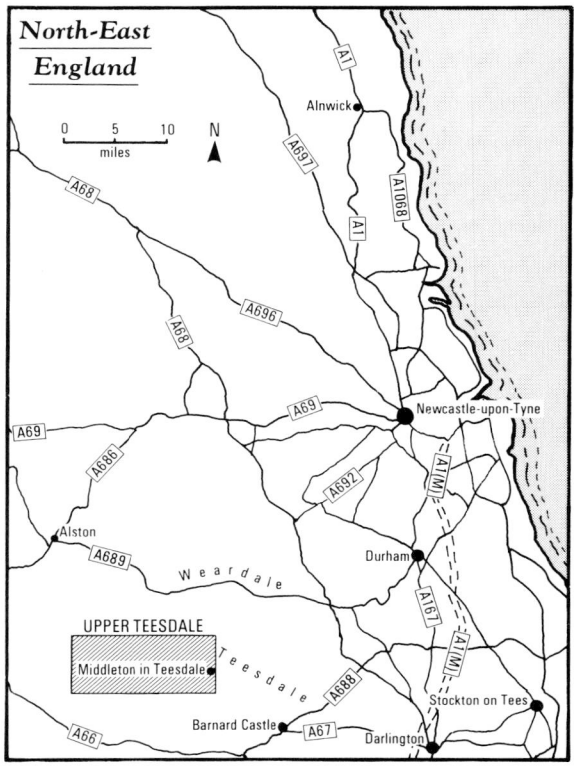

High Force

North-westwards from Middleton in Teesdale, the Pennine wayfarer has, at first, a charming stroll, them comes Low Force, more a series of stepped rapids where the Tees forces its way across platforms of rock. The setting is woodland, and in spring the spaces between the trees are filled with flowers. The word 'force' comes from *foss*, the norse word for waterfall.

Both sides of the river around Low Force are accessible thanks to the well-maintained Wynch Bridge, a footbridge first erected by Teesdale miners as a means of access to the mines south of the river.

A little over a mile upstream an outcrop of dolerite makes the stage for High Force, England's most dramatic waterfall. The best time to see this spectacle is after heavy rain when the river is in spate and comes crashing over the 70ft drop.

On a warm day the scent from the juniper bushes on either side of High Force reminds us that it is imported juniper berries which give English gin its flavour and aroma.

After much bitter argument, the infant Tees was held back by a dam at Cow Green. Gone for ever are the rare flowers which bloomed with fragile beauty on a special soil, which is only found in the area now flooded by the reservoir. 'Sugar limestone' is a form of limestone which was affected by high temperature in volcanic times, and has blended with surrounding soil to form an ideal growing medium for these semi-alpine flowers.

Cauldron Snout is now regulated by the dam, but can still provide enough spectacle to remind us of its former glory. The river cascades over a series of steps, weaknesses in an outcrop of dolerite. This is the Whin Sill, made of volcanic basalt, which spread across Northern England from High Cup in the west to the north-east coast. Nowhere is it more prominent than along its northern boundary, where it provides the base of Hadrian's Wall to the north, but here in Teesdale the sill is the spring board for these dramatic 'forces'.

Beyond Cow Green, and also south of High Force, a wilderness of bog and moorlands has been designated as a Nature Reserve to both protect and study this unique environment.

PLACES OF INTEREST
Wheelhead Syke Nature Trail   Near Cow Green Reservoir.
Cauldron Snout Waterfall   Cow Green.
High Force   B6277. 5 miles north-west of Middleton in Teesdale.
Low Force   B6277. 4 miles north-west of Middleton in Teesdale.
Bowlees Visitor Centre   Natural history of Teesdale explained in easy to follow, yet well-documented manner.
Gibson's Cave   Above Bowlees.

WALKS IN THE AREA
Even the most popular walks in Upper Teesdale are never crowded. Cauldron Snout, Low Force and High Force are all highly recommended.

The lower slopes of the fells north of the B6277 are criss-crossed by a network of rights-of-way and can offer hours of walking.

This is a remote and wild area well known for its high winds and harsh weather. Take heed of local conditions and make sure that someone knows where you have gone, no matter how short your walk may be.

Cauldron Snout

BARNARD CASTLE

Durham

OS Map: 1:50,000 Sheet No 92

Location

A1 to Scotch Corner and take the A66 (Penrith road) to Rokeby Park. Turn right for the A6277 into Barnard Castle. Or by the A67 from Darlington direct to Barnard Castle.

From M6 (Junction 40), take the A66 from Penrith to Bowes and turn left on the A67.

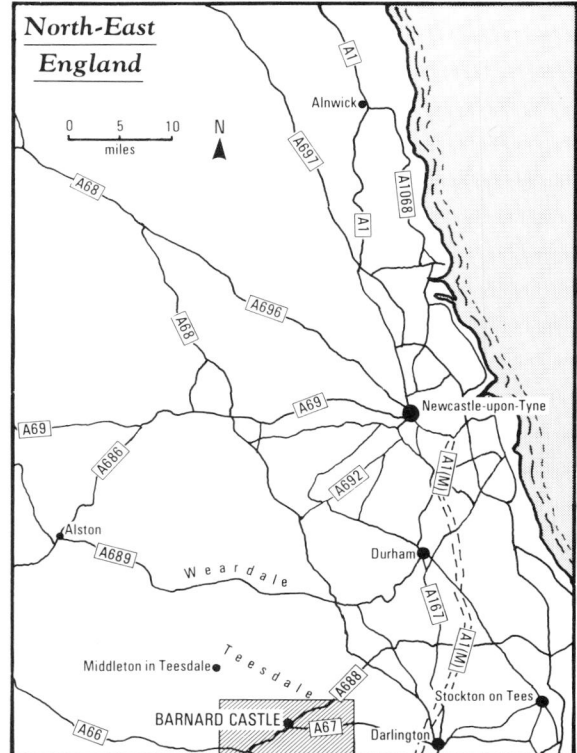

Barnard Castle takes its name from Barnard (Bernard), son of Guy Balliol who was granted lands in Teesdale by William II in 1093. Probably on the site of a much older fortification, the castle was extended and strengthened several times over the years. It saw much strife during the Wars of the Roses and the constant border feuding which went on before England and Scotland could live at peace with each other. The town still seems to cluster for safety around the skirts of its castle.

For centuries Barnard Castle has been the market place of the surrounding area, a feature of this commerce being the solidly-built covered market standing in Thorngate.

Many venerable buildings line the streets, or 'gates' as they have been called since the Norsemen brought their language to the area. Charles Dickens stayed at the King's Head in Horsemarket when he was researching *Nicholas Nickleby*, an indictment of the often cruel boarding school system of Victorian times. Dotheboys Hall, featured in the novel, is nearby on the outskirts of Bowes village.

Bowes Museum is south of the town, and is housed in a massive chateau-like building, built between 1869 and 1892 by the French architect Jules Pellachet. Originally it was intended for George Bowes, heir to the Strathmore fortunes who never saw its completion; it is now run by Durham County Council Museum Service. In an unexpectedly grand building for such a small town, the museum contains such diverse objects as local Roman relics, famous paintings, and even a mechanical swan! There is much to occupy the visitor in the town and it rarely gets crowded, but if it does and if maybe you want a change from looking at the castle or its surrounding streets, the riverside is always tranquil. Paths up and

Barnard Castle and River Tees

downstream offer miles of easy strolling, often at its best on a hot summer's afternoon or evening.

God's Bridge

PLACES OF INTEREST

Barnard Castle and town

Bowes Museum ½ mile east of the town centre.

Egglestone Abbey 1½ miles south-east of Barnard Castle. Ruins of thirteenth to fourteenth-century abbey.

Bowes A66, 4 miles south-west of Barnard Castle. Roman fort, twelfth-century stone keep. Dotheboys Hall.

God's Bridge Natural limestone bridge spanning the river Greta. Once carried a drove road. Access is from Pasture End Farm on the A66, 2¼ miles west of Bowes.

WALKS IN THE AREA

Rokeby Park Follow the river downstream by its southern bank. Visit Mortham Tower within Rokeby Park. Continue by field path through West Thorpe and cross the river at Whorlton. Turn left and return upstream on the northern bank.

The Tees and its woodland Walk upstream by the footpath on the north bank of the river as far as West Holme House. Turn right and follow the farm road to its junction with the B6278. Turn right for Barnard Castle.

Deepdale Woods This secluded wooded valley bisects the angle of the B6277 and A67 above Startford. A footpath wanders through its northern side as far as Low Crag.

Greta Bridge to Brignall Two paths climb the sides of this valley and both go as far as Brignall. It does not matter which one you choose for the ascent, but return along the other to make a more interesting route.

The North York Moors

ESK DALE

North Yorkshire

OS Map: 1:50,000 Sheet 94,
1 inch Tourist Map, The North York
Moors.

Location

The A169 Whitby – Pickering road crosses the
eastern end of Esk Dale and the A172 and A173
skirt its western access. A winding series of minor
roads along the valley connect these major roads.
Also the A171 Middlesborough – Whitby road
offers an easy and quick access to the roads leading
into the central part of the dale.

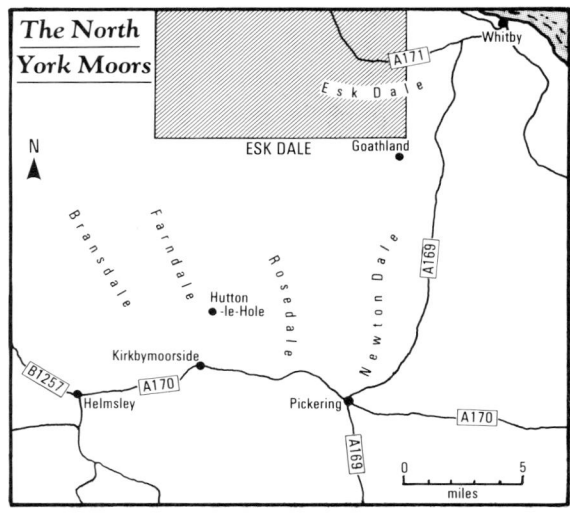

Here is a valley where time seems to stand still.
Quiet villages and ancient farmhouses are four
square against the elements, testimony to the
quality and design of the practical craftsmen of
yesteryear. Esk Dale is a valley that just asks to be
explored either by car, bicycle or better still on
foot. The National Park authority have done great
works by linking a series of waymarked trails up
and down the valley, but there are still miles and
miles of almost untrodden tracks throughout the
area.

The dale was carved by waters released from a
huge and deep lake dammed by a frozen North Sea
during the Ice Age. When the ice dam broke, the
outflowing waters must have been of cataclysmic
proportions to carve the steep sides of Esk Dale
and its tributaries. Ancient man settled on the high
moors and left us the enigmatic cairns of Danby
Rigg or the strange earthworks on Commondale.
This is an earth bank over two miles long, which
would have taken hundreds of man-hours to
build, but its purpose is still the subject of
conjecture.

Packhorse tracks, some still recognisable from
their flagged surfaces, ran the length of the dale
and crossed the river by the graceful Duck or
Beggar bridges.

Captain Cook, the navigator of the South Seas,
would have known Esk Dale very well indeed, he

Beggar Bridge

◁ *Eskdale from Danby. Little Fryup Dale in the distance,
with Danby Rigg to the right*

was born nearby at Marton and spent his school days at Great Ayton before learning seamanship in Whitby.

There is an almost unlimited choice of walks on little-known footpaths; those in the valley bottom are mostly linked by the waymarked routes and are highly recommended as they hardly come into the category of being overused. The side valleys offer tremendous scope and tracks across the intervening moors are a delight. Spring and autumn are the best times to walk anywhere in Esk Dale; the views are at their best in the special light of the two gentlest seasons of the year.

PLACES OF INTEREST
Danby Lodge   The Moors Centre
Captain Cook Birthplace Museum   Marton. In a public park to the south of Middlesbrough.
Captain Cook Schoolhouse   Great Ayton.
Commondale   (GR650110). Ancient earthwork.
Duck Bridge   (GR719078). Packhorse bridge.
Beggar Bridge   (GR785055). Packhorse bridge.
Falling Foss   (GR889036). Waterfall.
Mallyan Spout   (GR825010). Waterfall.
North York Moors Railway

WALKS IN THE AREA
Danby Rigg   Climb Danby Rigg from Ainthorpe. Drop down to Crossley House in Little Fryup Dale. Walk a little way along the road and at Stonebeck Farm turn left, down the track to Crag Farm. Left across the Esk and climb up to the valley road. Turn left, then straight on to Duck Bridge and follow the lane back to Ainthorpe.
Danby Low Moor   Follow the moor road as far as Rosedale Intake and join the path which climbs across the moor until it joins the track over Garrick Moor. Turn left on this track and walk down into Commondale. Left through the village as far as the railway station and left again on to waymarked footpath number 9 as far as Castleton, then by road into Danby.
Glaisdale   An easy circuit of this side valley may be made by first following the road from Glaisdale village, then footpaths on its far side.
Waymarked Trails   With the exception of footpath number 9 (Commondale to Castleton) and the Clitterbeck trails, the main complex of trails lie between Lealholme, Egton Bridge and Grosmont to Goathland, the latter being linked by the North York Moors Railway.

Commondale, Upper Esk Valley

FARNDALE

North Yorkshire

OS Map: 1:50,000 Sheet No 94,
1 inch Tourist Map, The North York
Moors

Location

This remote dale is best approached by the minor
road north from the A170 (Scarborough –
Thirsk) road via Kirkbymoorside. Alternatively,
Farndale may be reached from the Blakey Ridge
road from Esk Dale to Kirkbymoorside.

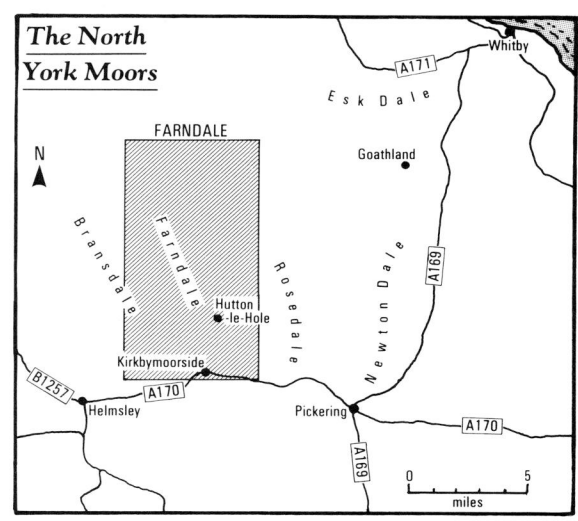

Farndale is justly famous for its daffodils, the best
known being those which bloom every spring
along the riverside between Low Mill and Church
House; but these gentle harbingers of sunshine are
also found in little pockets throughout most of the
dale. At one time thoughtless picking endangered
their survival, and they are now protected with a
section of the valley designated as a nature reserve.

As the seasons progress, golden yellow fades
and summery green takes over, then in autumn the
moors blaze with the purple of heather. It is hard to
say which is the best time for Farndale, certainly
the daffodils should not be missed, but autumn's
glory is magnificent.

Not so long ago, the moors and nearby valleys
resounded to the clamour of industry when
ironstone was mined for the smelters of Teesside.
Now worked out, the mines occupied most of the
high ground, and black smoke from kiln chimneys
hung like a pall over the moors. A railway track
1,200 ft above sea level ran around the edge of
nearby Rosedale and crossed the upper reaches of
Farndale before descending the steep Greenhow
Incline on its way north to Middlesbrough.
Ironstone miners no longer carouse late into the
night at Blakey House; the pub is now a much
more respectable place, but it still offers refreshment
to travellers across the moors.

Ancient tracks follow the crests of the moorland
ridges separating Farndale from its sister dales.
Some, but not all, are metalled and the one to the
west of Farndale, which aims almost arrow-
straight across Rudland Rigg to Ingleby Moor,
makes a safe high-level route in all but the most
inclement weather. Other possibilities for good
high-level walking can be found in the upper dale,
or on Spaunton Moor to the east.

PLACES OF INTEREST
Farndale daffodils
St Gregory's Minster   1 mile south-west of
Kirkbymoorside, off A170. Saxon church and
Viking sundial.
Lastingham Abbey   1¾ miles east of Hutton le
Hole via A170. Eleventh-century Benedictine
Abbey.
Rosedale Abbey   Twelfth-century Cistercian
Priory now incorporated within the parish church.
Hutton le Hole   4 miles north-east of Kirkby-
moorside. Attractive village. Folk museum.
Rosedale Iron Workings

Ruined ironstone kilns, Rosedale

Hutton le Hole

WALKS IN THE AREA

Rudland Rigg　Use this ancient track to connect suitable start and finishing points, either in Low Mill or Upper Farndale.

High Blakey Moor　Climb up to Blakey Ridge from Church House. Turn left along the old railway line and follow it as far as Greenhow Moor. Turn left on the footpath into Farndale and follow the valley road back to Church House.

Gillamoor and Lower Farndale　Walk down to the Dove (Farndale's river) by the footpath on the lower edge of Rumsdale Plantation. On joining the track from Ravenswick Farm, turn left and cross the river by a bridge. Climb the far side of the valley alongside another plantation. Follow this track all the way to Douthwaite and Grouse Hall Farms. Turn left at the latter and cross the dale again, by a field path and farm lane back to Gillamoor.

Blakey Ridge and Rosedale　Follow the old railway south-east from Blakey House as far as the steep road into Rosedale Abbey from Bank Top. Turn right and cross the moor by a footpath. Walk down to Low Mill, turn right along the path to Church House and then climb steeply up to the junction of the Farndale and Blakey Ridge roads with the railway track.

NEWTON DALE AND PICKERING

North Yorkshire

OS Map: 1:50,000 Sheet No 100
1 inch Tourist Map, The North York Moors

Location

The North York Moors Railway follows the dale, but there are no roads through Newton Dale itself. The A169 Pickering to Whitby road follows its eastern crest. Pickering is on the A170 Scarborough – Thirsk road, about seventeen miles west of Scarborough.

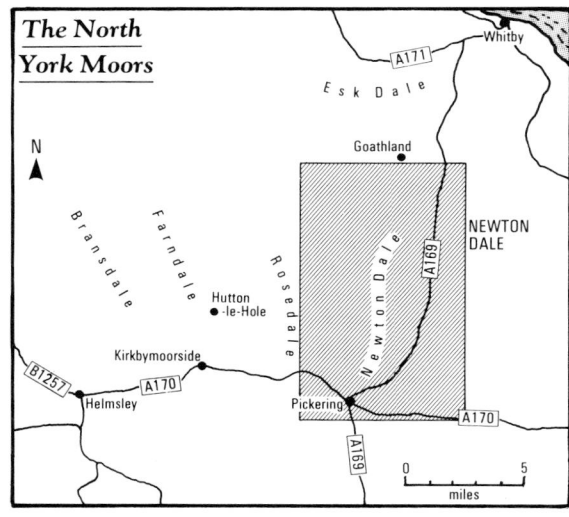

Visitors to the area are often surprised at the depth of Newton Dale; in places the valley sides are almost vertical and yet its river, Pickering Beck, is the gentlest of streams for most of the year. The reason is that Pickering Beck has had little to do with the formation of Newton Dale. In fact it was the River Esk, or more correctly, waters from ancient Lake Esk to the north, which scoured out this deep channel. Towards the end of the last Ice Age, ice covering the land melted before that in the North Sea. As a result, a deep lake flooded what is now Esk Dale. So vast was this lake that it overflowed across Goathland Moor and roared down what at first was a shallow valley, gradually deepening it with the flow of water until it formed more or less the shape we see today.

Pickering stands guard at the mouth of Newton Dale, an important centre since the Middle Ages, as witness its twin ruined castles. The one to the east of the town, built, so legend has it, by the Giant Wade, who also is credited with building Mulgrave Castle near Whitby. Not only was he a castle builder, but is supposed to have made the Roman road west of the dale which runs from Cawthorne near Pickering to Esk Dale.

Wade's Causeway, the Roman road, can be traced as far south as Cawthorne where a series of mounds and ditches are remains of Roman practice camps. Many were built over earlier camps, and some were possibly experimental as their shape differs from the normally square format.

The North York Moors Railway, which follows Newton Dale north from Pickering as far as the main line at Grosmont, makes an ideal form of transport for walks on either side of Newton Dale.

Hole of Horcum

Beck Isle Museum, Pickering

PLACES OF INTEREST
Pickering   Market town. Medieval Castle.
Beck Isle Museum of Farming
North York Moors Railway
Trout Farm
Cawthorne Roman Camps   (GR785900)
Flamingo Land Zoo   Kirby Misperton.
Dalby Forest   Forest trails. Information Centre.
Hole of Horcum   West of the A169. 5 miles
north-east of Pickering.
Fylingdales Early Warning Station

WALKS IN THE AREA
Newton Dale   Footpaths follow much of either
bank of Pickering Beck, access is from either
Pickering or Levisham (North York Moors
Railway).
Hole of Horcum   From Levisham or Lockton
villages or the scenic layby on the A169 above the
'Hole'.
Cawthorne Camps and Cropton Forest
Goathland Moor   Access from Wheeldale or
the Eller Beck Bridge (A169) – Goathland road.
Dalby Forest   Forest walks and drives — access
via Thornton Dale.

*Thornton Dale, near
Pickering*

HELMSLEY

North Yorkshire

OS Map: 1:50,000 Sheet No 100
            1 inch Tourist Map, The North York
            Moors

Location

Helmsley stands at the crossroads of the A170
(Scarborough – Thirsk) and the B1257 (Malton –
Stokesley) roads. Approach is from the south via
the A64, or from the north by way of Middlesbrough and the B1257.

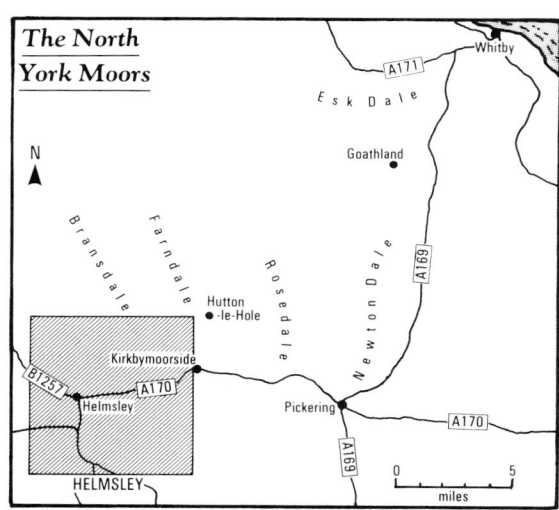

Stagecoaches no longer leave Helmsley for York
and London, but its market square still has a
couple of coaching inns, which despite a small
amount of twentieth century tidying up, still look
much as they did when they catered for the needs
of the coaching trade. Markets are held every
Friday and again have only been adapted to
modern needs, for a farmer's wife coming from
the nearby dales will still have some of the same
basic requirements as her great, great, grandmother.

The Normans first recorded the name of
Helmsley as *Elmslac* in the Domesday Book.
Robert de Roos built the castle, with its unique 'D'
shaped keep, between 1188 and 1227. Life was
quiet and uneventful for four centuries until the
Civil War, when after a long siege it was captured
by Parliamentary Troops under Sir Thomas
Fairfax from nearby Gilling. The present ruins
date from that time and are mainly the result of
'slighting', making the captured fortress untenable.
No doubt a great number of stones found their
way as free building material into local cottages!

The rich farm land of the Vale of Pickering
contrasts with the airy spaciousness of the moors.
Stately homes denote the wealth of this county and
tranquil ruins of one-time monasteries, set in deep
secluded valleys, speak in their turn of other forms
of prosperity.

Rievaulx Abbey, said by many to be Yorkshire's
finest, is an easy walk from the market square.
Built by Cistercian monks, it was their finest
creation and a demonstration of their wealth. This
wealth, built up by centuries of careful husbandry
of vast sheep flocks, iron workings and fishing
interests, was confiscated in 1538 by officers
acting on behalf of Henry VIII. The monks were
cast out into the world and their beautiful abbey

Rievaulx Abbey

desecrated.

Since then, time has softened the destruction and left us the beautiful shell of this one-time seat of monastic learning. Try to visit Rievaulx in autumn, and go first to the nearby terrace where mock Ionic and Tuscan temples complement the exquisite vista.

PLACES OF INTEREST
Helmsley Castle
Rievaulx Terrace
Rievaulx Abbey
Nunnington Hall
Kilburn White Horse
Sutton Bank
Shandy Hall
Castle Howard
St Gregory's Minster, Kirkdale

WALKS IN THE AREA
Rievalux Abbey from Helmsley Simply follow the signposted path behind the Feversham Arms, through Duncombe Park and Whinny Bank Wood as far as the abbey. Climb up to Rievaulx Terrace for the best view before returning along the same route.

Collier Hag Wood and Ash Dale Take the Roppa road for a few hundred yards out of Helmsley and then left into Elton Gill. Turn right and follow the stream north along a footpath, then right where the side stream flows out of Collier Hag Wood. Follow the latter until a path leads uphill on the right to Middle Baxton's Farm. Left on the road for ½ mile then right by a lane as far as Ash Dale Plantation. Left on a path for the 1¾ miles back to Helmsley.

Rye Dale Riverside paths follow both banks of the Rye as far as Rye House Farm. It is possible to link up with other tracks as far as Nunnington and beyond.

Riccal Dale Footpaths and forest drives follow both sides of this heavily-wooded dale. Several cross-valley tracks may be used to link the main paths and combinations of routes can developed to suit most requirements.

Helmsley village

The Yorkshire Dales

THWAITE (SWALEDALE)

North Yorkshire

OS Map: 1:50,000 Sheet Nos 91 and 98

Location

From Hawes and the A684 follow the Buttertubs road to Thwaite. Or by the B6270; 20 miles west from Richmond (A1) or 12 miles east from Kirkby Stephen. (Kirkby Stephen is 12 miles from Tebay — Junction 38, then A685).

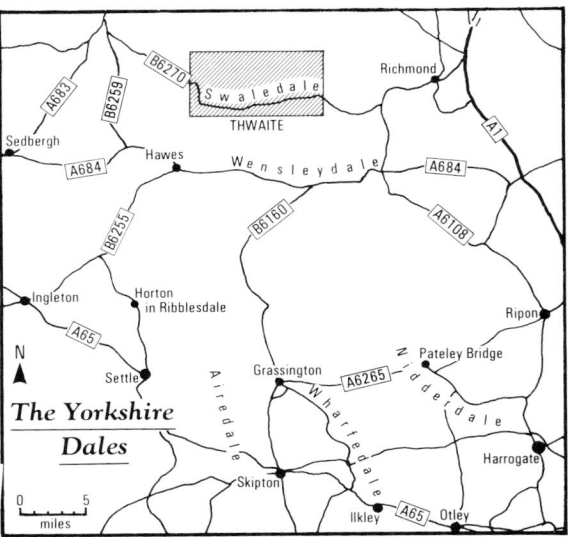

Narrowest of all the main Pennine dales, Swaledale was once important for its lead mines, but now it is the quietest and grandest, reckoned by many to be the best of all the dales. Almost anywhere along its upper reaches, Swaledale can offer views unsurpassed the length and breath of the country. Its river, the Swale, starts among peat bogs, 2,000ft up on Birkdale Common, almost on Yorkshire's boundary with Cumbria. The Swale soon becomes a wild exuberant stream and keeps this youthful appearance almost as far as Reeth. In fact it is not fully mature until it slows down in the

Arkengarthdale

◁ *Horton in Ribblesdale church with Penyghent in the distance*

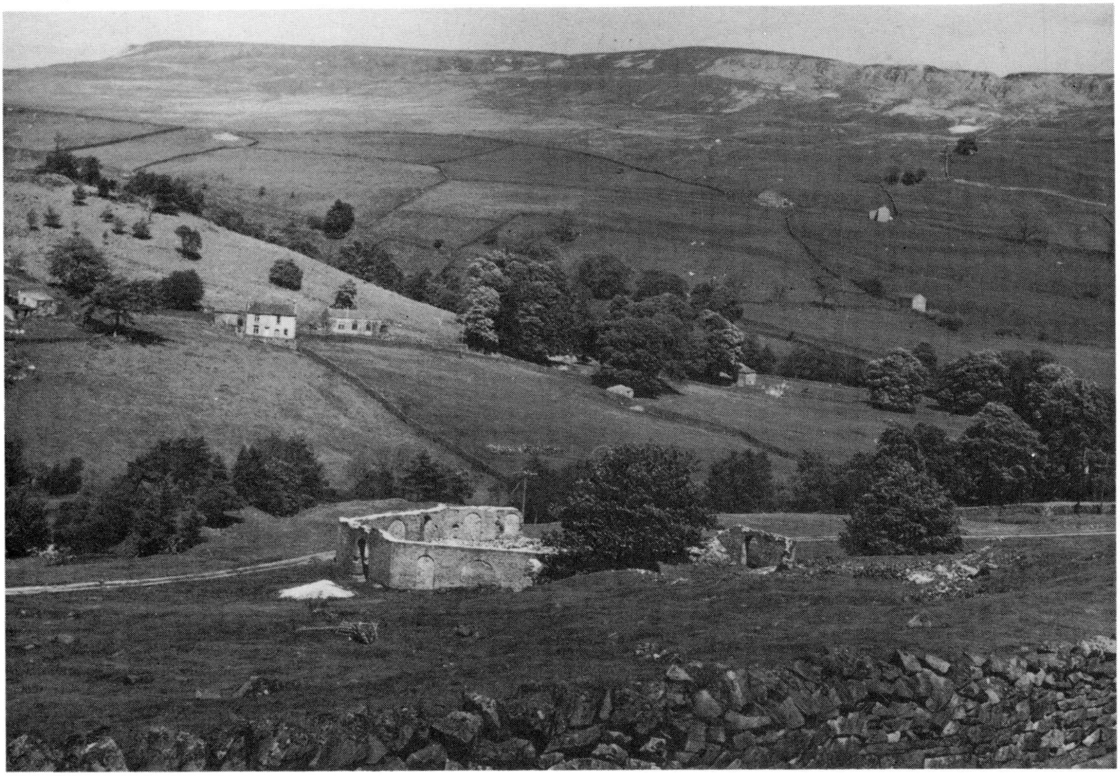

Muker

broad Vale of York.

The acid moorlands of the enclosing fells are in stark contrast to the lush pastures of the valley bottom. Moors support few sheep and modern interest is mostly confined to raising grouse. Habitation is restricted to the valley bottom; villages still retain a flavour of their Viking heritage. Stonebuilt farmhouses standing four square against the elements are built in a traditional design which has remained unchanged for many centuries. Many still have the family and animal accommodation under one roof, snug places insulated by a hayloft above the cowbyre. This is a practical design made of necessity in a dale where winters can be long and hard.

Every village in the dale has its special character and charm, but Thwaite is superior to them all. Approached up-dale over a humpbacked road bridge, the cluster of houses break all the rules of modern town planning, but as a result hit the senses with their appeal. *Thwaite* is old Norse, meaning 'a clearing in woodland', but today there is very little woodland throughout the dale, except for shelter belts. One of the eye-catching features of Upper Swaledale is the number of barns or 'laithes' which dot the fellsides. This is another and more tangible legacy of the Viking settlement of the dale. Almost within living memory, a method of farming husbandry still common in

Norway and the Alps was practised in the upper dale. Based on these barns, hay was stored in the upper storey with the lower section housing three or four cattle throughout the winter. Nowadays cattle are kept in and around the valley farms all year round, with the barns used mainly for hay storage.

PLACES OF INTEREST
Kisdon Force Stepped waterfall 1½ miles north of Thwaite.
Buttertubs Small pot holes by the Hawes road.
Arkengarthdale Remains of lead mines.
Reeth Centre for lead mining in Swaledale.
Swaledale Museum Reeth
Maiden Castle (GR022981). Ancient earthwork.

WALKS IN THE AREA
Kisdon Hill Pennine Way to Kisdon Farm. Turn left at the farm for the path around Kisdon Hill as far as Keld. Return by the Pennine Way alongside the River Swale.
Swaledale riverside walk A series of footpaths follow the river downstream from Thwaite as far as Grinton and can be followed as far as you chose.
Gunnerside A series of miners' tracks contour the valley to the north of the village and follow both sides of Gunnerside Gill.

HAWES (WENSLEYDALE)

Yorkshire

OS Map: 1:50,000 Sheet No 98

Location

The A684 conveniently links the A1 and the M6. From the A1, join the A684 at Leeming Bar and Hawes is at the dale head. If using the M6 leave this at Junction 37 to follow the A684 through Sedburgh over Garsdale Head.

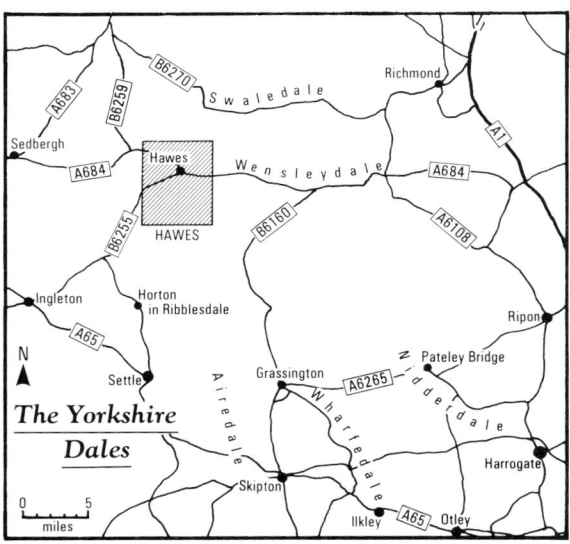

The Yorkshire Dales

The old name for Wensleydale was Yoredale after its river the Ure, but now only a few of the older people use that name. Hawes lies in a sheltering fold of the fells almost at the end of the rich pasture of the valley bottom; this is where local farmers congregate for Tuesday markets. The weekly livestock sales account for about 10,000 sheep and lambs, and 12,000 cattle changing hands each year, with the major sheep and lamb sales taking place from August to October.

Cheese, and in particular the local Wensleydale variety, was traditionally made by farmers' wives. Although you can occasionally find the true farmhouse product, most the Wensleydale cheese sold locally is made at Gayle. Not that this is in any way an inferior product; it is, however, a pity that the traditional craft is dying out.

One craft which remains as strong as ever is that of rope making. The small hand operated ropeworks, close by the old station yard in Hawes, has been producing rope halters and other short lengths of specialised ropes for many years. Visitors are welcomed to the ropeworks where they can watch the various stages of this fascinating craft.

The nearby old station buildings have been converted into a Yorkshire Dales National Park Information Centre and also the Upper Dales Folk Museum. The latter is based on the Marie Hartley and Joan Ingilby collection of artifacts and bygones from dale farms in the locality.

Hawes is a corruption of *haus*, an Anglo-Saxon word meaning a mountain pass (Hawes is almost at the top of Wensleydale). The use of this word is quite commonly encountered in the Lake District. Nearby Gayle has Norse associations; in fact the whole of Upper Wensleydale was settled by Norsemen. They have left their mark with place names ending in 'sett'. Villages and hamlets like Burtersett, Countersett and Marsett all tell of the onetime norse 'saetre' (meaning a small mountain farm) which once stood on the spot.

The only heavily-used path in the area is the Pennine Way. This passes through Hawes and crosses the dale on its way to Shunner Fell and Swaledale. Miles of other quiet and little-used footpaths line the dale bottom or wander over the fellsides. These offer lots of scope, whether it be a tough all-day walk or a short ramble from the car.

PLACES OF INTEREST

National Park Information Centre Old Station Yard, Hawes.
Upper Dales Folk Museum Old Station Yard, Hawes.
Hawes Ropeworks Old Station Yard, Hawes.
Hardrow Force Highest above-ground waterfall in England.
Semerwater 1½ miles south of Bainbridge. Natural lake.

WALKS IN THE AREA

Gayle to Burtersett Walk uphill from Gayle by the Duerley road. Beyond the last houses a signposted path on the left leads over the fields to Burtersett. Return by way of further field paths north of the village, across Bainbridge Ings to Hawes.
Widdale A footpath, starting about a ¼ mile west of Hawes, turns left away from the A684, crosses Spillon Green to join the Appersett road in Widdale. Turn left and follow the road past its junction with the B6255. Walk on for a little over

Hardrow Force

¼ mile and turn right on to a footpath which crosses the valley and climbs to Appersett Pasture. Follow it as far as Appersett village. Follow the A684 back to Hawes.

Abbotside Common Take the Pennine Way as far as Hardrow. Turn right and climb the Thwaite road for about 1½ miles. About 200yd beyond a roadside barn on the left, turn right to follow the fellside path across Abbotside Common.

Continue downhill to Sedbusk and return to Hawes by field paths.

Cam Pasture and Burtersett Follow the Pennine Way south by the green road to Cam Pasture. At the T junction with the Roman road beyond Dodd's Fell, turn left and walk as far as the metalled road above Bardale Head. Turn left along the latter, then right to cross Drumaldrace and left down across Burtersett High Pasture into Burtersett.

AYSGARTH (WENSLEYDALE)

North Yorkshire

OS Map: 1:50,000 Sheet No 98

Location
The A684 Northallerton – Kendal road runs through Aysgarth and the village is about 23 miles east from the M6 (Junction 37), and 18 miles west from the A1 (Leeming Bar).

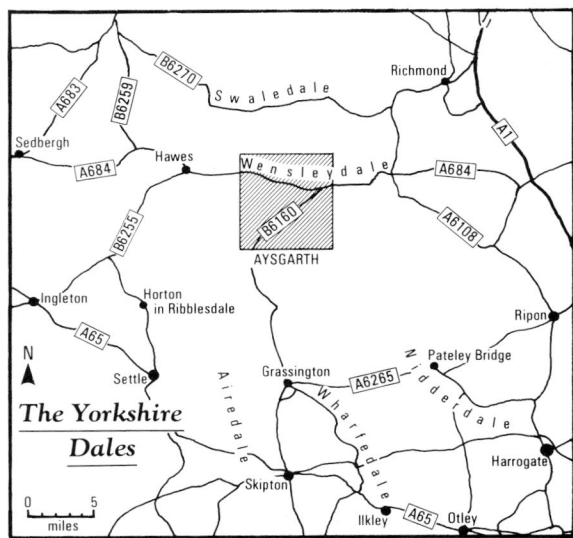

Aysgarth's best known features are the waterfalls or forces, to give them their local name, which step the river Ure a mile or so either side of the village bridge. This typical dales village has been featured on more than one occasion in the highly successful TV series *All Creatures Great and Small.* Life goes on at an unhurried pace despite the busy A684 and the quota of visitors who come to enjoy the delights of the river bank.

History has touched this tranquil dale; it was at nearby Castle Bolton that Mary Queen of Scots was imprisoned for six months in 1568. During the Civil War, Colonel Clayton held the castle against Cromwellian troops for over a year in 1645, before starvation forced the garrison to surrender.

Valley walking is probably better around Aysgarth than elsewhere in the dales. Quiet tracks run up and down stream and also nearby Bishopdale

is virtually unexplored. Fells climb to remote heights above the dales, and all have a network of ancient tracks.

North of Aysgarth, relics of lead mining are encountered; for centuries this industry brought prosperity to the area. Lead mining reached its zenith during the nineteenth century when the rapidly growing industrial towns of the north demanded huge quantities of lead for use in house building and plumbing, a demand which soon outstripped the available supplies. Cheaper imports and dwindling resources led to eventual closure of the mines.

Aysgarth Falls

Ennerdale, Lake District

Duddon Valley, Lake District

Hadrian's Wall at Housesteads, Northumbria

Rievaulx Abbey, North York Moors

Castle Bolton with Bishopdale in the distance

Many of the moorland tracks were created to give access to the old lead mines, and walks along their routes can often give an insight into the mining methods employed in days gone by. Ruined shafts and spoil heaps are easily identifiable, but what of the scarred ravines in the upper valleys? Most of these are 'hushes', a system whereby dammed-up waters were released to wash, or hush, away surface layers. With this method the mining prospectors could tell what riches lay beneath. Even today, samples of shining ore or spar crystals can be found in and around streambeds. **Do not on any account try to enter the mines, as the timbers which once shored them up have all rotted, with the result that the shafts are now in a dangerous condition.**

WALKS IN THE AREA
Aysgarth to Askrigg   A riverside walk as far as Askrigg starts at the old station car park. Cross the valley and the A684 to return by the old road through Thornton Rust.

Bishopdale   Numerous tracks and footpaths line the sides of this quiet valley.
Aysgarth Woods and waterfalls   Follow the signposted paths from the car park.
Stake Allotments   Walk south from Aysgarth and uphill by road as far as Thoralby. Turn right through the village and climb Thoralby Common to Stake Allotments. Turn left along the green road across Stake Moss and join the B6160 road at its highest point (1,376ft). Turn left and follow this road as far as Myers Garth, on the right just beyond a roadside telephone box. Left again to join the valley path past New House, Rookery Cottage and eventually Thoralby.

PLACES OF INTEREST
Aysgarth Falls
Carriage Museum   A collection of horse-drawn vehicles housed in Aysgarth Mill.
Aysgarth Church
National Park Information Centre
Nature Trail
Castle Bolton   4½ miles north-east of Aysgarth.

HORTON IN RIBBLESDALE

North Yorkshire

OS Map: 1:50,000 Sheet No 98
1:25,000 Three Peaks Outdoor Leisure
Map

Location

From the West Riding or north-east Lancashire aim for the A65, follow this as far as Settle and take the B6479 along the Ribble Valley to Norton.

If travelling by the M6, leave it at Lancaster (Junction 34) and follow the A683 along the Lune Valley. Turn right at the A687 just south of Tunstall, right at the junction with the A65 which is followed as far as Ingleton, left on the B6255 to Ribblehead and right for the B6479.

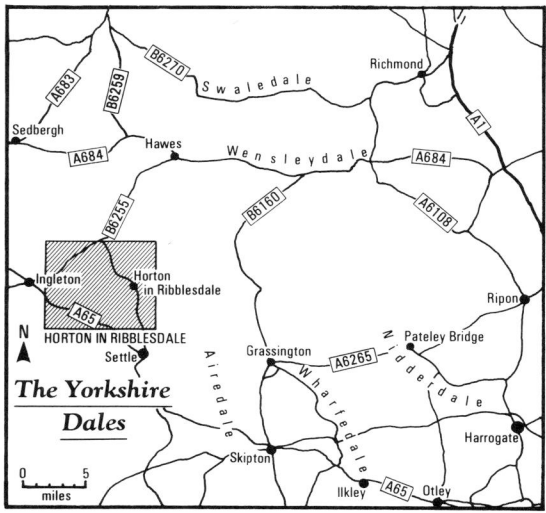

On fine summer weekends Horton in Ribblesdale can look almost like a transit camp. This is a favourite place to start and finish the gruelling Three Peaks Walk. Twenty-four miles and 4,750ft of ascent on a route which crosses Penyghent, Whernside and Ingleborough, a tough challenge over some of the highest fells in the Yorkshire Dales. The Pennine Way also passes through Horton, so as well as hosting Three Peaks walkers, Horton is an obvious place for Pennine Wayfarers to take stock of the situation. Almost 100 miles from the southern end, it is not uncommon for first-time walkers going north, often overburdened with excess gear, to call it a day on reaching Horton.

Those who decide to spend some time in Horton and explore the alternatives to the tougher walks are usually in for a pleasant surprise. Miles of limestone moors and remote fells, criss-crossed by footpaths and ancient green roads, can occupy many hours with enjoyable walking.

Green roads, a major feature of this area, are the old arteries of communication between the upper dales' farms and villages. Designed as drove roads for cattle movement or pack-horse tracks, their grassy surfaces offer miles of easy and comfortable walking. Many have been upgraded into motor roads, but there are still several which would be recognisable even today to travellers of a century ago. Two excellent examples leave Horton; one crosses Birkwith Moor on its way to Langstrothdale.

The other is over Foxup Moor to Littondale. Short stretches of both green roads are followed by the Pennine Way and probably offer the easiest walking of the whole route.

This is limestone country, and a quick glance along the valley side will soon give the visitor an appreciation of how the area is exploited by quarrying. Fortunately we can quickly leave the vicinity of the quarries, but cannot help feeling disappointment in the fact that these operations must take place in such a lovely area. It is an unfortunate fact that limestone, which gives us such wonderful scenery, is a necessary commodity for road building and cement making.

PLACES OF INTEREST

Pot Holes (**Note** Do not attempt to explore any caves and pot holes in the area unless you are experienced in this dangerous sport).

Norber Boulders (Between Clapham and Austwick) Curiously situated boulders perched on other rock formations, left by retreating glaciers.

Penyghent Hill 2,273ft

Horton Church Typical dales church. The slate, limestone and lead used in its construction all came from local sources.

Ribbleshead Viaduct Carries the controversial Settle – Carlisle railway across some of the most dramatic scenery in the Pennines.

White Scar Cave Public show cave 2 ¼ miles north-east of Ingleton by the side of the B6255.

Penyghent Pinnacle

WALKS IN THE AREA

The best and least used walking areas are across Moughton and Sulber Scars to the west.

Penyghent can be climbed by the most enjoyable and least used route by way of Brackenbottom Farm and Fawcett Moor.

Providing you do not try to enter them, the cave system and pot holes on Horton Moor to the north of the village, can be reached along the green lanes mentioned earlier.

By linking up quiet roads and tracks, it is possible to walk downstream as far as Settle.

MALHAM (AIREDALE)

North Yorkshire

OS Map: 1:50,000 Sheet No 98
1:25,000 Outdoor Leisure Map,
Malham and Upper Wharfedale

Location

From the West Riding: A650 via Kieghley and
A629 to Skipton; or A65 via Ilkley to Skipton.
From Skipton follow the A65 to Gargrave and
turn right for the minor road — signposted — to
Malham.

From north-east Lancashire: A56 from Colne
to Skipton and then A65 as above. (Skipton may
be bypassed by taking the minor road from
Broughton to Gargrave).

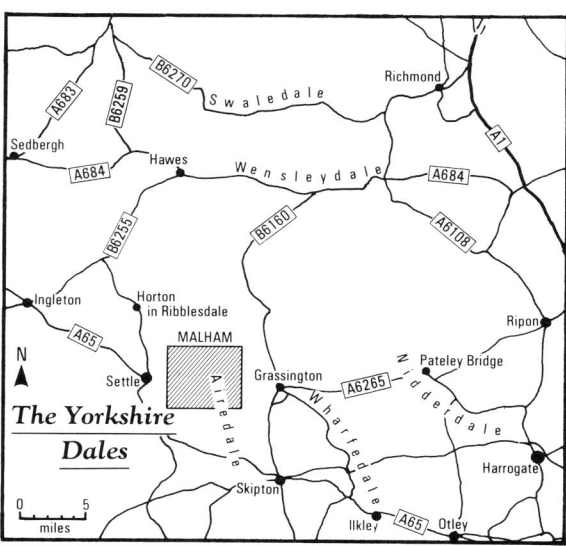

The Yorkshire Dales

Although the honeypots of Malham Cove and
Gordale Scar attract more than their fair share of
tourists, as witness the necessary footpath repairs
in the area, the reason for the inclusion of Malham
in a guide to the Byways of Britain is that there is
ample scope for those wanting to escape from the
crowds. There are miles of often solitary walking
to be found in and around this beautiful area.

For anyone who has yet to discover Malham,
the main attractions are the Cove and Gordale
Scar. Dramatic Gordale Scar, about a mile north-
east of Malham, is a collapsed cave system and the
Cove is a huge amphitheatre of limestone cliffs at
the base of which bubbles a stream. This is not, as
some believe, the source of the Aire, but a
tributary which has travelled a short distance
underground. The main source of the Aire starts
further away at Malham Tarn, only to disappear
underground and reappear about ½ mile south of
Malham village. Charles Kingsley used Malham
Cove as the setting for his novel *The Water Babies*,
a work which showed something of the way in
which children were exploited in the nineteenth
century.

Away from the Cove and Scar, the crowds soon
thin and the walker is left to enjoy the moorland
delights surrounding Malham. Truly remote
country opens up on the heights above Malham
Tarn. This is a place where, even on the hottest
summer day, there will be a breeze of sorts. This is
a countryside of huge vistas and cloudscapes. To
the west of the village, Ewe Moor leads on to
Kirkby Fell and eventually down to Settle. North,

the 'flatlands' of Malham Lings and the uniquely-
formed tarn soon give way to rocky heights where
the curlew will be the only company a solitary
walker can expect to find. East across Malham
Moor, the ancient track of Mastiles Lane leads
into Littondale by way of Kilnsey Crag.

PLACES OF INTEREST
Malham Cove
Malham Tarn
Gordale Scar
National Park Information Centre Malham Car Park
Gargrave Leeds – Liverpool canal
Ewe Moor Remains of lead and zinc mining activity.
Janet's Foss and Nature Trail

WALKS IN THE AREA
Ewe Moor from Malham Cove Climb the path up the left side (facing) of the cove. Turn right across the limestone 'pavement' and then left up the dry valley to Malham Tarn. Turn left along the road as far as the crossroads. A footpath climbs the fellside opposite, follow it and turn left after about 1½ miles, then left again on joining the Settle path.

Mastiles Lane Walk up the road just past Gordale Scar, or climb the steep rocky outcrop and waterfall of Gordale Scar and join Mastiles Lane near Street Gate. This rough road, walled for most of its length, runs as far as Kilnsey.

High Mark from Malham Tarn From Street Gate on Mastiles Lane aim north-east for High Mark. A full day can be spent wandering amongst the crags and clints of Flock Rake as far as Parson's Pulpit. Return by way of Great Close. **Note** There are few if any footpaths above High Mark, so do not attempt this walk in bad weather.

Wedber Wood and Janet's Foss This often-neglected path is well signposted from the centre of Malham village, and follows Gordale Beck upstream to Wedber Wood and the delightful waterfall of Janet's Foss. Above the Foss a field path leads to Gordale Scar. Plaques in and around Wedber Wood explain the geology and plant life seen on the walk.

Limestone pavement above Malham Cove

Mastiles Lane

KETTLEWELL

North Yorkshire

OS Map: 1:50,000 Sheet No98
1:25,000 Outdoor Leisure Map,
Map, Malham and Upper Wharfedale

Location

Kettlewell is in Upper Wharfedale, about two miles north of the junction with Littondale. Road access is from Ilkley and the West Riding conurbations by A65 to Addingham, then B6160 to Kettlewell. Or from Skipton and north-east Lancashire by B6265 and join the B6160 at Threshfield.

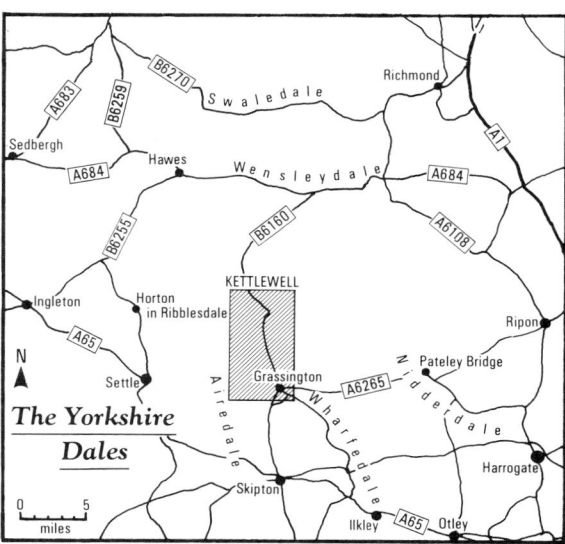

The Yorkshire Dales

Some of the best dales scenery of all the Pennines is in the upper reaches of Wharfedale. Delius, the Yorkshire composer, managed to capture its feel and tranquillity by describing its meadows and woodlands or the wild beauty of the moors, in many of his compositions. His *North Country*

Sketches speaks evocatively of the march of the four seasons in this wild yet gentle dale. He never admitted that this piece was based on any particular dale or moor, but those who listen to it and know Wharfedale, especially the part around

Kettlewell, can recapture happy memories of this fine bit of Pennine scenery.

Kettlewell's name has nothing to do with kettles; it is Norse for 'bubbling spring'. Standing at the junction of two ancient and important moorland routes, it was once a staging post on the coach route from London to Richmond by way of Skipton. In those days travel was far from comfortable; whichever way the coach left Wharfedale, it faced a steep climb. The route used by the modern B6160 across Cow Pasture above Cray is steeper than 1 in 7, but the route over Park Rash is even worse at 1 in 4. In coaching days it meant that passengers not only walked, but helped to push the coach.

One of the best features of the dale is the way in which traditional hospitality has been maintained, from innkeeper to innkeeper, to the present time. Comfortable accommodation is plentiful, the only problem being that once visitors have discovered their favourite place, they tend to keep coming back time after time, but by booking in advance, or even taking pot luck, the right place can usually be found, and the welcome is always warm.

The dale sides are steep, but well-defined and ancient paths climb to open fells which offer unlimited scope for good high-level wandering. In contrast, valley walking through meadows and along the riverside is gentle.

PLACES OF INTEREST
Kilnsey Crag
Dales' Centre Grassington
Upper Wharfedale Museum Grassington
Stump Cross Cavern (B6265)

WALKS IN THE AREA
Kettlewell to Buckden A pleasant riverside stroll.
Conistone Moor This path climbs steeply above Crookacre Wood, and aims south-east to Conistone Moor. Return by the moor lane to Conistone village then follow the road back to Kettlewell.
Cam Head and Buckden Pike Take the Cam Pasture lane out of Kettlewell and follow the moor edge beyond Cam Head to Buckden Pike. Return by way of Cam Gill Beck and Starbotton village. **Note** This walk is not recommended in mist or bad weather.
Middlesmoor Pasture, Old Cote Moor, Firth Fell, Buckden Use the Arncliff path due west from Kettlewell. At the top of the climb turn right to follow the crest of the ridge across Old Cote Moor to Firth Fell. Join the path from Litton to Buckden by turning right to walk downhill to the Buckden village. Follow the valley path back to Kettlewell.

Kilnsey Crag

Kettlewell,
◁ *across the River Wharfe*

PATELEY BRIDGE (NIDDERDALE)

North Yorkshire

OS Map: 1:50,000 Sheet No 99

Location

From Ripon take the B6265 south-west to
Glasshouses and turn right on the B6165 —Pateley
Bridge is about 2½ miles from here. Or from
Harrogate follow the A61 north to Ripley and
then turn left on the B6165. From Skipton take
the A59 east to Dangerous Corner and then left on
B6451 to Summer Bridge. Turn left for Pateley
Bridge.

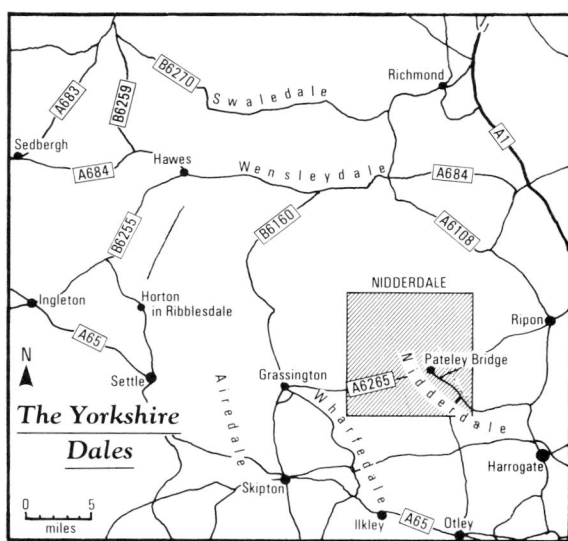

Despite being so close to Harrogate, Nidderdale is
comparatively unknown. A pleasant dale, wide
and welcoming, it has plenty of features to
surprise every visitor.

Pateley Bridge, the attractive sun trap, hosts
picnickers on a fine summer's day and many come
to watch the high standard of the local cricket
team, or maybe just to enjoy the tranquil scene.
Without doubt the best-known natural features
of this dale are the curious weather-worn rocks
above Pateley Bridge. These are Brimham Rocks;
they are made from different strata of millstone
grit with varying degrees of hardness. As a result of
this difference in hardness the rocks have been
worn into all manner of fantastic shapes. They
first became popular in Victorian times when
visitors to the nearby spa town of Harrogate came
to see them as a change from taking the waters.
Following this popularity, a whole list of fanciful
names have been given to the rocks. Names
ranging from the 'Dancing Bear' to the 'Idol'
describe the strange shapes which abound in their
moorland setting.

Nidderdale was once the scene of industries
associated with lead mining. Ore from the extensive
veins deep beneath the western moors was graded
and smelted around Pateley Bridge, but little now
remains apart from the name of Smelthouses, the
village below Brimham Rocks where the ore was
converted into usable metal. Stump Cross Caverns
close by on the B6255 were discovered by lead
miners.

When Gouthwaite and Scar House Reservoirs
were being built for Bradford Corporation, a light
railway was installed to move materials up this
remote dale. When the reservoirs were completed

'The Dancing Bear', Brimham Rocks

How Stean Gorge ▷

the line continued to operate, carrying goods and passengers. This was the only municipally-run railway in the country, but it closed in 1929.

Moorland birds and waterfowl were quick to realise the attractiveness of Gouthwaite Reservoir and today it and the surrounding area has been designated as a nature reserve.

To complete the range of attractions for all interests, How Stean Gorge, a narrow side valley at the head of Nidderdale, has been skilfully adapted as a Visitor Centre by the provision of bridges and walkways.

PLACES OF INTEREST
Stump Cross Caverns
Foster Beck Mill   Fishing.
Nidderdale Museum   Pateley Bridge.
Brimham Rocks   (National Trust)
How Stean Gorge   Visitor Centre

WALKS IN THE AREA
Brimham Rocks   Several footpaths lead from the valley to the rocks. The best approach is from Pateley Bridge, following a series of linking paths below the B6265 as far as Cliff Top. The area of the rocks is entered across the small wooded valley.

Nidderdale   A riverside path follows the Nidd all the way from Gouthwaite Reservoir, through Pateley Bridge and Summer Bridge to Birstwith. Walk as far as you wish, but make sure that you know the times of the infrequent bus service or arrange transport back.

In Moor   A pleasant moorland walk can be enjoyed from Middlesmoor, at the head of Nidderdale, as far as Scar House Reservoir. Return by following the river along one of the three easy tracks down the valley.

Panorama Walk — Pateley Bridge   This walk is well signposted from the centre of the village and offers some of the finest views in Yorkshire.

Dacre Bank to Pateley Bridge   Probably the least used footpath in the dale, but still easy to follow by a route which starts close to Dacre Banks Youth Hostel and climbs to Heyshaw before turning north and descending Guise Cliff. Walk through Guisecliff Wood and then down to the road where a short walk leads to Pateley Bridge.

BOLTON ABBEY (WHARFEDALE)

North Yorkshire

OS Map: 1:50,000 Sheet No 104

Location

From Ilkley and the A65, take the B6160 to
Bolton Abbey. Or from Skipton or Harrogate via
the A59 to Bolton Bridge, the abbey and its village
are about ¾ mile north on the B6160.

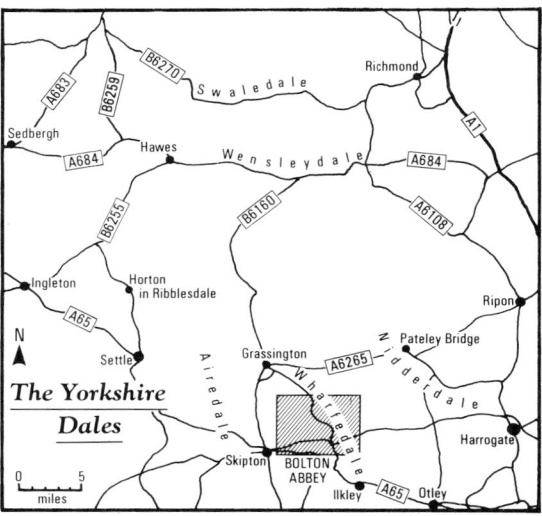

The Yorkshire Dales

Another popular area, but one where the majority
of its visitors are content to picnic or wander
around the ruins of Bolton Abbey. A few may
venture along the well-laid out paths as far as the
Strid, but for the enthusiastic walker the rest of the
area is open to their solitary enjoyment.

The abbey, or priory, to give it its correct title,
was once the home for a community of Augustinian
canons, but in 1539 the building was wrecked, its
treasures confiscated and the brothers sent away.
This act of apparent vandalism was carried out by
officers acting for Henry VIII, who following his
quarrel with Rome, dissolved all the major
ecclesiastical establishments in England. The nave
was spared destruction and is still used as the
parish church for Bolton Abbey village.

The dale and most of the surrounding moors are
owned by the Chatsworth Estates on behalf of the
Duke of Devonshire. Walking is permitted on
most of the paths in the area, except during days
when grouse shooting takes place. These dates are
published by the Yorkshire Dales National Park
and are also advertised on notices pinned to
strategic gateposts and notice boards around the
dale.

A walk, especially in spring, through Bolton
Abbey Woods can be a delight. Wood anemones
and bluebells fill the gaps between newly-leafed
trees. At this time, the delicate green of the new
growth is a beautiful contrast to the autumn
grandeur later in the year.

The Strid is the Wharfe's most famous — some
say infamous — spot; this is where the river is
restricted in a deep narrow trench. The temptation
to 'strid' or stride across it should be resisted as it is
wider than most people can cross by a standing
jump.

The Dales Way, one of the best and certainly
most varied long distance footpaths, follows
Wharfedale from Ilkley to the Wharfe's source.

The way then crosses the high moors of Cam Fell
and on to the Lake District, finishing at Bowness-
on-Windermere.

Accommodation ranging from bed and break-
fast to stone tents can be found along the way, and
a bus service, 'Parklink — Wharfedale', runs
along the dale in summer.

The Strid

The ruins of Bolton Abbey reflected in the River Wharfe

PLACES OF INTEREST
Bolton Abbey ruins
The Strid
Nature Trails
Barden Tower
Yorkshire Dales Railway   Embsay
Ilkley Moor

WALKS IN THE AREA
Valley of Desolation   Cross the river opposite the priory ruins and turn left (upstream). Follow the signposted path into the Valley of Desolation.
Simon's Seat   Continue the previous walk by following the path across Barden Fell to Simon's Seat. Return by way of Howgill and the Barden road.

Barden Moor   Follow the footpath north-west from Bolton Abbey village through Westy Bank Wood. Cross over the Embsay – Barden road and walk along the track starting on the opposite side of the road. At Hutchingill Head turn left and walk downhill to Eastby. Turn left in the village and then right at a fork in the lane beyond the pub; follow this as far as a barn and where the lane turns sharply to the left, continue ahead on a footpath to Halton East. A quiet road leads back to Bolton Abbey.
The Strid and Bolton Abbey Woods   Well-signposted footpaths follow nature trails each side of the river between Bolton Abbey and Barden Bridge.

The Peak District

HIGH BRADFIELD
AND THE EWDEN VALLEY

South Yorkshire

OS Map: 1:50,000 Sheet No 110

Location

Situated due east of the Derwent Reservoir. From A57 (Ladybower Reservoir to Sheffield road) turn north at Moscar (GR235877). Pass the Strines Inn and take the next turn right for Low Bradfield and High Bradfield.

The Bradfield Moors represent the eastern extremity of the moorland belt, better known for the parts to the west. The latter consist of Kinder Scout and Bleaklow with their bleak peat hags and generally inhospitable terrain. At Bradfield, the moors are considerably lower, with a certain degree of cultivation, especially in the more sheltered areas. The moor has deeply incised valleys which cut into it, draining the area to the east. These are the Ewden Valley and Bradfield Dale, and the top end of the Loxley Valley. Both of

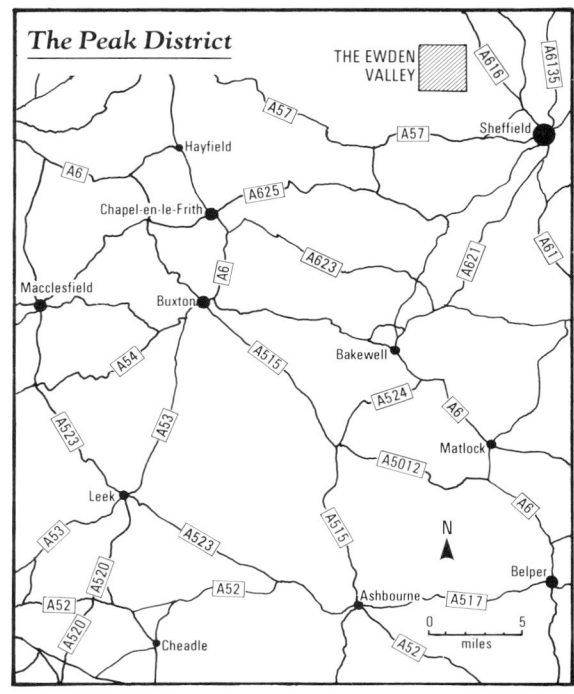

Gibraltar Quarry, High Bradfield

The Watch House, High Bradfield

these valleys have been dammed to provide water for the Sheffield area. There are two dams across the Ewden Beck and four across the river Loxley. The Dale Dike reservoir in Bradfield Dale was the scene of Britain's worst dam disaster. The dam collapsed, two days after its completion, on 11 March 1864, causing the death of 238 people, destroying over 600 buildings and 15 bridges.

Low and High Bradfield villages are pretty places, especially the former, while High Bradfield still retains the village stocks and a motte and bailey survives to the west of the village. It is a quiet area on the whole, except in Low Bradfield on a sunny weekend in summer. This is Sheffield's backyard but remains relatively unexplored by most visitors to the Peak. They miss the extensive views across the valleys, the peace and quiet and one of the most exhilarating walks in the Peak.

PLACES OF INTEREST

High Bradfield   Interesting thirteenth-century church with watch house at the church gate to deter bodysnatchers. Village stocks survive, also motte and bailey and Castle Hill.

Dale Dyke Reservoir   Bradfield Dale: site of Britain's worst dam disaster.

Bar Dyke   Defensive earthwork at SK246946.

Strines Inn   Fourteenth-century inn at SK222908.

Boots Folly   A distinctive tower on the opposite side of the valley from the popular Strines Inn. Access to the top now sealed off.

WALKS IN THE AREA

Park your car in High Bradfield. Proceed to the churchyard with its unusual 'watch house' (built to deter bodysnatchers). The signposted path starts behind the watch house to the right of the churchyard. Cross the churchyard and field beyond to enter the wood.

The path runs along a ledge above the steep valleyside, with its views down to Agden Reservoir. It descends slowly, turning sharp left to descend to the Rocher End Brook. Cross the brook and follow the yellow waymarked path across the fields beneath the old quarry. Climb the ladder stile and enjoy the pleasant stroll across flattish fields amid the oak trees with splendid views across to Bradfield Dale, over the reservoirs and on towards Boots Folly and the Strines Inn. Pass the ruined Rocher Head farmhouse, built in 1741, and take the farm track to the metalled road. Turn left and then right and proceed on to the Bar Dyke, possibly a Mercian defensive line against the Northumbrians. Just south of Bradfield Hall, turn right downhill past Wigtwizzle depot and through the wood to Broomhead Reservoir. The road runs down the side of the reservoir although views are spoilt by afforestation. Leave the valley to cross White Lee Moor to return to High Bradfield, with good views in all directions.

For a short walk, upon reaching the ladder stile, bear to the right and over another ladder stile. Walk beneath the old quarry and up the steps to join a cart track. Follow this until it reaches the road. Turn right and walk down hill to High Bradfield.

ALPORT DALE

Derbyshire

OS Map: 1:25,000 Dark Peak Outdoor Leisure
Map

Location

Situated off the A57 Glossop – Sheffield road to
the north of the Snake Road between Ladybower
Reservoir and the Snake Pass Inn.

The river Alport flows off Bleaklow, the upland
tract of grouse moor, peat hags and swampy
ground situated to the north of Kinder Scout. A
series of small streams collect in an area known as
the Swamp at Grains in the Water and flows down
Alport Dale and into the Woodland Valley and
Ladybower Reservoir. Amid the rough moorland,
Alport Dale remains an unspoilt oasis of peace and
quiet. It has a rugged character, particularly in the
winter when the cold chill of the wind strikes up
the valley and the river is full of rain or the
meltwater of a season's snow. Even when the
spring comes, the view down the dale often shows
streaks of snow and ice steadfastly remaining on
the north flank of Kinder Scout, sometimes until
June. This is however a delightful dale, unknown
to the majority of trippers attracted in their
hundreds to the nearby Derwent dams.

The valley is not very wide but its sides are high,
which is the essence of its grandeur, and it is this
grandness and the ruggedness which separate it
from gritstone dales of lower altitudes such as the
Dane Valley. The upper parts of the valley sides
are walls of exposed and weathered gritstone. An
important feature to look for is the immense mass
of gritstone known as The Tower. It stands
detached from the main escarpment and apparently
is slowly sliding away from it on a bed of shale. You
can in fact take a path quite close to it, high above
and to the east of Alport Castles Farm.

This farm is the home of the annual Alport
Lovefeast which is held on the first Sunday in July.
It commemorates the clergymen who were thrown
out of their living in Derby for refusing to accept
the Act of Uniformity in 1662. A remote barn
enabled them to continue their religious persuasion
far from the established church. The church
service is still held in the same barn.

Doctor's Gate Roman road, Coldharbour Moor

PLACES OF INTEREST

Derwent Dams   Three large dams impounding large tracts of water. Cycle hire facilities at Fairholmes, immediately below Derwent dam. A road runs up the entire length of the reservoirs.

Snake Pass   Carries the A57 between Manchester and Sheffield. Wild, open country with Snake Pass Inn, a former coaching inn, near the top.

Alport Castles and Tower   Dramatic gritstone escarpment and massive detached section caused by a huge landslip.

Doctor's Gate   Remains of a Roman road, now known as Doctor's Gate, can be seen running up Coldharbour Moor. Park at the top of the Snake Pass where it is crossed by the Pennine Way. Walk north up the Pennine Way about ¼ mile to a guidepost, which marks Doctor's Gate. Turn left or right to see the stone causeway complete with curb stones.

WALKS IN THE AREA

Despite the rigorous countryside around the valley, a walk up the dale is very easy. Park your car at Alport Bridge and climb over the stile. The path runs up the side of the river to another, wooden stile, and climbs up the hillside to the road that runs up the dale. This road reaches the A57 a little to the west of Alport Bridge and can be used as an alternative. It gives a more gradual slope, if needed. The road surfaced with stone chippings is a right of way also, as far as Alport Castles Farm. If you prefer, upon reaching the farm, you can take the path up the east side of the valley to Alport Castles at the rim of the valley, to see The Tower. The moors beyond are now open access where, for most of the year, you can wander at will.

If you are fit enough and kitted out properly, there is a circular route you can take to Alport Bridge. From Alport Castles, cross over Birchinlee Pasture and drop down through Ditch Clough Plantation to the road adjacent Howden Reservoir. Walk down past Howden Dam to the path which leaves the road at Wrenhey Coppice, half-way down Derwent Dam (GR168911). Take this path passed Lockerbrook Farm, Bellhagg Barn and Rowlee Farm to reach the A57, three-quarters of a mile down river from Alport Bridge. It needs to be stressed that these bleak and often inhospitable moors should only be crossed if you have adequate clothing, boots, maps and compass.

The Woodlands Valley from Alport Dale

WIN HILL, HOPE

Derbyshire

OS Map: 1:25,00 Dark Peak Outdoor Leisure
Map

Location

Win Hill is situated at the eastern end of the Vale
of Edale, with its northern flank partly inundated
beneath Ladybower Reservoir.

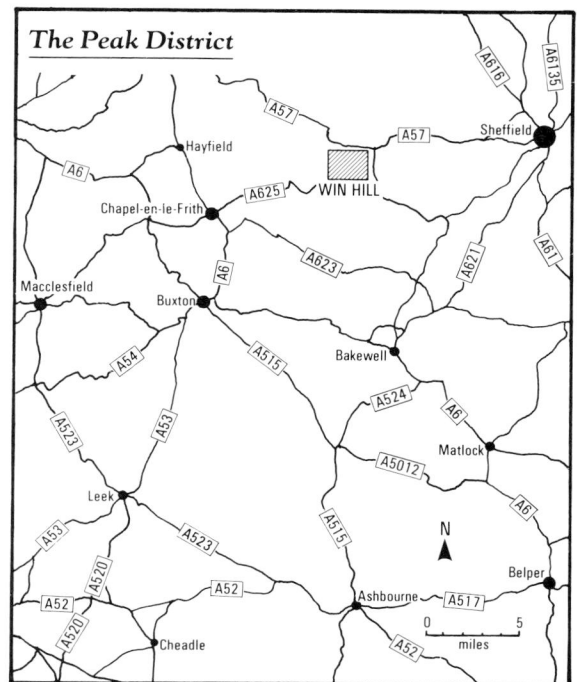

The Peak District

There are many short walks in the Peak and this
area is well known to some ramblers, especially
from the Sheffield area. It is, however, typical of
many in that it is not widely known. Win Hill
stands to the east of Lose Hill, the two conical hills
separated by the valley of the river Noe. Lose Hill,
with its ridgepath to Mam Tor and Rushup Edge
via Black Tor is reasonably well known, and the
two hills will be familiar to many visitors to the
Peak, whether they ramble or not. The Win Hill
path is perhaps not so generally well known.

Those who do walk around it soon begin to
share and appreciate its secret: the views from the
footpath, which are magnificent. Above Aston
village, there are uninterrupted views over to
Shatton and Abney Moors to the south. The Hope
Vale spreads below you with Castleton and Cave
Dale clearly visible and even the Winnats just
visible against the flank of Lose Hill. Along the
east side, the view stretches over Ladybower
Reservoir to the moors beyond and across the
Derwent Valley to Stanage Edge. To the north lies
the Woodland Valley and to the west, Edale, its
valley and Kinder Scout.

As one descends the path towards Hope village,
with its cement works beyond, a pronounced path
can be seen coming across the side of the hill to join
the descent to Hope. This is the former Roman
road descending to _Navio_, the Roman fort at
Brough. It connects Brough with another fort at
Glossop via Doctor's Gate, and good sections of it
lie preserved on Coldharbour Moor.

Although generally speaking the views are
excellent, there is one exception. This is on the
northern flank of the hill where there is a section of
path which follows the edge of Wiseman Hey
Clough Plantation. The trees preclude any view of
Ladybower, but the section is not too long and one
soon reaches the north flank of the hill and the
view over Edale and Kinder Scout.

PLACES OF INTEREST

Castleton Village Old lead mining village with Norman castle; several caves open to the public. Famous for ornaments in locally mined Blue John Stone.

Edale Village The start of the Pennine Way. National Park Information Centre.

The Winnats Impressive gorge at the head of the valley behind Castleton.

△
The path from Aston to Win Hill

The Edale Valley from Win Hill

WALKS IN THE AREA

Hope to Win Hill Park in Hope near to the Cheshire Cheese Inn situated alongside the road to Edale. From the pub, walk back towards Hope. Notice the mill dam on the river to your left, now becoming obscured by foliage. Just beyond here, bear left over the river Noe at Kilhill bridge and take the unmetalled road to the right which heads for Aston. The roadway is quite distinct and passes under the Sheffield – Manchester railway, and heads for Farfield Farm. Make sure you stop and look around you. The view gets better with altitude!

Eventually the road reaches a T junction. Turn left and walk up the lane beneath the shady foliage at Aston. Continue to GR187839, where there are two stone troughs at the junction with an unmade green road to your left. Follow the green road until it reaches open fields and head for the ladder stile at the far right of the upper end of the field. Beyond here, the path ranges to the right, climbing uphill up a pronounced holloway, carved by countless packhorses of a bygone era.

The holloway emerges on the top of the flank of Win Hill (where the views on a good day are magnificent). Join a well-worn track which heads for an afforested portion of the hillside with views to the east down to Yorkshire Bridge and up the Derwent valley to Ladybower Reservoir. Upon leaving the wood, with views up the flooded Woodland valley, the view becomes obscured by Win Hill on your left and the forest on your right. The path hugs the wood for about a mile and then bears left at GR173861. Follow this well-worn track which rounds the flank of Win Hill and emerges with a magnificent view both up and down the Edale valley; over towards Castleton village; to Bradwell and on towards Great Hucklow with gliders shimmering in the sunlight, rising on thermals above Hucklow Edge.

From here the path is downhill for about 1½ miles back to Hope. The total length of this path is about 5 miles, and it offers significant views over this part of the Peak. It does not have the restfulness of running water which paths down the Peakland valleys or dales can offer. Nonetheless, for a bracing walk with magnificent scenery it takes some beating, but must remain subservient to the Mam Tor to Lose Hill path used by thousands of visitors. Perhaps it is this which makes its inclusion a necessity.

PADLEY GORGE
AND THE LONGSHAW ESTATE

Derbyshire

OS Map: 1:25,000 White Peak Outdoor Leisure
Map covers majority of area

Location
Situated off the Grindleford – Sheffield road (the
A6011) above Grindleford station.

The Longshaw Estate of some 11,000 acres
belonging to the Duke of Rutland was sold in
1927, and much of the estate was purchased and
given to the National Trust. In addition to the
shooting lodge and its grounds, the estate included
a significant area of the eastern moors including
Padley Wood and Padley Gorge, through which
Burbage Brook descends towards the river Derwent
at Grindleford. It is an area well-known to
ramblers from the Sheffield district but not so well
known generally.

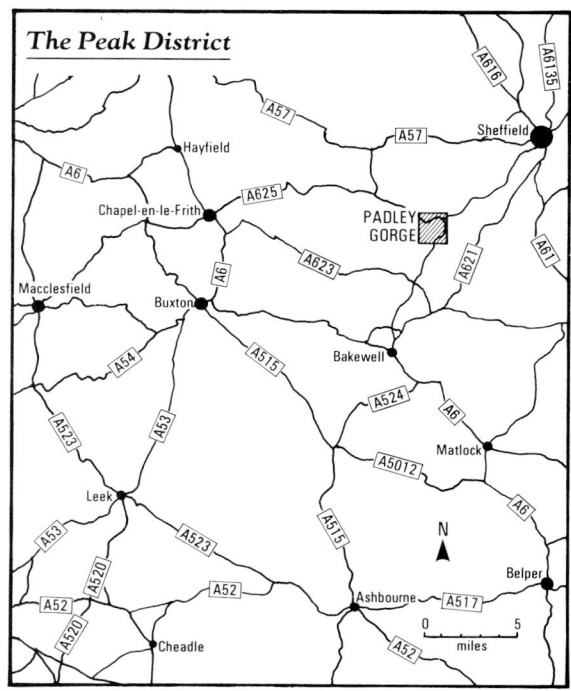

Burbage Brook

Padley Gorge, with is rushing white water
tumbling through the gritstone rocks and its
pleasant path, slowly climbing up the valley,
should not be missed. However, the beauty of the
estate is that there is much more to see. There is the
house itself, built in local gritstone and set next to
its lawn and lake against a backcloth of open
moorland. The house is privately let but the
visitor is still catered for with a National Trust
Information Centre, a shop and a cafeteria,
together with walks in the grounds.

Beyond the immediate grounds of the house
there is the path to Carl Wark, an Iron Age
hillfort, set in a bleak and open site with commanding views in all directions. This path also
leads on beyond Carl Wark up on to the edge of
the moor and on towards the Stanage Edge path, a
linear route that runs for miles up the edge of the
eastern moors. This path overlooks the Derwent
valley with extensive views into the Peak.

By joining the Hathersage road at the Fox House
Inn and turning towards Hathersage, one crosses
the Burbage Brook on a sharp bend where there is
also a curious rock formation. It is known as the
Toad's Mouth Rock and is situated on the north
side of the road. A few hundred yards beyond, the
road cuts through the gritstone edge at Surprise
View, with extensive views up the Derwent

Valley, the Vale of Hope and beyond. Just below here is a gate on the left and access onto the old cart track to Bole Hill Quarry, which provided much material for the building of the Ladybower Reservoir dam. At the trackside there are also literally hundreds of millstones now largely forgotten, relics of a bygone era.

PLACES OF INTEREST
Longshaw Lodge and Estate Former shooting lodge of Dukes of Rutland, now owned by the National Trust. Estate includes the beautiful Padley Gorge. Information centre and National Trust shop adjacent to the lodge.
Carl Wark Iron Age fort situated in a commanding position; defensive wall of large blocks of stone.
Hathersage Churchyard Contains the grave of Little John, Robin Hood's companion.
Padley Chapel Scene of annual pilgrimage to commemorate two Catholic martyrs.

WALKS IN THE AREA
Park off the road at SK263805 near to Fox House Inn. Walk along the pavement at the side of the A625. Ahead on the skyline you will see the Carl Wark hillfort. Proceed round the bend and cross the bridge over the Burbage Brook, past Toad's Mouth Rock and on for about a mile to Millstone

Edge and the appropriately named Surprise View. At SK248801 a stile on the left leads you off the road. It is easily identified by a National Trust sign marked 'Bole Hill'.

Walk down the well-marked path, past an old quarry and old millstones, and then the larger workings which supplied stone for Ladybower dam. The path crosses through a well-wooded area with extensive views across the Derwent Valley. Eventually the path descends through the wood to Upper Padley and Grindleford station, where you can join the main road from Grindleford to Fox House Inn. Walk up the road a little until you are above the railway line. Here a path leads off on your left into the wood. It is clearly defined and leads down to the Burbage Brook. The path crosses the brook and climbs up the valleyside a little, before leading you upstream through the wood. Eventually the path enters open fields and your car is roughly dead ahead. Cross the little wooden bridge and walk up through the plantation to rejoin the A625 near your car.

This area is well-known to Sheffield people, and also well used by them. It is included to bring the area to a wider audience. However, a word of advice! The Padley Gorge is well known for its waterfalls and rushing white waters, but it loses a lot of its beauty when the water level drops after prolonged dry weather.

Carl Wark and Higger Tor

EYAM MOOR, HIGHLOW BROOK AND BRETTON CLOUGH

Derbyshire

OS Map: 1:25,000 White Peak Outdoor Leisure
Map

Location
Situated north of Eyam village and north-west of
Grindleford.

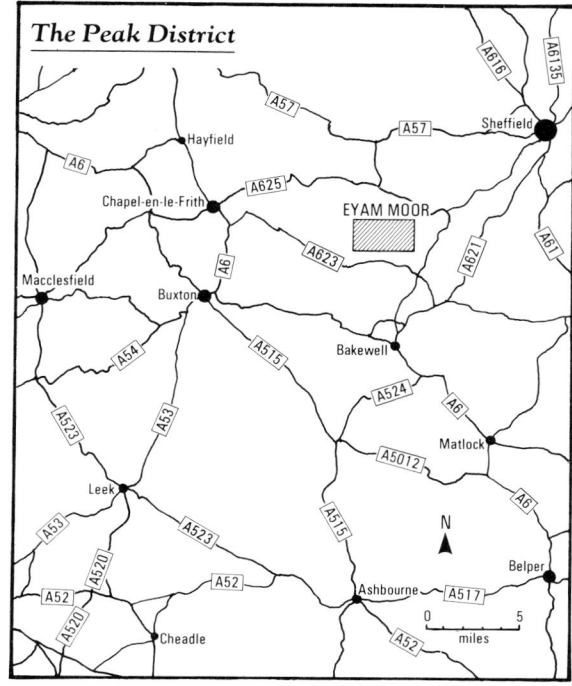

The Peak District

North of Eyam village lies an upland area, roughly
ten square miles in extent. It is bounded by
steeply-sloping ground on all sides, although the
western and southern edges are most dramatic.
Much of the area is uncultivated moorland, and
across it lies the valley of the Highlow Brook. This
deeply-cut valley is an attractive and relatively
little-known area. Two brooks, one flowing down
Abney Clough and the other flowing down
Bretton Clough, unite at Stoke Ford and then the
waters flow roughly eastwards towards the Derwent.
The area is well-wooded in the lower slopes of the
valley, with some cultivated land breaking the
hold of the fern and heather.

The walk described is one of contrasts, especially
true in the summer months. The walk along the
unmade roadway across Sir William Hill is
delightful for its display of how roadside verges
can be prolific in flowers when pollution is absent.
There is a fine view over Eyam towards the
Middleton and Longstone Moors. This section
contrasts greatly with the path across Eyam Moor

with its vegetation cover of heather and fern
although the view across the Derwent towards the
edges, Carl Wark and Millstone Edge Quarry is
particularly memorable.

From Hazelford the scenery changes yet again as
one turns up the valley, entering the larchwoods
and slowly descending to the river. This quiet and
secluded valley is reminiscent of the Gradbach
area and the Upper Dane Valley, although the
latter area is slightly superior to this one.

Bretton Clough

Plague Cottages, Eyam ▷

PLACES OF INTEREST

Eyam The Derbyshire plague village where 257 inhabitants died in 1665-6. Various cottages connected with the plague have plaques to commemorate this. In the church is a finely carved cross, complete with its head, of Celtic origins. Seventeenth-century hall with village stocks adjacent.

Hathersage In the churchyard is the grave of Little John, Robin Hood's friend. He is reputed to have been a nailer who lived in Hathersage.

Foolow A delightful village with a village pond, a fourteenth-century cross and (adjacent to the cross) a bull-baiting stone.

WALKS IN THE AREA

Park at SK210778 where the Eyam Edge road bears to the right and the partly-metalled road across Sir William Hill continues straight on. Walk along the track past the transmitter and drop to where the roadway joins this old track again.

Where the roads meet, take the path to the left across Eyam Moor, heading for Leam Wood and the road to Hazelford. The path is quite distinct as it crosses the moor. A look at the map indicates the numerous prehistoric cairns and stone circle on the moor — all unfortunately off the right of way. Upon reaching the road turn left and walk along the road, turning left along the track to Tor Farm. At the farm, continue on through the gate and across the fields. Skirt the larch plantation and head for a gate at the corner of the last field. Enter the larch wood (Highlow Wood) and follow the track down to the ford. Here the well-rutted track climbs up the hill through an oak wood to emerge amid the ferns on the side of Bolehill. As you gain height up Bolehill, the scenery gets progressively better. There is a good view across the valley towards the sixteenth-century Highlow Hall and Abney Clough. Behind you the eastern edges come back into view again. Eventually the path begins to drop down to Stoke Ford where Abney and Bretton Cloughs unite.

Turn up the path which climbs up Bretton Clough. It eventually leaves the woodland and at Bretton Clough Farm (now in ruins), the path starts to cross the flat fields of the valley bottom. Turn up the tributary valley of the Bretton Brook (on your left) and eventually climb out of the valley at Nether Bretton. Here an unmade track heads back across the side of the Bretton Moor to emerge on the Eyam Edge road with the start in sight. There are fine views from the whole of Eyam Edge. At the westerly end is a gliding club and on a fine day several gliders take advantage of the thermals above Great Hucklow.

MONSAL DALE

Derbyshire

OS Map: 1:50,000 Sheet 119
1:25,000 White Peak Outdoor Leisure
Map

Location

Situated north of the A6 trunk road between
Bakewell and Buxton.

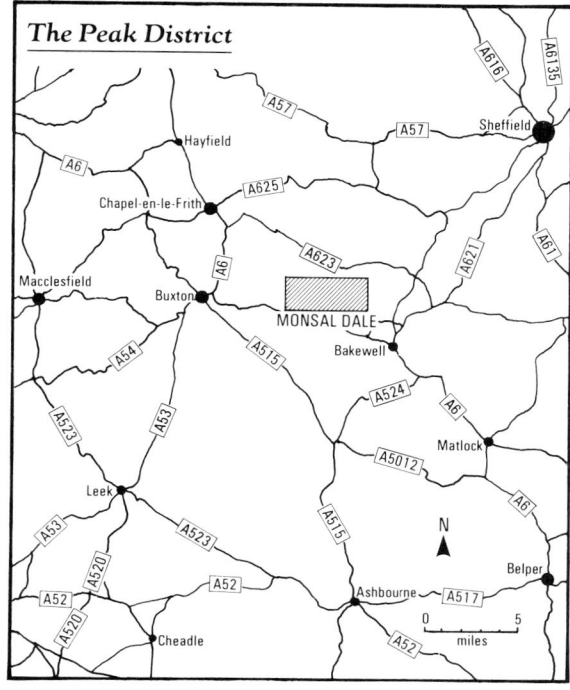

The Peak District

The limestone massif which constitutes much of
the central and southern part of the Peak District is
severed by the deeply entrenched valley of the
river Wye. The waters rise and collect from
various minor streams to form the Wye, which
flows through Buxton and down a series of dales
towards Bakewell and Rowsley where it joins the
Derwent.

Monsal Dale is perhaps the prettiest dale in the
Peak, certainly vying with the better known and
more popular Dovedale. Its well wooded gorge,
sheer-sided in places, and crystal clear water
undeniably have contributed to its popularity.
The view from Monsal Head down to the old
Midland Railway viaduct must be known to
almost all visitors to the Peak.

A recent innovation has been the establishment
of a footpath on the old railway line down the
valley. This was a bold decision by the planners,
for the tunnels had to be sealed. The path over the
tunnels is narrow and not for those who are not
sure footed. It is, however, fine for all the family if
you take care. The view down into the dale affords
a beautiful and fascinating scene of familiar sights
looked at from above. As yet, most visitors to the
dale use the valley path and the Monsal Trail, as it
is known, remains relatively quiet. There are one
or two places where a slip would seem likely to
cause an immediate slide down the grassy banks to
a vertical drop into the river but the path is
definitely worth trying.

Monsal Dale

Disused railway viaduct,
Millers Dale

PLACES OF INTEREST

Tideswell A delightful Peakland village with a marvellous fourteenth-century church often described as the 'Cathedral of the Peak'.

Litton and Cressbrook Mills Two early-established textile mills on the river Wye. The latter's mill-pond fills the dale which here is known as Water-cum-Jolly Dale.

Monsal Head Well-known viewpoint into Monsal Dale.

Magpie Lead Mine Substantial surface remains of a typical deep Derbyshire lead mine, but situated on private ground.

WALKS IN THE AREA

Taddington Dale to Monsal Head Park at the bottom of Taddington Dale in the car park (GR 171706) and take the path that leaves the valley bottom and climbs up a dry valley to Taddington Field Farm. Take care to ensure you are not walking up the adjacent Deep Dale. From

the farm take the lane into Taddington. Just before the church is reached, take the track that heads north-eastwards, over the A6 and across the fields to High Dale. Descend into this dry dale and climb out the other side heading for the top of the dale above Litton Mill. The view from here is superb, with almost everything between Millers Dale and Cressbrook being in view far below.

Descend towards the mill. The valley side is a nature reserve which should be respected. Turn downriver along the old railway track, taking the path which has been laid out above the two tunnels. Upon reaching the viaduct at Monsal Head, leave the railway for the delightful walk down the river meadows to your car. This part is very popular, but there could hardly be a more fitting final section to such a good walk. If your timing is right, you may cross the viaduct and take the steps on the left which climb up through the wooded valleyside to emerge adjacent to the pub at Monsal Head.

THE UPPER DANE VALLEY

Staffordshire and Cheshire

OS Map: 1:25,000 White Peak Outdoor Leisure Map

Location

Situated to the west of the A53 road between Leek, (Staffordshire) and Buxton, (Derbyshire). The river flows off Axe Edge and rises to the north-west of Flash village.

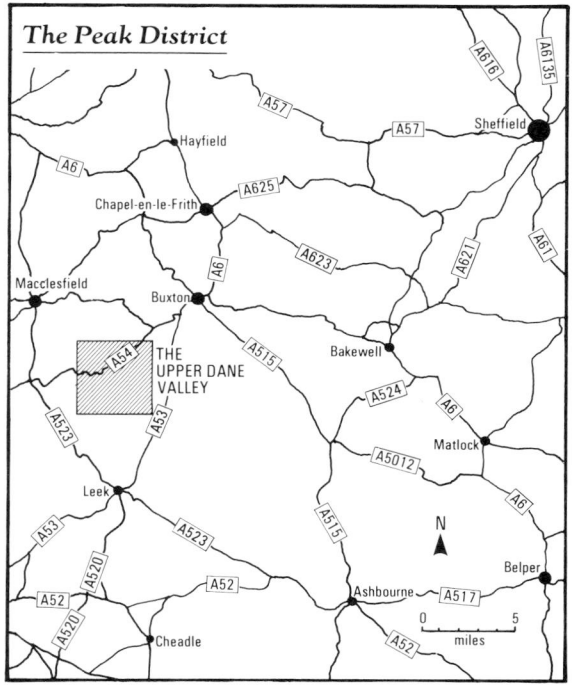

The Upper Dane Valley is a delightful area surrounded by gritstone edges and moorland. The waters of the rivers Dane and Black Brook tumble towards Gradbach and on to Danebridge in a broad and deep valley, now a mixture of green fields plus stands of wood and heather.

The valley cuts deep into Axe Edge, the moorland belt between Buxton and Leek. It affords easy access to the Derbyshire plateau from Cheshire and was used by packhorse trains for centuries. Names like Panniers Pool Bridge and Tinkerspit Gutter are a reminder of these times. The network of packhorse routes still survives and enables this area to be discovered easily. Many are green roads but some have been surfaced and narrow lanes, little used by vehicular traffic, surround the valley. They are ideal for the rambler and curious motorist alike.

PLACES OF INTEREST

Ludchurch   Huge landslip above Back Forest at Gradbach.
Flash Village   The highest village in England.
Cat and Fiddle Inn   The highest inn in England with a full licence.
Forest Chapel, Macclesfield Forest   Annual rush bearing ceremony on the Sunday nearest to 12 August.

Gradbach Mill, now a Youth Hostel

The River Dane near Three Shires Head

WALKS IN THE AREA

Danebridge to Gradbach From Danebridge, a path at the eastern end of the bridge runs up river contouring around and gradually gaining height. It eventually reaches open fields at Back Dane and then heads for Gradbach, dropping down close to the river as Back Forest is reached. The path stays close to the river to Casters Bridge, where Black Brook joins the River Dane. A path (probably medieval) from here climbs up into Back Forest. Use this to retrace your route to Danebridge. It runs close to the river path at first before climbing high into the wood. Upon reaching a large rock outcrop the path continues towards Paddock Farm. However, take the path to the left first and look out for a track on the right which leads to the concealed Lud Church. Beyond Paddock Farm the path turns towards Swythamley Hall, below the Hanging Stone. Return to the start via Park House and Snipe Cottages.

Danebridge to Wildboarclough A longer path can be used as an alternative from Casters Bridge. Continue across the fields upriver to Gradbach Youth Hostel, housed in a former silk mill (GR994661). Cross the river and take the packhorse route via Burntcliff Top and Tagsclough. Continue heading for Wildboarclough, nestling below the high rounded peak of Shutlingsloe. The path reaches the road near the Crag Inn at GR983685. Take the road down the Clough Brook, turning left at the T junction after 1 mile Cross the A54 and at Allmeadows Farm take the path back to Danebridge across the flat fields above the River Dane.

Danebridge to Barleyford and Wincle Grange From near to Danebridge Post Office a path drops to the river and proceeds down river across the meadows to a long footbridge high above the river below Whitelee Farm. The weir here provides a source of water for the Feeder, which runs down to Rudyard Lake. Continue down the Feeder —built like a canal— and cross Barleyford Bridge at GR944637. Take the path back to Danebridge via Barleyford Farm, Dumkins and Wincle Grange. At the latter — a grange farm of the former Cistercian Abbey of Dieulacresse, near Leek —take the road for a few yards before taking the path which drops down to a small wood and then on towards Danebridge.

Axe Edge to Three Shires Head A short walk to Three Shires Head may be made from Axe Edge. Park near Knotbury at GR023683. Walk past Readyleech Green, through the gate and drop down to the brook. Follow the track down to the fine packhorse bridge known as Panniers Pool Bridge at Three Shires Head, where Cheshire meets Staffordshire and Derbyshire. You can see packhorse routes radiating away in four directions. Keeping the River Dane on your right follow the track downstream, climbing up and out of the valley. There are lovely views down to Back Forest and beyond. The track eventually becomes metalled and leads back to the starting point.

THE UPPER DOVE, HAMPS AND MANIFOLD VALLEYS

Staffordshire and Derbyshire border

OS Map: 1:50,000 Sheet No 119
1:25,000 White Peak Outdoor Leisure
Map

Location

Situated to the east of the Leek to Buxton road (A53) in the south-west corner of the Peak District.

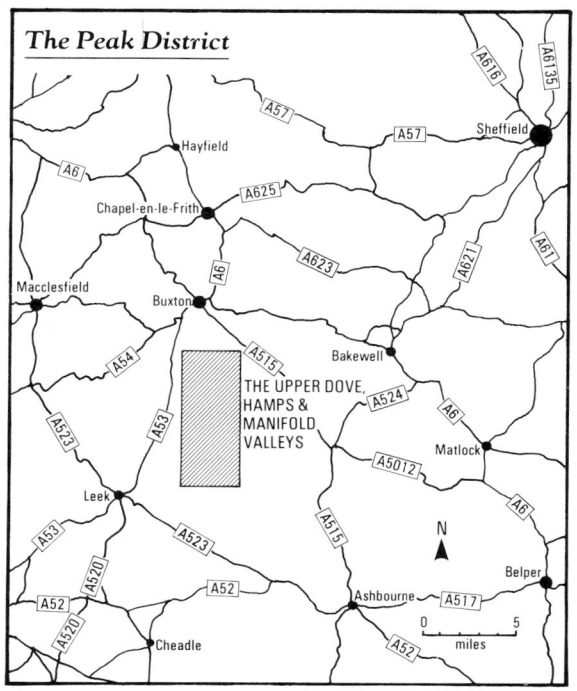

The Manifold Valley and Dovedale are extremely attractive and very popular areas. However, most visitors are content to confine their visit to the area between Hartington and Ilam. The upper reaches of the rivers Dove and Manifold, plus the latter's main tributary, the river Hamps, offer some delightful scenery, plus a measure of tranquillity, peace and quiet that is often lacking in the more popular lower reaches. The upper reaches are striking in the variety of the scenery, especially around Glutton, but lack the gorge-like appearance which makes the area south of Hartington so popular.

Earl Sterndale, Hitter Hill and Chrome Hill, Upper Dove Valley

PLACES OF INTEREST

Ilam Hall Country Park On the banks of the river Manifold, which bubbles up after a subterranean journey from Wetton Mill.

Buxton Spa town with interesting buildings, including The Crescent of 1780-4 and The Devonshire Hospital (central area open to the public and guidebook available). Also the Opera House and Pavilion Gardens should not be missed.

Leek Old market town with interesting fourteenth-century church. Brindley Mill is a restored cornmill open to the public.

Ashbourne Popular tourist town with interesting buildings including the church, Old Grammar School and almhouses.

WALKS IN THE AREA

Upper Dove The uppermost reaches of the various river systems on Axe Edge contain many former packhorse routes which are now footpaths. Park in layby adjacent to The Travellers Rest Inn at Flash Bar (GR032678) on the A53. Take the Longnor road and turn left (downhill) to Dove Head. On crossing the brook, take the track to the right to Brand Top. Take the path to the south of Howe Green, which runs down the Dove valley, to Washgate Bridge (GR052674), due south of Brand End Hill. Cross the packhorse bridge and head up the track to Tenterhill Farm. Just past the

Packhorse track, Washgate

farm turn right (north) along another old route. Head uphill to Colshaw and continue along minor roads back to the start.

Manifold and Dove Valleys Park in Longnor and take the path from Folds End Farm down to the river Manifold. Walk downstream to Brund via Lower Boothlow through the flat river meadows. Walk up the north side of Sheen Hill passing Sheen Lane Farm. Cross the Sheen – Longnor road and drop down to the river Dove at Pilsbury. The Dove Valley is deeply cut into the limestone at this point, contrasting with the Manifold. Walk up river to Crowdecote, emerging adjacent to the Packhorse Inn. Return to Longnor from here or from Beggar's Bridge, which is a little further upstream, if you prefer to keep off the road.

Hamps Valley Park in Upper Elkstone and take the track towards Under the Hill Farm, and on to Breech Farm. Turn west up the path (or adjacent road) and head for the Hamps Valley. Passing Meadows Farm on your left the path soon drops towards a footbridge over the infant river. Just before the bridge, a path turns up the valley, past an old dam built for the nearby Mixon copper mines. The path continues past New York Farm to Royledge. Bear right in front of the farmhouse and upon reaching the road use it to return to Upper Elkstone via Hob Hay.

Hoo Brook This tributary of the Manifold rises on Grindon Moor as a fan of small streams which unite at The Twist. It flows down a valley which gets progressively deeper as it heads towards Wetton Mill.

Park on Grindon Moor at GR062559 and take the track heading for The Twist. From here, continue through the narrow fields until the path emerges at the ford on the Butterton to Grindon road. There is a pub and shop in Butterton, just up the hill above the ford. Continue down the Hoo Brook, first on one side and then the other, to a footbridge, where the valley is crossed by the old packhorse route between Grindon and Warslow. Proceed from here down the steep-sided valley to Wetton Mill.

Wetton Mill is hardly off the beaten track, but never mind, the beauty of the scenery compensates for this and there is a tea-room here. Walk down the valley past the river swallet to Thor's Cave. Here turn up into Ladyside Wood which gives good views into the Manifold Valley and across to Thor's Cave. Follow the path through the wood and across the field to Grindon church. Return across Grindon Moor to the starting point.

THE CHURNET VALLEY
(CONSALL FORGE)

Staffordshire

OS Map: 1:50,000 Sheet No 119

Location
Situated in the south-west corner of the Peak District and near to Leek.

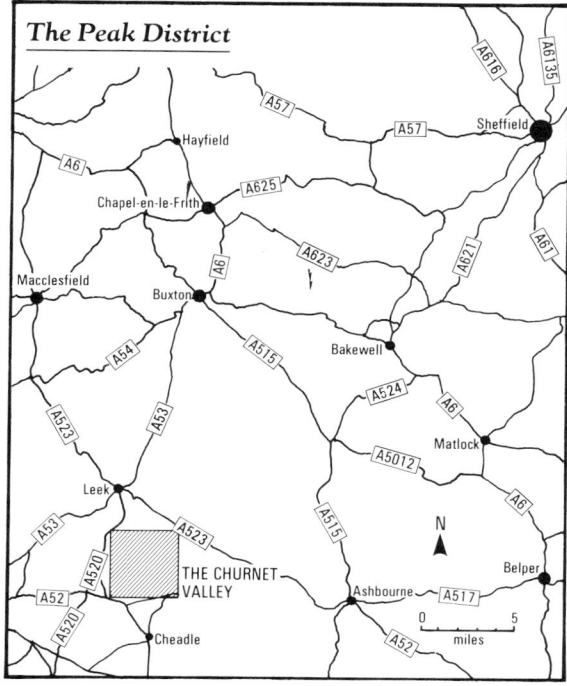

The Peak District

Although close to Stoke on Trent, this area is often referred to as 'the hidden valley'. One of the main reasons for this is the limited vehicular access. In its entire length as far as Denstone, the only roadway down the valley is the short section between Oakamoor and Alton. There are, however, roads crossing this well wooded area and several footpaths which lead down to it. In addition the Caldon Canal penetrates as far as Froghall, giving access on foot and linking various paths which cut across the valley.

In addition to being a particularly attractive valley in a scenic sense, early industrial activity has created other attractions for the tourist. At Cheddleton, a flint mill with two waterwheels survives by the restored Caldon Canal. A mile or so downstream, the former Cheddleton railway station houses the North Staffordshire Railway Society's museum and headquarters.

Between here and Froghall lies Consall Forge, a hamlet popular with ramblers, with the Black Lion Inn standing above a broad expanse of canalised river. The forge has long gone, but limekilns and old workers' cottages contribute to the tranquillity. The canal ended at Froghall where there used to be a thriving wharf for the limestone trade. The area is now landscaped as a picnic area and a passenger service along the canal in a horsedrawn narrow boat may be boarded here.

Cheddleton Flint Mill

Caldon Canal (left) and River Churnet (right) at Consall Forge

PLACES OF INTEREST

Cheddleton Mill Restored flint grinding mill with two working waterwheels and steam engine. Situated on A520 by Caldon Canal.

Cheddleton Railway Station Headquarters of North Staffordshire Railway Society with museum and rolling stock.

Froghall Wharf Former transshipment centre for limestone on Caldon Canal. Picnic area, old limekilns and passenger trips on the canal.

WALKS IN THE AREA

To explore the Churnet Valley you can walk along the canal towpath from Cheddleton or Froghall. A footpath to Consall Forge descends from Consall village (at SF991490) or from Belmont Pools (SK004500) on the Ipstones – Cheddleton road. Both cross fields before descending many stone steps to the hamlet. Another easy way into the valley is from Hazlescross near to Kingsley (SK003480). This well defined path crosses a field to reach the top of the wooded valley. It drops to a footbridge adjacent to an old flint mill, where it joins the canal towpath. Consall Forge is just a

few minutes away up river. A useful circular route can be made by parking at Belmont Pools or in Consall village, dropping down to Consall Forge and proceeding down the canal towards Froghall. Leave the valley at SK014483 and walk up past Booth's Farm to reach the minor road. Turn left and proceed to Belmont Pools. If you parked in Consall, continue down 'The Devil's Staircase' — two hundred steps — to Consall Forge and up the far side of the valley to your car.

For a car route, the minor roads between Hazlescross and Froghall and Oakamoor and Alton are recommended.

Perched on the hillside above the River Churnet is Alton Towers. This Disneyland-type attraction, set in 600 acres of parkland, now has over 2 million visitors a year, so it cannot be regarded as 'off the beaten track'. Nevertheless, almost (but not quite) within sight and sound of Alton Towers is Dimmingsdale with a series of pools which provided water for an old mill. Situated in a wooded tributary valley, it is a beautiful spot and often missed by visitors. It is referred to in the next section.

THE WEAVER HILLS AND DIMMINGSDALE

Staffordshire

OS Map: 1:50,000 Sheet No 128

Location

Situated west of Ashbourne. Both Wootton and Farley are accessible from Ellastone, three miles along the B5032 from Mayfield.

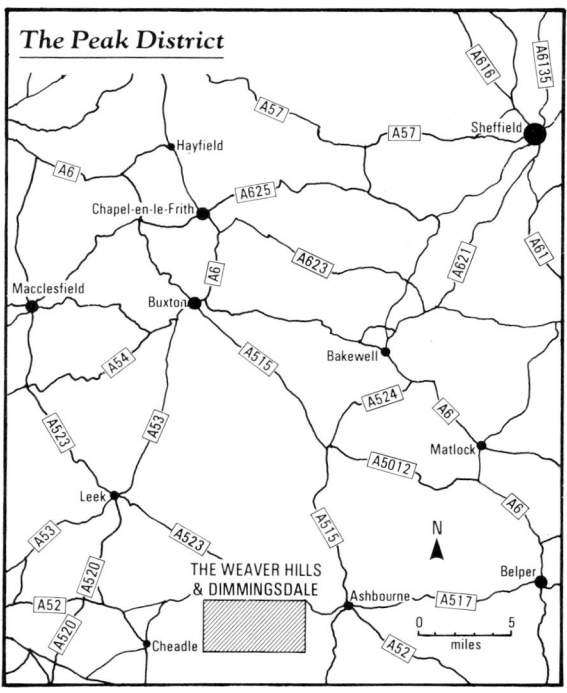

This area links the Weaver Hills, the last remnant of the Pennines, with the Churnet Valley between Alton and Oakamoor. The Weaver Hills are a very neglected area of the southern Peak District, which is astonishing, given the view on a clear day. The summit is over 1,200ft high and the view stretches across the Trent basin and over to the Wrekin in Shropshire. See how many power stations you can count! There are six to be seen on a clear day. The ridge is the most southerly outcrop of limestone in the Peak District and its smooth-sided and treeless outline can be seen for miles.

Ellastone, nestling beneath the Weaver Hills

Swaledale, Yorkshire Dales

Arkengarthdale, Yorkshire Dales

Long Mynd, Shropshire

The walk described below also includes the tiny villages of Wootton and Stanton. Both consist of sturdy sandstone cottages nestling under the south-eastern flank of the Weaver Hills and the walk is a pretty link between the two.

The Churnet Valley between the villages of Alton and Oakamoor is especially scenic — indeed the view to Alton Castle from the floor of the valley is almost reminiscent of the Rhine Valley. Today, however, the majority of visitors to this area are heading in their thousands for Alton Towers, once a stately home and now one of Europe's leading pleasure parks. However, away from the hustle and bustle of Alton Towers, the secluded Dimmingsdale, with its beautiful scenery and delightful pools, offers a complete contrast.

The Weaver Hills

PLACES OF INTEREST

Croxden Abbey Situated south of Alton, near Great Gate, are the substantial remains of this former Cisterian Abbey, now cared for by English Heritage.

Alton Village A walk around this attractive village is worthwhile. Look out for the circular lock-up, the castle — rebuilt in the nineteenth century, the restored railway station, lodge to Alton Towers etc.

Rocester Combine your visit to Croxden Abbey with a ride past the JCB excavator plant in Rocester village. Look out for the ducks and geese on one of the lakes which surround the factory.

WALKS IN THE AREA

Wootton and Stanton Park in Stanton village and walk from SK124460 on a path running due west to Raddlepits. Join a minor road here and walk down the road to Wootton. More interesting paths incorporating the Weaver Hills west of here exist, but are currently blocked. Walk through the village to where an old track to Stanton can be joined at SK112450. Follow this to the junction with a lane just south of Stanton village, and back to the starting point. Alternatively, at this junction, turn right and walk down the hill to a sharp bend where the road reaches a brook. A path leaves the road and runs in a north-easterly direction along Dydon Brook. The path eventually climbs up above the stream in Dydon Wood and terraces around with views down towards the stream. This attractive path reaches the road a mile east of Stanton village. Several small streams cross the path in Dydon Wood, making this as wet as it is attractive, even in summer, so wellingtons are recommended for this section.

Dimmingsdale and Farley Park in Oakamoor at the country park. From the site of the old railway station take the path to the former prison at Moor Court and walk down the lane to Farley village. Virtually opposite the beautifully-appointed hall, take the path which crosses the fields and head towards Abbey Wood. It emerges at the roadside adjacent to an unusual Italianate-style house, where a further path runs down to Lords Bridge, over the river Churnet and the old railway line. Here there is a similar style house and a well defined path which leads up to Dimmingsdale.

Follow the dale up to the minor road at Oldfurnace and turn right to return to Oakamoor.

The Welsh Borders

LONG MYND AND THE SOUTH SHROPSHIRE HILLS

Shropshire

OS Map: 1:50,000 Sheet Nos 126 and 137
1:63,360 Sheet Nos 118 and 129

Location

From Shrewsbury, south along the A49 to Church Stretton. Or take the minor road via Longden, Pulverbatch and Bridges. Or the A488 to Bishop's Castle.

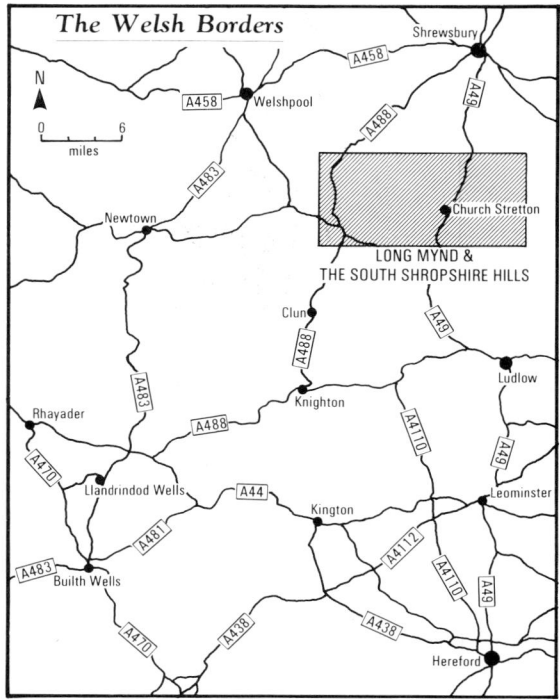

South of Shrewsbury lie a series of hill ranges running north-east to south-west. Each have a different character, due to the diversity of rock formations here. Stretching south from the Wrekin is a line of volcanic upthrusts culminating in the peaks of The Lawley, Caer Caradoc and Ragleth. The flanks of Caer Caradoc are occasionally broken by outcrops of dark rock, and the summit ridge was turned into a defensive fort by Iron Age man. On a clear day there are extensive views.

The views eastwards from the Caradoc range extend beyond Cardington Hill and across the farmland of Ape Dale to the dark wooded escarpment of Wenlock Edge. This unbroken outcrop is 15 miles (24km) long and is composed of Silurian limestone. Looking west, the Caradoc Hills are separated from the smooth upland bulk of the Long Mynd by the Church Stretton valley. This deep narrow fault between two masses of high land was utilised by Roman engineers who constructed a road from Wroxeter (*Viroconium*) to Leintwardine (*Bravonium*). This important highway through the hills is a glen almost of highland character, and attracts many visitors to Church Stretton which lies beneath the slopes of the Long Mynd. The Long Mynd (the second syllable is an abbreviation of the Welsh 'mynydd' or mountain) is a mass of very ancient rocks — slates and sandstones. These produce an upland which is very much smoother then the Caradocs. The most attractive part of the Long Mynd is along the south-eastern side, where a series of steep-sided valleys called batches or hollows dissect the ancient surface. Looking westwards from the Long Mynd, the countryside begins to assume its borderland characteristics. During Ordovician times coarse sediments were laid down, and there was occasional volcanic activity. The harder beds

now stand out and one of them, the near western edge, is called Stiperstones. Its broad summit ridge is punctuated by tor-like outcrops of quartzite rock. The major crags are Nipstone Rock, Cranberry Rock, Manstone Rock and the Devil's Chair. Legends abound in this part of the world. The Black Pool on the Long Mynd is reputed to be haunted by the spirit of a White Lady. Dead Man's Hollow is haunted by the ghosts of shepherds and travellers who perished on these lonely heights. On Stiperstones, it is said that devils gather on midwinter nights to select a leader.

Linley Hill is completely opposite in character; a good place for a quiet, uninterrupted walk. Westwards, beyond the valley of West Onny, is the rugged circular cone of Corndon Hill, which is the real outpost of Wales.

PLACES OF INTEREST

Church Stretton The town developed as a Victorian resort, as seen in the architecture. The combination of tranquillity, lovely countryside and invigorating air fostered its development as a spa hydro despite the lack of mineral springs.

Acton Scott Farm Museum About 4 miles (6.4km) south of Church Stretton, on a by-road signposted from the A49.

◁ *Offa's Dyke near Kington*

Caer Caradoc, the Lawley and The Wrekin from Burway Hill

Mitchell's Fold Stone Circle   A stone circle, which originally consisted of sixteen stones, now has ten standing.

Caer Caradoc Hillfort   A marvellous vantage point, this Iron Age hillfort lies on the narrow rocky ridge overlooking the Stretton Valley. The camp enclosure is 6¼ acres (2.5 ha) in extent, and is protected by a ditch, a stone bank and natural rock outcrops.

Shipton Hall, Corvedale   A handsome Elizabethan house with some modernisation carried out in 1789. The building contains a splendid staircase, and some fine Tudor panelling in the library. The formal gardens are also delightful.

Ratlinghope   A remote community which nestles in a valley on the west side of the Mynd; it consists of a few cottages and farms and a restored church.

Norbury   Situated at the southern end of Linley Hill, the village lies between the valleys of East and West Onny.

WALKS IN THE AREA

Bridges   Walk past the Bridges Youth Hostel and turn left through a gate before a stone bridge. Follow the stream, the Darnford Brook, up to Lower Darnford Farm and climb up to the Port Way beyond the ruined building. Turn left and follow the track to the minor road. Bear left and walk to the sharp bend, then take the path that descends to New Leasowes. The route continues by track to Leasomes Bank Farm to Gatten Lodge. Just beyond the Lodge a path strikes up to the summit ridge to the Stiperstones, where a clear route passes the Devil's Chair, Manstone Rock and Cranberry Rock to descend to the road. Cross over, and follow the fence through the plantation to a prominent rock outcrop. Descend to Rock House over scree and heather. Follow the track left down to the road, descend to the stream, and the ascend steeply to the lane. Follow the lane past Ridge Farm, and at the second gate walk uphill to the beech trees on Linley Hill. Turn left, follow the track and footpath to Birchope, and the farm lane to the road. Return along the road to Bridges. Distance: 13½ miles (21.6 km).

Black Marsh   Start at the crossroads; take the lane past Holly Cottage and footpath on to Stapeley Hill. Follow the clear track to Mitchell's Fold Stone Circle and continue to the road. Keep straight ahead when the road turns left and follow the track. At the corner of the plantation a steep ascent climbs to the summit of Corndon Hill. Head south along the forest fence and descend to a path above Corndon Farm. Bear right down to Corndon Cottage and then left to Corndon Malt House. The path descends to the Oak Inn at Old Church Stoke. Turn left, follow the road, and join the path beneath Roundton Hill to Hurdley. Continue by path to Hyssington, Yewtree Farm, and then by a lane and path to reach the main road by Welsh Lodge. Walk ½ mile (800 m) up the main road, and take the path over Mucklewick Hill and down to Gritt Farm. Return by Shelve Hill to starting point. Distance: 13 miles (20.8 km).

Lawley Hill   This is a linear walk, starting from SO506991. Take the path starting from the third bend in the road. Walk over Lawley Hill. Descend to the road and turn left; immediately turn right across the fields to a road. Turn left and then right, through a gate, and a steady climb up to the summit of Caer Caradoc. Walk south along the ridge and descend to the valley between Caradoc and Helmeth Hill. Follow the lane back to the A49 and Church Stretton. Distance: 7 miles (11.2 km).

Minton   Take a short lane at the north end of Minton village and climb up the broad bulk of Packetstone Hill, across the moor to Port Way. Turn right and walk for a short distance along the road. Bear right and follow the ever-deepening valley of Callow Hollow to Oakleymill waterfall. Just beyond, turn right and over the rise to Small Batch Valley. Bear left through pine woods to the road. Turn right and return to Minton. Distance: 6 miles (9.6 km).

CLUN FOREST AND BEACON HILL

Shropshire and Powys

OS Map: 1:50,000 Sheet Nos 137 and 148
              1:63,360 Sheet No 128

Location
Reached by the A488, Shrewsbury – Knighton road: alternatively, the A49, Shrewsbury – Craven Arms road, then B4368 Clun – Newcastle: or the A49, Ludlow – Craven Arms road.

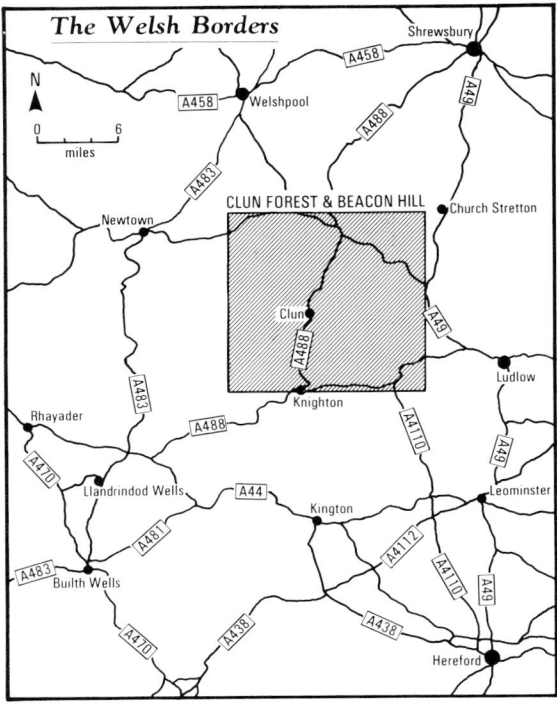

Shropshire has a great diversity of landscape, and much very fine scenery. The rich northern farmland overlooked by the Wrekin merges into sharp hill ridges, sharply-cut valleys and high heather-clad moorland. In the extreme south-west, the remote Clun Forest district drives a wedge deep into Celtic Wales. Its hills are not so much a range, more a succession of swelling heights divided by valleys to rise to the bleak open moorland of Beacon Hill and Kerry Hill in Powys.

In Norman days this border hill country was virtually independent, dominated by the Norman barons. The word 'forest' was originally given to an area of land over which the king had complete jurisdiction in the matters of hunting and game conservation. Special courts were set up which rigidly enforced these laws. There is no doubt that in Norman times the ancient Forest of Clun was well-wooded, but there was also much high open country and moorland. The natural woodland was much reduced by the need for building materials, as shown by the wealth of pleasant half-timbered houses in the area. Today, there are several man-made forests in the Clun area, the work of the Forestry Commission.

Clun Forest is a well-defined wedge of rolling hill country pushing into Wales. It lies approximately between the river Camlad in the north down to the rivers Clun and Teme. West and north-west of Knighton is a wide, sparsely-populated area of hill pasture and moorland, ideal country for lovers of solitude. It has few roads, but many footpaths and sheep tracks.

The railway linking Shrewsbury with Craven Arms, Knighton, Llandrindod Wells down to South Wales is an aid to the rambler here: it is possible to alight at one of the many unmanned halts and walk the whole day in country well off the beaten track. Check train times carefully.

One characteristic of the area is a lack of sizeable settlements. Towns like Bishop's Castle, Clun and Knighton tend to be small, homely communities. The pattern of rolling hills, woodland and rural settlements combine to form some of the loveliest countryside in the British Isles. The rambler has a tremendous range of unspoilt scenery. In particular, the exhilaration of following the dips and ascents of the Offa's Dyke long-distance footpath should not be missed. From its upland crests, the walker has superb and expansive all-round views. In parts, the Dyke is a massive bank of striking proportions, its line and scale constituting a permanent record of the skill of King Offa's engineers and labourers.

PLACES OF INTEREST
Knighton   This market town is situated on the River Teme, which the boundary between Shropshire and Powys, and is almost at the mid-point of the Offa's Dyke long-distance footpath. It has a steep main street with a Victorian clock-tower and a fifteenth-century narrow timber-framed building, 'The Little House'. There are wide-ranging views westwards along the Teme.

Clun   Clun is a charming huddle of houses at the centre of the pleasant River Clun valley, which grew up to serve a castle built in 1170, the stonework of which is crumbling and in a dangerous condition, so entry is prohibited. The two parts of the town are linked by a tiny packhorse bridge. A typical border church with an interesting interior, almshouses dating from 1618, and a Local History Museum in the Town Hall can be found on the north side of the Clun.

Stow Farms and one or two cottages support a tiny church with a weather-boarded belfry and interesting interior. A track climbs from the church to the broad ridge of Stow Hill, where an ancient green road affords lovely views.

Cantlin Stone High on the moorland of Clun Forest stands the Cantlin Stone, together with a nineteenth-century cross. On the stone, the faint inscription 'WC decsd here Buried 1691 at Betws' can be made out. The WC was William Cantlin, a travelling pedlar, who collapsed and died here. His body was buried in Betws-y-Crwyn churchyard.

Betws-y-Crwyn Church This remote church resolutely faces the winds blowing across the Clun Forest hills. The building contains some fine woodwork including a sixteenth-century screen and a Jacobean pulpit.

Stokesay Castle A unique, well-preserved example of a thirteenth-century manor house. The building now consists of a long gabled hall and a solar wing at the south-end. The Great Tower stands at the south-east of the building and another tower is at the north corner. A walled-enclosed courtyard lies on the eastern side and is entered by a fine Tudor half-timbered Gatehouse. A substantial moat surrounds the house.

Offa's Dyke on Edenhope Hill

WALKS IN THE AREA

Offa's Dyke Leave Clun on the Knighton Road, turn right beyond the church to a crossroads. Park here and then follow the lane to Burfield Farm. Walk through fields to the head of the valley bear left on a path up to Offa's Dyke. Walk south on the crest of the dyke over Llanfair Hill, and descend to a line of pine trees. At the ruin of Garbett Cottage turn left along a track and down to a small valley. Return past Upper Treverward to the start. Distance: 6½ miles (10.4 km).

To lengthen this walk, continue along Offa's Dyke to Selley Hall, and climb Cwmsanaham Hill. Descend the rocky slope to the head of the steep valley; leave the Dyke path on the left. Follow the route down to the Bwlch roads and continue straight on, climbing gently to meet the route as described above. Distance: 10 miles (16km).

Rhespass Take the B4368 out of Clun, cross the river to Whitcott Keysett, and park. Follow the lane north for a short distance and take the path ascending to Cefns ridge to Three Gates and over Hergan Hill. Follow the Dyke to Middle Knuck and the track on the left to Knuck Bank. Turn right at the crossroads and walk for ½ mile (800m). Turn left and walk ¾ mile (1.2km), then descend left to the valley on a path, and follow the stream beneath Mount Bank to Rhespass. Continue down the lane to meet the road at Bridge Farm. Rejoin the Dyke path and follow it along the slopes of Graig Hill to the road. Turn left and return to the start. Distance: 10½ miles (16.8km).

Knucklas Pass under the railway viaduct at Knucklas, turn right and then left up the track alongside the stream. Join the road and follow it to the junction. Turn right and continue straight on to descend to Llancoch. Bear right, and after a few yards, turn left and ascend to the ridgeway. Bear left and follow this route to Beacon Hill. Walk along the ridge track above Fron Rocks to the next track junction and turn right. Descend to the Fron, and ascend to the track along Wernygeufron Hill. Continue to Lloiney in the Teme Valley. Walk to Knucklas. Distance: 14½ miles (23.2km).

Hopesay Start at Kempton on the B4385. Take the path over Burrow to Aston on Clun. Follow the valley footpath on to Hopesay Common (excellent views). Continue along the hill top to the road and turn left to Round Oak and along the lane at Grist House. Return to Hopesay village. Follow the track by the church keeping left at the top of the hill to join the wide track back to Kempton. Distance: 8 miles (12.8km).

RADNOR FOREST AND THE GLASCWM HILLS

Powys

OS Map: 1:50,000 Sheet Nos 147 and 148
1:63,360, Sheet Nos 128 and 141

Location

Reached by the Knighton – Penybont road; or by the B4355, B4357 and B4372 roads, Knighton – New Radnor; or by the A44, Kington – Rhayader road.

Radnor Forest is an upland island of Silurian shales and mudstones, rising to a plateau. The highest points are Great Rhos, 2,166 ft (660 m) and Black Mixen, 2,135 ft (650m). The smooth slopes of the Forest have deeply-carved valleys running outwards from the central mass. These sheltered dingles are occupied by small streams. On the steep western sides of Harley Dingle, erosion of the soft deposits has caused the prominent scars marked as the Three Riggles. On the opposite side of the valley, small craggy outcrops line the rim of Great Creigiau and Whinyard.

For some time, afforestation has been undertaken especially along the eastern and northern sides of the Forest but there are still wide stretches of grassy moorland where flocks of sheep and wild ponies graze. There are no roads, but a number of tracks and footpaths allow ramblers access to this remote area, where often they will be alone in the folds of these hills. Buzzards are numerous, as are ravens; in summer, wheatears, curlews and whinchats are common.

South of Llanfihangel-nant-Melan, there is a large tract of hill country rising to the Glascwm and Llanbedr hills. This is a sparsely-populated, remote area; its upland heights are criss-crossed by lonely tracks which once carried great herds of Welsh cattle and flocks of sheep to markets in England. The stretch of road leading to Cregrina is still marked 'Hungry Green', a relic of the droving era when sheep and cattle could feed here. The area has few roads, and the small communities with their ancient churches lie hidden in the valleys. The beautiful valley of the river Edw is, however, accompanied at every turn by a narrow road, and another road runs along the valley of the Clas Brook to Glascwm.

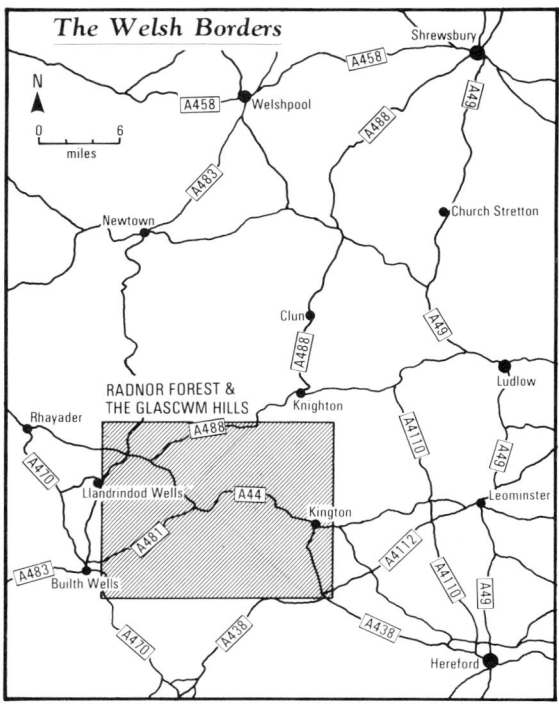

The Welsh Borders

PLACES OF INTEREST

New Radnor   Remains of a castle motte and a section of old town wall earthworks. An excellent centre for walks or touring the area.

Old Radnor Church (St Stephen)   Magnificently situated, with an exceptional rood screen and organ case, and ancient stalls. The font is sixth or seventh century.

Llandegley   A village with sulphur springs and an interesting well house north of the village.

Llandrindod Wells   Attractive nineteenth-century architecture, good facilities for touring and holidays.

Giants Grave, Glascwm   A large barrow about 97 ft (30m) in diameter on the route of the drovers' road to Glascwm.

Four Stones, Walton   Four glacial boulders arranged to form a square 17 ft (5.2 m) in diameter. Its purpose is not known, and could be ceremonial, or possibly a route marker.

Presteigne   Has a large number of elegant buildings, including a fourteenth-century church with magnificent Flemish tapestry; a seventeenth-century inn, and many half-timbered houses.

View north from castle mound, New Radnor ▷

WALKS IN THE AREA

New Radnor From the road junction in the centre of New Radnor, ascend the steep lane, and follow the path below Whimble and on to the head of the dingle. Bear right along the forest edge and then head right towards the summit of Bache Hill. Return to the forest edge, and follow the path round to the southern side of Bache Hill. Take the path through the afforested area and descend to the track leading to Ferndale. Turn right and walk down the track below Knowle Hill back to New Radnor. Distance: 6 miles (9.6km).

A longer walk from New Radnor Follow the previous route beyond Whinyard Rocks to the head of the dingle. Bear left and follow the track to the summit of Black Mixen. Walk across the moor north-west to Shepherd's Well at the head of Harley Dingle. Accompany the forest fence for a short distance to meet a footpath emerging from the forest. Follow this across the moor; it eventually meets the track from Llanfihangel Rhydithon. If conditions are clear, take the route which heads south-east over Esgairnantau and descend to the Warren Plantation valley. Climb up to the saddle between Great Rhos and Fron Hill, and descend steeply to Harley Dingle and thence to New Radnor. Distance: 10 miles (16km).

Alternatively, the Llanfihangel track may easily be followed to the 'Water-break-its-neck' waterfall, to Vron Farm, and then return along the road to New Radnor.

The Smatcher Walk down the main street of New Radnor, the Knighton road. Take the track on the right, and the footpath over The Smatcher. Descend to a track on the right towards the valley. Return by footpath alongside the Summergil brook. Distance: 4¼ miles (6.8km).

A walk from Llanfihangel-nant-Melan Llanfihangel-nant-Melan, Black Yatt, Glascwm, Gwaunceste Hill, Bryn-y-Maen, Forest Inn, Llanfihangel. NB: There is a youth hostel at Glascwm. Distance: 10 miles (16km).

A walk from Painscastle Painscastle, Bryngwyn Hill, Allt Dderw, Rhulen, Rhulen Hill, Llanbedr Hill, Painscastle. Distance: 11 miles (17.6km).

A short walk from Llandegley Llandegley, Llandegley Rocks, Bwlch-y-cefn Bank, Bwlch-Llwyn Bank, Llandegley Rhos, Larch Grove, Llandegley. Distance: 6 miles (9.6km).

The Cotswolds

VALLEY OF THE WINDRUSH

Oxfordshire

OS Map: 1:50,000 Sheet No 163

Location

From Stow-on-the-Wold the A429 goes south-west and the A424 south-east. The A40 joins these two roads between Burford and Northleach. Burford is roughly equidistant on the A40 from Oxford and Cheltenham.

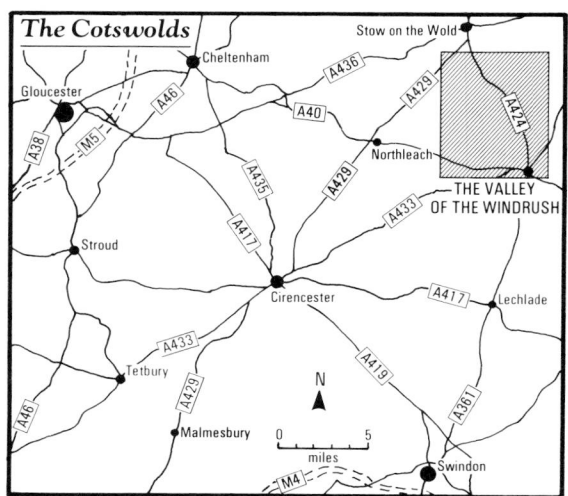

The two roads A429 and A424 follow the highest ground. Between them is the River Windrush, and east of the A424 is the River Evenlode.

Though almost in the Oxford Vale, this is still Cotswold country. Slopes are gentler and river valleys broader. This has been considered prime land for centuries. The number of Roman villa sites and manor houses testify to it. There are well-drained slopes for crops, and rivers that never run dry as they are fed by the many springs in the hills; ridges for the highways and sheltered valleys for the dwellings. In this small area, hardly a dozen miles across, there are almost two dozen villages and hamlets, though one could be forgiven for thinking the area deserted, so peaceful is the rural scene away from the main roads.

Burford, like many other Cotswold towns, was a wool town and has a handsome main street leading down to the River Windrush. Of little importance in Roman times, as the Roman roads passed at Asthall and Northleach, Burford became important in Anglo-Saxon times when a new route was established using the ford. This gave the town its present name as the *burh-ford*, a fortified ford. The large number of buildings that were once coaching inns testifies to the growth of traffic on the route through the town.

'Stow-on-the-Wold where the wind blows cold'— the concise local saying underlines the difference between the two towns. Stow is the only Cotswold town to scorn the valley shelter, probably as a result of the confluence of the many roads at this point.

The memory of a vanished forest is preserved in the names Milton-under-Wychwood and Shipton-under-Wychwood. Both villages are north of Burford by about five miles. Once the forest was three thousand acres of wilderness and woodland, the home of witches, brigands and outlaws.

◁ *Naunton in the Windrush Valley*

Stow-on-the-Wold

Lower Swell, near Stow-on-the-Wold

PLACES OF INTEREST

Bourton-on-the-Water A popular tourist village with a host of attractions; model railway, motor museum, butterfly exhibition, birdland, model village, and perfume blending laboratory.

Cotswold Countryside Collection Northleach.

Cotswold Wildlife park Near Burford.

Tolsey Museum Burford. A collection of seals and charters for the town.

Bibury Arlington Mill Museum. A mill with a working waterwheel and a collection of arts, crafts and agricultural implements. Arlington Row. A fine row of seventeenth-century weavers cottages. A modern working trout farm.

WALKS IN THE AREA

Westcote From Westcote take the bridleway north-east to Westcote Brook. Cross and turn left. Recross the brook and head west then south-west to Gawcombe. Join the road and turn left back to Westcote.

Herbert's Heath From Fifield go north-east through the woods at Herbert's Heath to the road near Bruern Abbey. Do not take the road but turn almost back on your tracks towards the woods. At the far side of the woods turn right for Idbury. From Idbury take the footpath back to Fifield. For a shorter walk, do not enter the woods at Herbert's Heath but turn left direct to Idbury.

Windrush Mill Take the path from Windrush Mill over the water meadows to Sherbourne. Return the same way, or by the minor road. For a longer walk, take the lane towards Clapton for two miles. There is a track east to New Bridge which crosses the Windrush to Great Rissington. In the village take the drive south. Continue on the bridleway to join the road and reach Great Barrington. Return by road to Windrush.

ROMAN COTSWOLDS

Gloucestershire

OS Map: 1:50,000 Sheet No 163

Location

The area is about 5 miles south-east of Cheltenham,
and is bounded by the A417 Cirencester –
Gloucester road, the A429 and the A40, from its
junction with the A429, back to Cheltenham.

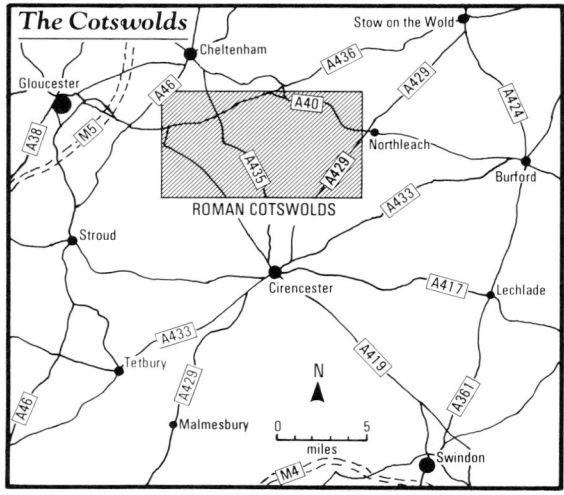

From the escarpment which drops steeply down
to the Severn valley, this area provides the
contrast of the gentle roll down towards the
Thames.

Indeed, the streams now run to join that river.
Seven Springs, almost on the escarpment looking
down to Cheltenham, has a tablet claiming in
Latin to be the source of the Thames. The River
Churn, which rises here, is longer and further from
Lechdale than the now-acknowledged head of the
Thames at Thameshead south-west of Cirencester.
Here the Rivers Churn and Coln meander between
the hills. The Churn joins the Thames near
Cricklade and the Coln near Lechlade.

Many idyllic villages lie on the rivers. Following
the Churn, the first village is Coberley where Dick
Whittington lived. The village church has a fine
collection of monuments to the Berkley family,
the oldest dating from 1295.

Next down the valley is Cowley which is a little

larger; the villages are joined by a path. The
surviving seventeenth-century manor house is
now a conference centre. The terraced gardens
have water gardens fed from artificial lakes filled
by the River Churn. Though the village church is
of Norman origin, it was drastically restored in
1872.

Climb over the hill south-west of Cowley and
cross the main road, the A417, and you have
crossed a major British watershed. The River
Frome rises at Brimpsfield and flows into the
Severn. King Edward II destroyed the castle and
hanged John Gifford, one of the fighting Giffords.
Near the church are the ruins of both the castle and

Cowley Court

a priory; little remains, for much of the village is built from stone plundered from the castle walls.

Again from Cowley, the next valley east is the valley of the Coln. This rises north of Andoversford and meanders through that small town to pass Yarnworth, famous for its Roman villa, past the lovely Stowell park, to cross the Fosse Way (A429) at Fossebridge. In between are the large Chedworth Woods and lovely riverside walks.

Chedworth village

PLACES OF INTEREST
Chedworth Roman villa. Possibly the finest villa site in Britain. A museum on site houses the better relics.

Denfurlong Farm Trail A working farm near Chedworth.

Carriage Museum Stroud. Carriages and fire engines.

Corinium Museum Cirencester. Local Roman finds.

Sudeley Castle Winchcombe. Fortified building set in beautiful parkland. Art collection in the house.

Railway Museum Winchcombe. British Rail memorabilia.

Pittville Pump Room Cheltenham. Regency mansion in a large park.

Town Museum and Art Gallery Cheltenham.

WALKS IN THE AREA
Stowell Park Take the path north-east from Fossebridge to Stowell Park. Use the lane south-west to cross the river and turn left near the woods. Path goes close to the river then out to a lane. Turn left on the lane to Fossebridge. (Splendid views of Chedworth Woods).

Roman Villa Take the minor road towards Stowell from Chedworth. Past the railway bridge, turn left on the bridleway which goes through Chedworth Woods. (Good view of the village before entering the woods.) Turn left at the road to the villa. Return by one of the many paths through the woods.

Severn Escarpment From Coberley, a quarter-mile west of the church, take the bridleway, then footpath, north-east to Seven Springs, crossing the A436 on the way. Continue north on a minor road then join the Cotswolds Way round Leck-hampton Hill, over Charlton Kings Common and on to the Devil's Chimney. (Good views of Cheltenham and the escarpment.) Follow the Cotswold Way to Ullenwood, turn left on the minor road, left on the A436, then right on the minor road to Coberley.

Brimpsfield From the southern end of the village, go east on a drive to Brimpsfield Park. Pass between the buildings and cross the river. Recross on a footpath and follow the stream down to Caudle Green. Go uphill through the village and turn left on a bridleway, which shortly leads into the woods, and follow upstream to Climperwell. Cross a minor road and turn right on a footpath and bridleway back to Brimpsfield.

SOUTHERN COTSWOLDS

Gloucestershire

OS Map: 1:50,000 Sheet No 173

Location

Twenty-five miles south of Gloucester and seventeen miles south-west of Cirencester; Junction 13 off the M5 is the turn off for Stroud, which is ten miles due north. Junction 17 off the M4 is eight miles south-east.

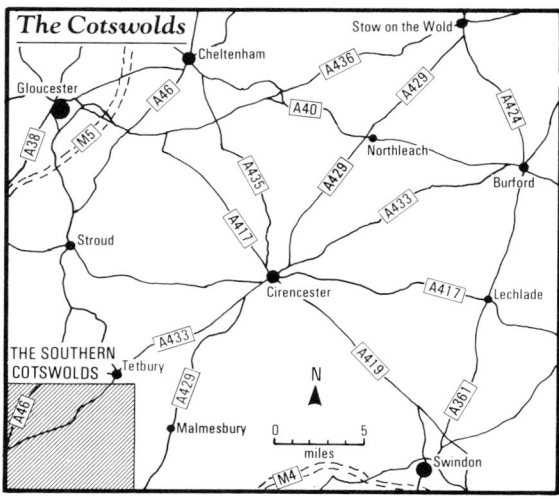

The Cotswolds should not be called hills. They are wolds, which is an old English word meaning upland common. Nowhere are the Cotswolds more than 1,000 ft high. Deep valleys hide from sight of the traveller on the roads high on the uplands; beautiful valleys with bubbling streams and shady arbours. An area which is rich in old villages, which prompted Wordsworth to write

> The pillared porch, elaborately embossed;
> The low, wide windows with their mullions old;
> The cornice richly fretted of grey stone;
> And that smooth slope from which the dwelling rose
> By beds and banks Arcadian of gay flowers,
> And flowering shrubs, protected and adorned.

The Cotswolds are oolitic limestone formed eons ago under the sea. Many cottages have fossils built into the walls. The streams which have cut the valleys flow out in all directions. The Thames and the Bristol Avon rise in this area, and the mighty Severn is fed by the River Frome which runs through Stroud.

This area is quite close to the now famous Highgrove House and to Westonbirt Arboretum. Westonbirt attracts plenty of visitors and, indeed, is well worth visiting but the walk round the outside will be quite peaceful.

South from Westonbirt is Sherston, on the B4040 Malmesbury to Chipping Sodbury road. Its wide main street testifies that this was a market town in its heyday, and the river deep in the valley south of the village is the infant Bristol Avon. Sherston has the Rattlebone Inn, which is named after John Rattlebone who is reputed to have fought with Edmund Ironsides when the Danes were defeated here in 1016.

Many of the fields are bounded by the drystone walls so famous as a part of the Cotswold scene, and on the higher ground the tree clumps are widely-spaced, giving the feeling of space and freedom.

One of the most delightful hamlets in the area is Easton Gray. There is a fine Georgian mansion and a lovely old bridge over the Avon which gives fine views of the river.

Oldbury-on-the-Hill church

PLACES OF INTEREST

Badminton House Palladian-style house, the home of the Duke of Beaufort. Stables and hunt kennels open.

Nan Tow's Tump Best preserved round barrow in the Cotswolds. By bridleway from Oldbury-on-the-Hill 1½ miles north-west.

Police Bygones Museum, Tetbury History of Gloucester Constabulary in three old police cells.

Westonbirt Arboretum A fine collection of British and foreign trees.

Horton Court Fine old manor house. Norman hall with small museum.

WALKS IN THE AREA

Sherston From Sherston church go south, cross the river, fork right then left on road. At the next junction go ahead, south, on a farm road. At the junction with the road and railway turn left on the road, for one mile of tarmac. Maintain direction on the Fosse Way to the River Avon. Turn left before the river. In a quarter mile, cross the river and soon swing left to Easton Grey. Cross the river bridge and take the path on the south bank and so back to Sherston.

Westonbirt In Westonbirt, 20 yd before the gate to the golf club, turn left between stone pillars. A road leads to a drive; cross over and maintain direction to the crossroads near the Hare and Hounds on the A433. Take the road to Leighterton and in a quarter of a mile at a crossroads go through a gate on the left across the junction on the outer edge of the wood. Soon find the Arboretum. There are woodland paths to explore; a guide to the paths is available.

Oldbury-on-the-Hill From the church at Oldbury-on-the-Hill (a Saxon church dedicated to St Arild) go north to Park Wood. From the north tip of the wood, head north-west to Saddlewood Farm, then to the A46. Turn sharp right just before the road; in one mile cross a minor road. Join a minor road but in a quarter of a mile turn right on a track, one mile to the A433 near the village.

Westonbirt Arboretum

The Mendips

CHEDDAR

Somerset

OS Map: 1:50,000 Sheet No 182

Location

The western parts of the Mendip Hills are only 5 miles south-east from Junction 21 of the M5. The A38 cuts through the hills 18 miles south of Bristol.

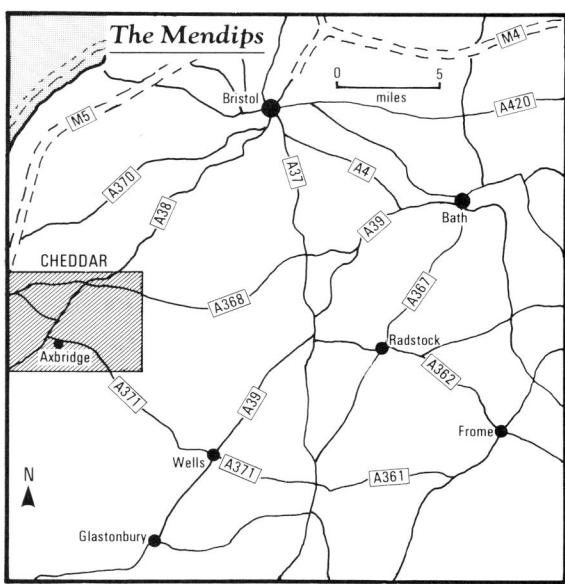

This western part of the hills shows evidence of a history from very early times almost to the beginning of the present century. Traces of neolithic man have been found in Cheddar Caves. Lead mining has been going on since pre-Roman times. A lead ingot was found stamped with the Emperor's head which dated the ingot six years after the first Roman invasion. Mining went on until the middle of the nineteenth century.

Charterhouse was the centre of the Roman mining interest. Not only lead was mined but also silver, and some British states had a silver coinage. Zinc, manganese and iron were also mined.

Little is known about the miners as nobody was interested in how they lived. Hannah More devoted herself to improving the life of the poor, and her records enabled some kind of historical record to be saved. The miner was recorded as being 'savage, depraved, brutal, and ferocious'.

Shipham was a mining centre then and it was recorded that no policeman would have dared try to arrest a Shipham man; he would have feared for his life. Traces of the mining can still be seen in the 'Gruffy Ground' just south of Shipham on Cuck Hill, and at Charterhouse.

On some maps Mendip Forest is shown. Probably at one time there was more woodland than now but forest means hunting ground or chase and King John kept a hunting lodge at Axbridge.

King John's Hunting Lodge, Axbridge

◁ *The southern face of Mendip, near Wells*

The core of the Mendips is carboniferous limestone. It dissolves easily in rainwater and so formed, over the centuries, the many caves and fissures now found. It also makes for dry walking on the tops.

It was one such fissure in Burrington Combe, now marked with a plaque, that the Reverend Augustus Toplady was sheltering from a violent storm one day in 1762. Here, the idea came for the well-loved hymn 'Rock of Ages'.

Not far above Burrington Combe is Beacon Batch, 325m, the highest point of the Mendip Hills; which provides a fantastic viewpoint on a clear day. Another good viewpoint is Crook Peak or Wavering Down, above Compton Bishop. These places are both very exposed to westerly winds, however.

PLACES OF INTEREST

Cheddar Caves, museum. Jacob's Ladder to a viewpoint.

Axbridge King John's Hunting Lodge, museum.

Brean Down Brean Down Nature Reserve. Tropical bird gardens. Sandy beach.

Weston-Super-Mare A Bristol Channel resort. Museum. Collection of helicopters at the Bristol Rotorcraft Museum at the airport.

WALKS IN THE AREA

Black Rock Nature Trail At the top of Cheddar Gorge.

The West Mendip Way 30 miles from Wells to Weston-Super-Mare. Guide book available from Weston-Super-Mare Rotary Club.

Beacon Batch From Burrington Combe car park follow the caves path, then go up the right hand side of the combe. Cross the combe, turning left to parallel the road. At a junction after 1 mile go right, climbing up the hill to the triangulation point at Beacon Batch. Take the next path right, 1 mile to the woods. Turn right inside the woods. Turn right again at the bottom of the hill and follow the track to Burrington.

Wavering Down Where the A38 cuts through the hills, at the highest point, there is a minor road west. Park here and go through a gate on the left of the road. Keep straight on for Wavering Down and Crook Peak. Return the same way (splendid viewpoints).

Axbridge From the church go south-west on a track to the River Yeo. Turn south-east, upstream, after crossing. At the next bridge re-cross and go north-east towards the reservoir. Take the first left and return to Axbridge.

Burrington Combe

WELLS

Somerset

OS Map: 1:50,000 Sheet No 182

Location
Wells is just over 20 miles south of Bristol on the A39. The M5 cuts the hills off from the sea between Junctions 21 and 22.

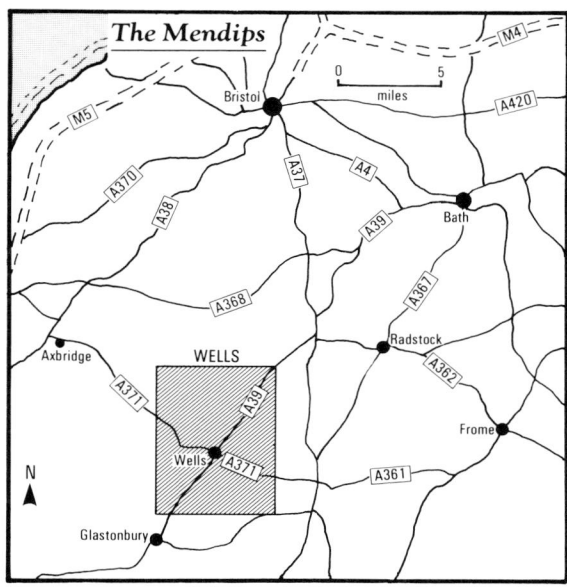

Wells lies sheltered on the south side of the Mendip plateau. King Ine of the Saxons decided to build a church at a point where there were numerous springs bubbling up from below the hills.

This is Somerset's only cathedral city, and it attracts many visitors to the cathedral itself and to the many medieval buildings, ecclesiastical and secular.

That Mendip is a plateau is beyond doubt. Visitors from higher parts will smile at the meagre height of 325m, but this is in contrast to the Somerset Levels, often only a few feet above sea level. The views from Mendip are extensive and magnificent.

Here on the southern edge, the views south-west across the Somerset Levels are extensive. The Quantock Hills can be seen 20 miles away, the massive square block of Hinkley Point power station can be picked out and from the western end, the Severn Estuary.

On the southern edge the escarpment is steep and cut deeply by Cheddar Gorge and Ebbor Gorge. The top of the plateau undulates before falling more gently on the northern edge.

Only 5 miles southerly along the A39 from Wells, is Glastonbury with its mysterious Tor. The Tor itself is a good landmark for miles around. This is the Isle of Avalon of ancient legend.

If visitors are confused as to why this was called 'island' and why Joseph of Arimathea 'landed', then the record of the old Abbey will provide the

Wells Cathedral

Glastonbury Tor

PLACES OF INTEREST

Wells Museum, theatre, cathedral, bishop's palace.

Wookey Hole Caves, museum. The Moors Nature Trail. Ebbor Gorge Nature Trail.

Chewton Mendip One of the finest of the Somerset churches.

Priddy An old sheep village high on Mendip.

Wootton Vines A working vineyard.

Glastonbury

  Abbey Ruins King Arthur's burial place.

  The Tor Splendid views from the top.

  Abbey Barn Somerset Rural Life Museum.

  Chalice Well Associations with healing and the Holy Grail.

WALKS IN THE AREA

Penhill At Penhill, from outside the entrance to the TV aerial site, walk south-west on a track. Turn right after about ½ mile, towards Penhill Farm. Pass the farm, and at the end of the next field go right heading towards a large wood. At the wood turn sharp left for ½ mile to a lane. Turn right on the lane. After about ½ mile take a footpath to the right. Follow the line of this footpath back to the start.

Kings Castle Wood From the centre of Wells, take the A371 road in the direction of Shepton Mallet. At the bottom of Tor Hill take the track left with wood and Tor Hill on the right. Follow the line between the woods and the houses; a little later on there is golf course on the right. Past the club house and the hospital, take a footpath to the right, heading south-east towards the corner of a wood. Follow the edge of the second wood then turn sharp right along the southern edge of the wood. Join a track, turning left, and still following the edge of Kings Castle Wood. On emerging at the main road go left for ¼ mile then right to enter The Park. There is a splendid view of the cathedral from this vantage point. Walk down the good path to town.

North Wootton From North Wootton, near the church, go north then turn left at the road junction. At the next road junction turn right on a track. Go through the wood ahead then across a large field to join a track, and swing right, entering woods. At a junction of paths turn right heading gently down towards a farm. Follow the path south from the farm to pass Park Wood, and emerge on to the road at North Town. Follow the road back to the church. This walk could be combined with a visit to Wootton Vines.

answer. The monks started the drainage to improve Abbey lands.

Somerset is derived from the translation of the name of a tribe using the area in ancient times. They were 'summer settlers' who brought their cattle to the area in summer to grow fat on the rich land. In winter the area was far too wet, most of it was shallow lakes and pools and strangers were in dire peril of getting lost or bogged down.

This is the area where King Alfred found refuge following defeat by the Danes. The majority of people lived on, or in, the hills. Traces of Neolithic man have been found in the caves on Mendip. Neolithic man probably hunted on the plateau.

MELLS AND FROME

Somerset

OS Map: 1:50,000 Sheet No 183

Location

Frome is on the A361, which runs from Swindon to Taunton, and the A362. It is 11 miles south of Bath and 17 miles south-east of Bristol. From London the M3 and A303 pass Mere, which is 10 miles south.

Frome is at the eastern edge of the Mendip Hills. Eastward again, as the hills decline, is a gently undulating area before the sharp western edge of Salisbury Plain.

This is a gentle area, with lovely wooded valleys such as Vallis Vale, a favourite walk for the Frome townspeople, or Asham Wood where a bridleway follows an infant stream.

Another stream comes down from Mells and there is a bridleway between that village and Great Elm just over a mile away.

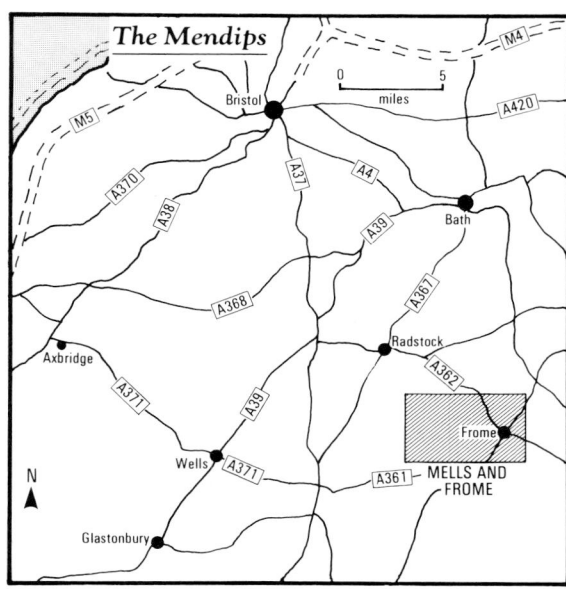

This last little corner of the Mendips is criss-crossed with a jumble of roads and dotted with hamlets and villages. Some of the finest attractions in Somerset are the fine churches. Mendip has its share and this section some of the best.

Mells has for many years been considered one of the showplaces of the county. Leland, and the novelist George Birmingham, wrote glowingly of the village and its church. From 1924 to 1934 Canon J.O. Hannay was rector of Mells. He came from the west of Ireland and was disappointed at the lack of mountains. He did, however, leave a striking description, which was unstinting in its praise, of his first sighting of Mells church.

Just over two miles south-east, Leigh-upon-Mendip also has a fine church. Travelling back towards Frome, Chantry has an interesting Victorian church and Whatley has a small church with a graceful spire. R.W. Church was rector for nineteen years before being offered the Deanery of St Paul's by Gladstone in 1871. Dean Church was buried at his own wish at Whatley, where he had spent so many happy years.

South of Whatley is Nunney with its small and ruined, yet imposing, castle. It was never inhabited after the Civil War. In the reign of Henry VIII Leland described it as 'a pretty castle'. In 1954 it was described as 'still impressive and stands

Cheap Street, Frome

broooding in a kind of magnificent dilapidation, giving the authentic medieval air to the village'.

Just west of the A37 and Shepton Mallet, the first hint of the Mendip escarpment begins. Close to each other on the south slopes are the villages of North Wootton and Pilton, where there are vineyards to be visited.

WALKS IN THE AREA

There are many footpaths in the area, which can provide, with careful use of a map or local guide, walks of anything from a short stroll to an all-day ramble.

PLACES OF INTEREST

Rode Tropical bird gardens and pets corner. Many exotic birds free in the grounds.
Frome The old town. Gentle Street and Cheap Street, Museum.
Longleat Longleat House and safari park.
Farleigh Hungerford Castle Fourteenth century.
East Somerset Railway At West Cranmore.
Oakhill Manor World of models.
Vineyards At Pilton and Wootton.
Shepton Mallet Museum, art and cultural centre.

Nunney Castle

The Chilterns

THE NORTHERN ESCARPMENT

Buckinghamshire

OS Map: 1:50,000 Sheet No 165

Location

Follow the A4010 High Wycombe to Aylesbury, or the A413 Uxbridge to Aylesbury roads. From Aylesbury, Wendover is 4 miles and Princes Risborough about 7 miles. The area is west of the A413.

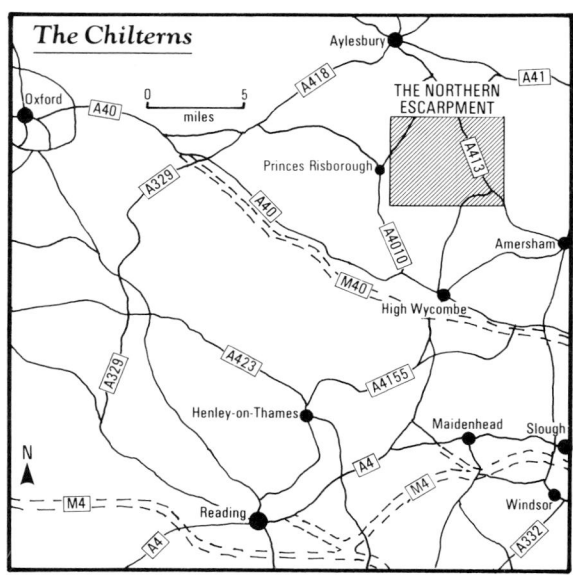

Here is an area of peace, tranquillity and great beauty. The green hills and wooded valleys are crossed by narrow lanes leading to peaceful villages.

So far off the beaten track is Little Hampden that the road ends at the village after rambling rustically through farm land. It eventually ends at the tiny hamlet, which has a few cottages, an inn and a church. The tiny church has a red roof, the nave is Norman, the porch fifteenth-century. The porch has a striking feature in the two oaks forming the doorway; the natural curve of the wood has been used to form a pointed arch. The principal possessions of the church are wall paintings, mostly dedicated to St Christopher and over 700 years old.

It is possible to walk from here to Coombe Hill, the highest point of the Chilterns. The view across the beechwoods and valleys towards Wendover is particularly good.

Just across the valley, south-west, is Great Hampden and a place of beauty holding an important part of English history. Hampden House is private. It was the home of John Hampden who was first to refuse to pay Ship Money, an action that was to lead to the Civil War.

John Hampden later fell in the Civil War leading his own Buckinghamshire Militia against a Royalist Troop. His monument was not erected until one hundred years after his death. The church is thirteenth-century and is full of interest, chiefly to do with the Hampden family.

A lovely circular walk in these tranquil surroundings, from the Hampden Arms in Great Hampden, crosses some of the parkland before the church and visits some easily identifiable parts of Grims Ditch. The virtually unspoilt pastoral scene must be much as John Hampden saw it.

Coombe Hill Obelisk

Beech woods near Princes Risborough

PLACES OF INTEREST

Princes Risborough Manor (National Trust) Seventeenth-century house with Jacobean oak staircase. (Open by appointment only).

Smock Mill Windmill Farm Lacey Green. The oldest mill of its type in the country. Dates from 1650.

Home of Rest for Horses Westcroft Stables, Speen Farm.

Buckinghamshire County Museum Aylesbury

Tring Nature Reserve Nature Conservancy Council.

Tring Zoological Museum

WALKS IN THE AREA

Little Hampden From near the end of the road go right on a bridleway to Dunsmore. At the crossroads, turn left down a lane, then a footpath to Coombe Hill. From here join the Ridgeway almost due south. Where The Ridgeway goes sharp right downhill, descend to the first cross track (¼ mile) then turn left and return to Little Hampden.

Great Hampden From near the Hampden Arms go to the road junction. Go right down the 'Private No Through Road' (this sign is for vehicles); the drive swings right and there is a footpath. Follow this footpath straight to the church grounds by way of a kissing gate. Turn left on the drive near Hampden House and join Grims Ditch. (Good view of the house). On entering the woods turn left, still on Grims Ditch. Turn left on the road then soon right; after 150m turn left over a stile. At the crossroads maintain direction following footpath signs; a good path leads to the road which returns to the start point.

Wendover Leave Wendover town by the B4010 west over the railway; at the first bend turn left off the road. Follow the white acorn marking the Ridgeway. Climb to Coombe Hill (splendid views). From the monument turn left to Dunsmore, at the duck pond turn left. Keep to the meadows northerly down to Wendover.

SOUTH-EAST CHILTERNS

Buckinghamshire

OS Map: 1:50,000 Sheet No 175

Location
Beaconsfield lies just off the M40 thirty-two miles from Oxford and twenty-five from London. Junction 7 off the M4 lies seven miles due south.

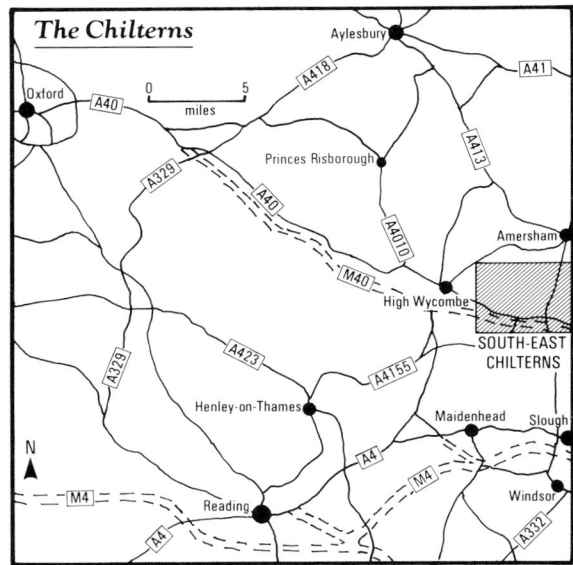

This area is rich in mature beechwoods of cathedral-like proportions. Indeed, just three miles south of Beaconsfield are the famous Burnham Beeches, a very picturesque and popular area which is criss-crossed with paths and tracks. The 400 acres were purchased by the City of London in 1880 for public use. Then the area was described as 'woodland and waste'; some of the trees are 300 years old.

Here on the southern edge of the Chilterns, the land flows gently down to the Thames. The hills continue south of the river but they are known as the Berkshire Downs.

The Chilterns are mostly limestone and the range extends from the Barton Hills in south Bedfordshire, through Buckinghamshire and into Oxfordshire. At the Goring Gap the River Thames breaks through the line of hills, flowing from north to south.

Wooded hill tops and sheltered valleys are the main feature, respectively known locally, as 'ridges' and 'bottoms'.

Beaconsfield has a delightful old centre which carries the A40, but the M40 has taken much traffic out of the town. There are some lovely buildings in the London End and the parish church and Old Rectory are worth closer inspection.

The area, once up from the river valley, has gentle countryside with cool glades and shady tracks. Round Seer Green there are plenty of level footpaths, whereas Penn stands high on a ridge and boasts that twelve counties can be seen from the church tower. Sir John Betjeman describes Penn as 'the Chelsea of the Chilterns'.

Water meadows may be noted near Chalfont St Giles from the paths beside the River Misbourne. Though often quite easy to find a quiet footpath to be alone, one is never far from habitation or a hospitable village pub. The area is crossed by many minor roads and dotted with villages.

From Beaconsfield the B474 goes to Penn.

Friends Meeting House, Jordans

Quite near, by minor roads, is Jordans where the world-famous Friends Meeting House can be found. It is impossible not to be moved, standing inside this simple but beautiful building.

PLACES OF INTEREST
Bekonscot Model Village   Beaconsfield. A world-famous model village.

Churchwood Reserve   Hedgerly. An RSPB sanctuary.

Jordans Meeting House   Quaker Meeting House.

Milton's Cottage   Chalfont St Giles

Chiltern Open Air Museum   Newlands Park, Chalfont St Giles. Collection of buildings and picnic area.

Royal Army Educational Corps Museum
Wilton Park. Open by appointment only.

WALKS IN THE AREA

The area is a delight for walkers with many well-marked paths.

Seer Green From Seer Green station car park take Williton Lane opposite. At the end, turn left on a road. Take the next left, on a drive at first, then by field paths to Butlers Cross. Take the road towards Chalfont St Giles. After 200 m turn sharp left (west) to Rawlings Farm. Enter Hodgemoor Wood and keep left with the boundary close on the left. Take a left fork, cross the Horse Trail and go left on the Forest Walk to a road. Head south-westerly on the road for 250 m then turn right. After ¼ mile head through a plantation. Follow south to the road and thus to Seer Green.

Penn From the Red Lion at Tylers Green head towards Beaconsfield. 70 m past a garage turn right (south-east), to the road near Parsonage Farm. Go ahead down the lane, but take the sharp left turn. After 150 m take a stile right uphill; at the lane go left. Past the school go left across a field and right on the road to Penn church. Turn right at the main road and left at the Crown (superb view of Penn Bottom). Enter the wood following arrows. Fork left and leave the wood. At the next wood turn left and maintain direction back to Tylers Green.

Chalfont St Giles From the church at Chalfont St Giles, take the footpath down the western side of the River Misbourne towards Chalfont St Peter. Stay right of the tennis club, behind the pavilion. Just beyond, turn right into an alleyway leading to Boundary Road. Turn right again back to the meadow land, north-west to pass Windmill Farm and reach a road. Turn right then left after 200 m. A footpath cuts off the corner to the next road. Go northerly (right) along this road and just past Little Bowstridge turn left on a track; after 50 m turn right over a stile. Follow this path, parallel to the road, to Three Households. Turn right, back to the start.

Beaconsfield

SOUTHERN CHILTERNS

Oxfordshire

OS Map: 1:50,000 Sheets Nos 174 and 175

Location

Wallingford is on the banks of the Thames. The A4130 comes in from Wantage to the west while the A329 comes up from Newbury sixteen miles south. London is 47 miles away, Oxford 12, and Newbury 16. Wallingford may also be reached via the A423 from Henley-on-Thames or the A4074 from Reading.

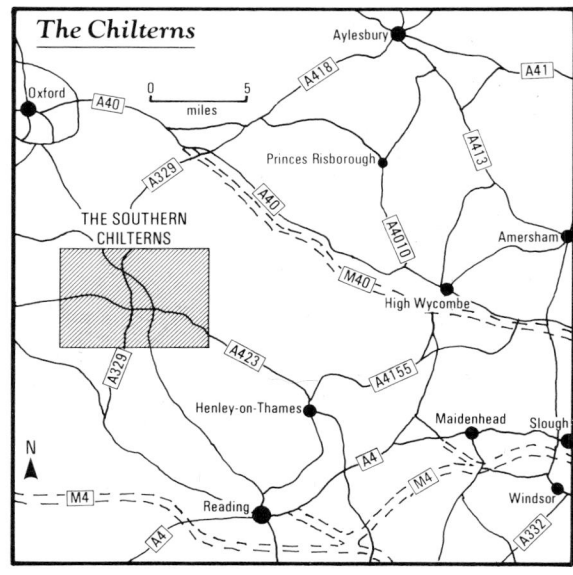

Wallingford is a Thameside town rather than a Chiltern town, but it is a convenient starting place from which to visit the southern part of the hills before they cross the river and become Downs. There is also the advantage of riverside walks with the opportunity of hiring a boat at Wallingford.

The town is unremarkable, except for the fine market square with its pillared town hall and cast-iron drinking trough. The Danes destroyed Wallingford in 1006. William the Conqueror crossed what must have been a ford in 1066 and King Henry II granted the town's first charter in 1155.

A fine stone bridge of twenty arches carries the road over the Thames to Crowmarsh Gifford. Three miles south, just off the A4074, is the village of Ipsden lying in a shallow valley, a typical Chiltern 'bottom'.

Higher up the valley is the Wellplace Bird Farm which rather belies its name by having local small animals as well as exotica such as bush babies and monkeys.

South-east by two miles is the village of Checkendon. At this point the beech woods are thickening and Checkendon is snugly surrounded by sheltering woods.

This really is an ideal corner of the Chilterns. The great motorways of the M4 west and the M40 north-west reaching out for the West Country

Wallingford Bridge

Wallingford town hall and church

PLACES OF INTEREST

Wellplace Bird Farm and Pets Corner 4 miles east of Wallingford.

Castle Priory Thames Street, Wallingford. The former home of Judge Blackstone, may be viewed by appointment.

Basildon Park (National Trust) Near Pangbourne. The house was built in 1776. Fine furniture, plasterwork and paintings.

Child Beale Wildfowl Park Church Farm, Lower Basildon. Exotic birds and rare breeds. Riverside walk and children's playground.

Westbury Farm Vineyard Purley, near Pangbourne. Fourteen-acre vineyard. Open to groups for winetasting and talks on English wines.

Mapledurham House and Watermill Built late sixteenth – early seventeenth century in red brick. Paintings, furniture and fine plasterwork. Restored watermill nearby.

WALKS IN THE AREA

Wittenham Woods From Shillingford bridge, one of the most graceful of the Thames bridges, take the road past North Farm on the Berkshire side of the river. Continue to Wittenham Woods. In the wood a turn left climbs up to Sinodun Hill, an ancient earthwork. The climb is rewarding for the completeness of the triple banks and the extensive views. From here retrace a little way then turn right to the triangulation point at Brightwell Barrow (113 m). Follow the footpath to Brightwell Farm and the main A4130. Just on the Wallingford side of the cutting go left up and over the hill to rejoin the original track near North Farm.

Grims Ditch From Crowmarsh Gifford take the bridleway south of the road then the footpath south to the corner of a line of trees. Cross the A4074. Grims Ditch now heads easterly, climbing. Cross two minor roads and a drive. On emerging from the woods near Nuffield turn right (south) to Upper House Farm. Turn right almost immediately, descending to Mongewell Woods. At the second road turn right, follow the road to the original crossing point and retrace to the start. The walk could be started from here if the car is parked carefully.

Wallingford From the Berkshire side of the river at Wallingford, riverside paths go both up and downstream. Once away from the town there are few people about. The Ridgeway long distance path crosses the Thames at Goring on its way from Ivinghoe to Avebury.

and Oxford, and the Oxford-Newbury dual carriageway, have enabled all the bustling traffic to speed away and leave it in peace.

The hills rise gently from the river with many pleasant and often unexpected views. The area is criss-crossed by minor roads, footpaths, and bridleways enabling rider, driver, or walker to enjoy the magnificent surroundings in peace and tranquillity.

An ancient earthwork, Grims Ditch, runs in an almost unbroken line from near the village of Nuffield almost to the river. It carries The Ridgeway long distance path but on this section only the hardy types, walking the whole way, are to be found. The Ridgeway follows most of the northern escarpment, sometimes on the original Icknield Way and sometimes on the parts, such as this, contrived to be more attractive.

South of England

THE NORTH HAMPSHIRE DOWNS

Hampshire

OS Map: 1:50,000 Sheet No 174

Location

From the east, M3 to Basingstoke and A339 to Kingsclere, or B3400 from Basingstoke to Overton, then B3051 north towards Kingsclere. From the west, A342 to Andover then any of the minor roads north-east. From the north or south, A34 and A339 to Kingsclere.

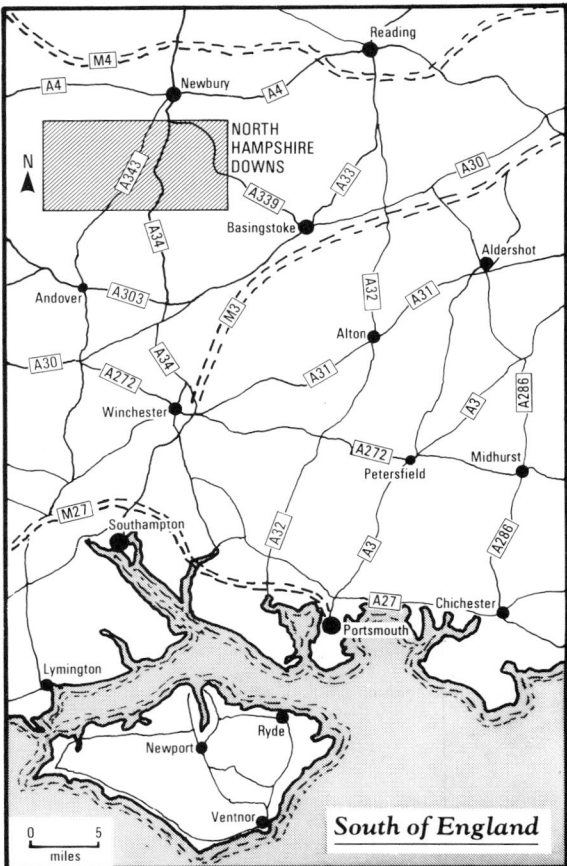

South of England

This swathe of north-facing chalk downs, the western outliers of the North Downs, are best known to the inhabitants of nearby towns, such as Wantage and Newbury in the Vale of Pewsey to the north, or Andover and Basingstoke to the south. There is, however, a spot which should be known to most, and this is Watership Down, immortalised by Richard Adams in his novel about a colony of rabbits living on the down. This is an actual place and is typical of the chalk escarpment, about 1½ miles south-south-west of Kingsclere.

Modern roads, especially trunk roads, run more or less north – south, with the exception of the A339. This is in strange contrast with roads which have been here since ancient times. A Portway, which predates the Roman roads, runs roughly east – west along the crest of the downs and three Roman roads run with the impunity of a conqueror, straight as a die, north-west and north-east from a crossroads outside Andover. Another Roman road comes up from Winchester to join the north-east road at *Calleva* near modern Silchester. *Calleva* (GR645625) was one of Roman Britain's major cities and its excavations are worth seeing.

Over to the west, Combe Gibbet (GR365622) on Inkpen Hill is a grim reminder of punishments meted out to highwaymen and others in the more troubled times of a couple of centuries ago. The gibbet, while it looks old, is not the original, but a weathered replacement, fortunately for ornament and not for use.

The best walking is along the escarpment of the North Downs, using the route of the Portway. Villages and their linking tracks to the south also make for good walking and most have interesting and friendly pubs.

Combe Gibbet

Old Malt Cottage

PLACES OF INTEREST

Combe Gibbet (GR365622). Inkpen Hill summit.

Watership Down (GR495568). Locale of the book of that title.

Calleva Roman Town (GR645625). Extensive excavations, remains of major Roman city. Artefacts in Reading museum.

Stratfield Saye Home of the Duke of Wellington. Open to the public.

Basing House (GR663526). 1½ miles east of Basingstoke. Surprisingly modern-looking outer fortications of a manor house which was besieged several times by Cromwellian troops in the Civil War (see also Alresford).

Beacon Hill (GR458573). Earthworks. Country park.

WALKS IN THE AREA

Watership Down Approach by the bridleway from White Hill. 1½ miles south of Kingsclere via the B3051.

Beacon Hill (GR458573). A short uphill stroll from the layby car park on the A34.

Combe Gibbet (GR365622). Can be approached from several directions, but the best is from the Portway which is joined from any of the villages to the north or south.

Linkenholt and the Portway Start from Linkenholt village (GR364581) and follow the track north-west up Hart Hill Down. Through Combe Wood and take the third turning on the right by a path over Sheepless Hill. Climb to Inkpen Hill and turn right, pass the gibbet and walk along the Portway as far as you like returning to Linkenholt by way of Faccombe.

The Portway between Ashmansworth and the A34 This little used section of the Portway winds in and out of quiet downland and forest. If you cannot arrange transport back to the start, then either reverse the walk, or better still, return by the quiet lanes between Lower Woodcolt Farm (GR443548) and Crux Easton village.

ALRESFORD

Hampshire

OS Map: 1:50,000 Sheet No 185

Location

Alresford is at the crossroads of the A31 and
B3046 about 7½ miles east-north-east of Winchester and 18 miles south-south-west of Basingstoke.

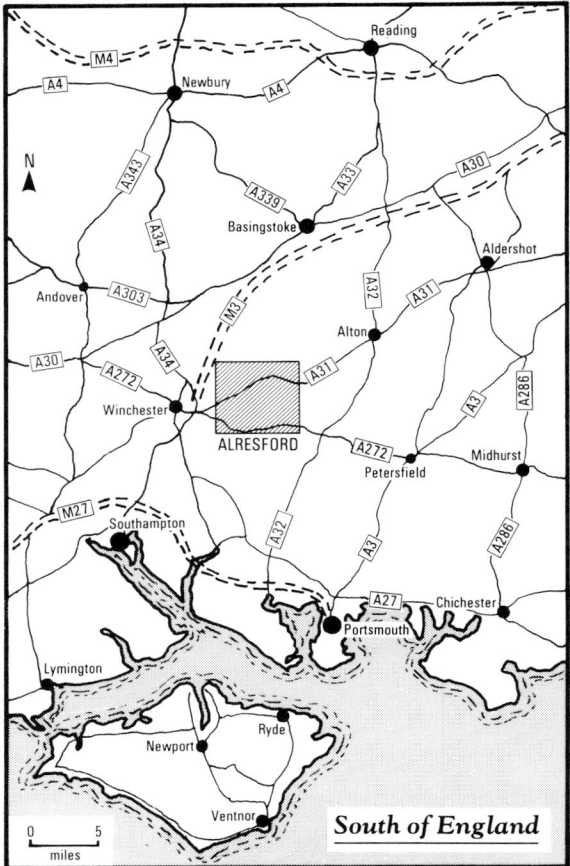

South of England

Alresford, or to give it its local pronunciation,
'Arlesford', is an enigmatic mix of confusing titles.
For one thing, Old Alresford is a newer place than
'New' Alresford, also there is much local argument
over why and when the 'r' was switched and how
the older part of the town became 'new'. Answers
to these questions vary, but what's in a name? This
is a sleepy little town that manages to keep much of
its ancient charm despite the incursions of modern
development.

Alresford has a long history. Ancient man tilled
the first fields on the surrounding downs, and later
Roman settlers built a farm and villa to the north
of the town. A brave lady of Tichbourne Manor, in
defiance of her uncaring husband, crawled, while
ill, around the bounds of his estate and forced him
to carry out his promise of food for the local poor.
This act is still commemorated by the annual
distribution of the Tichbourne Dole. In Victorian
times the Tichbourne fortune was the subject of a
scandalous claim.

*The Old Fulling Mill,
Alresford*

Wars have been fought on the broad acres of the surrounding countryside. One of the turning points in the Civil War took place in fields near Cheriton, a battle won decisively by Cromwell's reorganised army. In 1644 following the siege of Arundel castle, Royalist and Parliamentary troops marched on parallel courses until they reached Cheriton. The Royalists stationed themselves on the Alresford or northern side of the dry valley where the A272 Winchester – Petersfield road now runs. The London Regiment of the Parliamentary forces were billeted in fields around the group of cottages on the main road still known as 'Little London'. The battle which took place was decided by a foolish blunder on the part of the Royalists. They made a cavalry charge towards the London Regiment's position, down the sunken lane between Alresford and the bend in the A272 between Bramdean and Cheriton. The narrow lane, unchanged to this day, is hardly wide enough for two horsemen to ride side by side, so all that the Parliamentary troops had to do was pick the Royalists off one by one.

Napoleonic prisoners were kept in Alresford where a number of them died and their graves can still be seen in the churchyard.

Plans for the US Army's part in the Normandy invasion were made in a house at the bottom of Market Street. Fuel for the invading armies and the pipeline to carry it to them were stored nearby. This amazing plan, known as PLUTO (Pipeline under the ocean), made sure that the thousands of gallons of fuel needed for the allied tanks and vehicles was never far behind the front line.

Despite all these historical events, Alresford remains a predominantly agricultural area. Watercress is grown in the pure waters of the River Itchen, which is one of England's best trout streams. When the railway line was open for commercial traffic, whole trainloads were shipped out and the line became known as the 'Watercress Line'. Closed in February 1973, the line has been reopened by a voluntary society still using the title.

PLACES OF INTEREST

Watercress Line Steam line run by enthusiasts.

The Old Fulling Mill Old mill house built over the river (private house and not open to the public). Can be seen from the riverside footpath at the bottom of Market Street.

Alresford Church Napoleonic graves.

Tichbourne House

WALKS IN THE AREA

Alresford to Bramdean Follow the bridleway south-east from the golf course. Cross the 1644 battlefield and walk as far as Bramdean. Return by way of Cheriton and Tichbourne.

Alresford River Walk North of the town by way of the watercress beds and the Old Fulling Mill.

Alresford Park to Abbotstone Start at the west end of Alresford and follow bridleways to Abbotstone. Return by way of Old Alresford.

Alresford to Winchester A series of linked footpaths and bridleways, part of the Pilgrim Way from Winchester to Canterbury, follow the Itchen valley from Alresford to Winchester.

Ancient holloways near Alresford

SELBORNE

Hampshire

OS Map: 1:50,000 Sheet No 186

Location

From Portsmouth take the A3 north as far as Petersfield and turn left on to the A325 (Farnham road). A mile beyond Liss turn left on the B3006 (Alton road), Selborne is a further three miles. If travelling south by the A325 the B3006 is ¾ mile on the right beyond Greatham. Or take the A32 Farnham – Alton road) as far as East Tisted and turn right on to the unnumbered road for three miles.

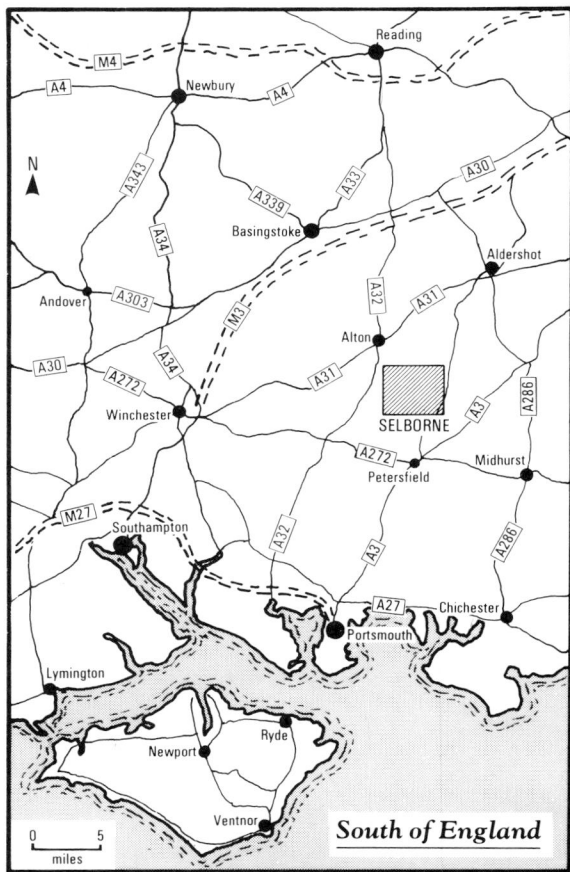

South of England

Selborne today, apart from its surfaced road, would be instantly recognisable to its most famous son, Gilbert White (1720-93) the naturalist, who spent most of his life here.

Born at Selborne, Gilbert White was destined for the life of a country gentleman, whose interest in wildlife would be centred around what was worth shooting for the table. He quickly tired of this, and began to record details of the local natural history, by writing letters to his friends Thomas Pennant and Daines Barrington. Fortunately most of the letters survived and were incorporated into the masterpiece *The Natural History of Selborne*. As well as recording the most

Gilbert White's church, Selborne

minute details of natural history, his keen eyes also noted much of the human story which unfolded around him in his travels in and around Selborne village.

In a time when foreign travel was a rarity, he developed the nucleus of a theory that certain birds migrate in winter. Noticing their absence, at first he thought they hibernated, and to test this he dug out the burrows of sand martins. Finding empty nests he concluded that the birds had followed the sun southwards; the fact that they had gone as far as Africa was only proven many years later.

That other famous son of Selborne, Captain Oates, who died in tragic circumstances on Scott's ill-fated expedition to the South Pole, is commemorated together with White in the Gilbert White Museum housed in 'The Wakes' on the main street.

We are lucky that succeeding generations have preserved much of the area around Selborne, especially the Hanger (a hanger is a wooded, usually with beech, chalk scarp) and Selborne Common, which are now owned by the National Trust.

Carefully graded footpaths, including White's zigzag track, climb Selborne Hanger. The nature trail and the Gilbert White museum are a must; not only do they explain the life of the brilliant man, but they also help us to understand present day agricultural demands and their effects on our environment.

PLACES OF INTEREST
Nature Trails on Selborne Hanger
'The Wakes' Gilbert White's house— now a museum.

Alton (5 miles north-west by the B3006). Busy agricultural town. On the Pilgrim's Way. Hop fields. Church door has bullet holes fired by Parliamentary troops in 1643.

Chawton House (1 mile south-west of Alton). Home of novelist Jane Austen for the last eight years of her life.

Romany Museum and Workshop Selborne.

WALKS IN THE AREA
Selborne Hanger and the Common Follow signposts from the village.

Oakhanger Stream From Selborne Church follow the farm lane to Priory Farm and then along the stream bank as far as Oakhanger. Return by field path to Candovers. Turn left on a bridlepath going south and enter the woods above Oakhanger Stream. About ¼ mile south of Wick Hill Farm turn right on a woodland path back to Selborne.

Temple Manor and its orchards This lies to the east of Selborne and is reached by either a field path or a quiet lane.

Noar Hill Makes an attractive alternative to Selborne Hanger. Noar Hill is to the south of the village and is reached by a path which starts behind the cottages by the fork between the East Tisted and B3006 roads.

'The Wakes', Selborne

OLD WINCHESTER HILL
AND THE MEON VALLEY

Hampshire

OS Map: 1:50,000 Sheet No 185

Location

Old Winchester Hill (GR640206), is about half a mile due west of the unclassified Warnford – Clanfield road. To reach Warnford from Alton and Guildford follow the A32; or from Petersfield take the A272 to the crossroads by the West Meon Hut public house and turn left on to the A32. From Winchester take the A32 eastwards beyond West Meon Hut and turn right.

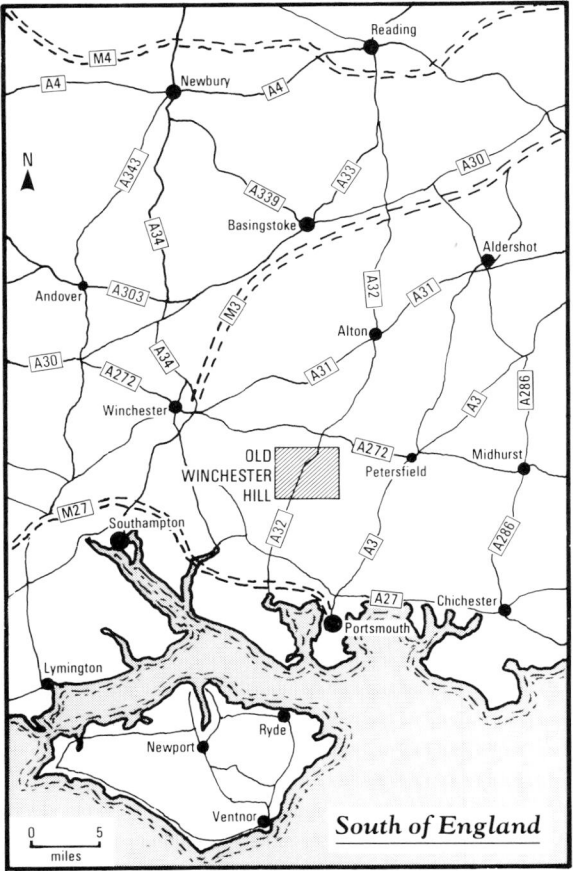

South of England

Old Winchester Hill is certainly older than at least the oldest visible parts of Winchester, but where the name came from is something of a mystery. The hill is capped by the extensive earthworks of an Iron Age fort, so it was certainly inhabited long ago, but by whom and what the connection was with Winchester, some 12 miles away to the north-west, is open to conjecture. The present inhabitants of the hill are mostly the foxes, rabbits and badgers which live in the scrub-filled combe on the north side of the hill.

Not only is the hill an interesting place as regards its ancient fortifications, but the chalky

A quiet backwater in West Meon

soil, untouched by the plough, is a unique haven for a wide range of special chalk downland flora and fauna. So important is the hill in this respect that the whole area between the road and North Combe has been designated a nature reserve. Plaques explaining the various features are sited by the roadside near to the car park. There is also a nature trail beginning at the car park.

From the walker's point of view, there are several routes which converge on the hill, either from the Meon Valley in the west or from East

Meonstoke church

Meon, about halfway from Petersfield. It is also on the new and logical westward extension of the South Downs Way.

Royalist cavalry under the command of Lord Ralph Hopton, shadowing Colonel Waller's Parliamentary army, camped on Old Winchester Hill on the night before the battle of Cheriton in 1644.

Villages in the Meon Valley have the A32 and its traffic to contend with, but most preserve their attractiveness nonetheless. Their river, the Meon, is a pleasant enough trout stream but has never been able to vie with its more up-market brothers in the west of the county.

Man has lived a settled life for many centuries in this tranquil area. A prosperous Roman or perhaps Romanised Briton lived a comfortable life in a large villa near West Meon, but the inhabitants of Lomer village (GR593234) were not so lucky. This extensive village, which can still be identified by mounds, was abandoned in the Middle Ages following the Black Death.

PLACES OF INTEREST
Old Winchester Hill   Earthworks and nature reserve.
Lomer Village   (GR593234). Deserted medieval village.
Meon Valley   Pretty villages and friendly pubs.
Petersfield   Market town.
Marwell Zoo   Off the A333 west of Colden Common.

WALKS IN THE AREA
Warnford   Follow the field path by way of the Peake Farm to the western end of the hill.
Exton   Either by field paths to the north of Shavard Farm, or via lanes and field paths east of Harvestgate Farm.
East Meon   A cart track leads west to Henwood Down and then by field path and road to Whitewool Farm, beyond which a lane and footpath leads up to the Warnford to Clanfield road. Turn left for the hill.
Lomer Village from Exton   Follow the quiet lane north-westwards out of Exton and across the upper slopes of Beacon Hill. Turn right and then left at the staggered crossroads, and then left again on to the farm track for Lomer Farm. The village is identifiable by mounds in the field to your left. This is private land and permission must be sought before entering. Return by the same route, varied by using the field path which cuts a corner off the road beneath Beacon Hill.

BUTSER HILL AND PETERSFIELD

Hampshire

OS Map: 1:50,000 Sheet No 197

Location

Petersfield lies at the crossroads of the A3 and
A272, 19 miles east of Winchester, 16 miles
south-west of Farnham and 16 miles north-east of
Portsmouth. Butser Hill, an outlier of the South
Downs, is 3 miles south-west of the town,
overlooking the A3.

Petersfield, a pleasant market town, still manages
to convey a rural atmosphere despite being a
popular dormitory for industrial Portsmouth. It is
even home for a growing number of commuters
who daily travel into London by Inter-City trains
on the Portsmouth line.

Nearby Butser Hill, by contrast, is no longer a
place where people need to live. This is the site of a
prehistoric fort where our early forefathers gathered,
safe from attack and also away from the swamps of
the forested valleys.

Today all that has changed; the valleys are
drained, the trees mostly planted, and life is very
different from what it was thousands of years ago.

An interesting experiment is being carried out
on Butser Hill. A little to the north of the summit,
an Iron Age farmstead has been developed where
farming methods, crops and animals similar to
those common 4,000 years ago are being reared.
Wattle huts and pit storage systems have been
made, with exceptionally interesting results, to
give an insight into this ancient culture. Access is
restricted to the site, but there is a demonstration
area close by, near the entrance of the Queen
Elizabeth Forest, which explains the work that is
going on.

As a walking area this is virtually unknown by
anyone living outside the district. Butser we have
mentioned and is worth a visit; the valley is mostly
devoted to dairy farming and so field paths are
easy to follow. Butser is typical downland, but to
the north of Petersfield beyond the village of
Steep, the landscape is so convoluted that it has
been given the apt title of the Hampshire Alps.
Woodlands abound, and the Queen Elizabeth
Forest to the east of the busy A3 is one of the most
natural-looking plantations in the country. It also
has the added advantage of a Nature Trail.

South of England

Shire horse ploughing matches are popular in the area

Experimental Iron Age farm on Butser Hill ▷

PLACES OF INTEREST

Butser Hill Iron Age Farm   Interpretive exhibition.

Country Park.

Queen Elizabeth Forest Trails   Permanent wayfaring course

Heath Pond Boating Lake   (By the A2126 ¾ mile south-east of Petersfield town centre.)

Portsmouth Dockyard   HMS *Victory, Mary Rose* Tudor warship and Gosport Submarine Museum.

Haslemere Educational Museum

Hurst Mill Gardens   (Private, but open on advertised days in summer).

Ashford Chase Gardens   (Private, but open on advertised days in summer).

WALKS IN THE AREA

Butser Hill from Petersfield   Car or bus to Stroud village and then follow the bridleway through Ramsdean and by way of Twentyways Farm to Butser Hill. Walk downhill and cross the A3 to join a signposted way through the Queen Elizabeth Forest to Buriton and field path north to Petersfield.

The 'Hampshire Alps'   There are several enjoyable routes through these 'alps', the best approach is via Steep and Ashford Chase to Wheathorn Hill.

Buriton and the forests   Follow the track east from Buriton then south through Ditcham Woods for about 3¾ miles as far as the railway line near Woodcroft Farm. Cross the line and walk north on the Charlton – Buriton road until it diverges left away from the railway. Follow the road for about another 180yd when a path on the right climbs steeply up to Head Down Plantation; follow this path all the way back to Buriton.

The Rother Valley Railway   This disused railway track makes an interesting but unofficial long (or short) distance footpath between Petersfield and Midhurst. It can be used to link footpaths or quiet roads to attractive villages.

East Meon   A whole complex of footpaths and bridleways, mostly across pastureland, can be linked across Barrow Hill to East Meon. The return route should be to the north of the village around Park Hill to join the A272 near Bordean House.

Infrequent buses travel along the A272, so unless you can be sure of linking to this service it might be safer to arrange to park cars at either end of the Butser Hill from Stroud and East Meon walks.

THE SOUTH DOWNS
ABOVE MIDHURST

West Sussex

OS Map: 1:50,000 Sheet No 197

Location
Midway between Petersfield and Petworth on the A272 and Haslemere and Chichester on the A256.

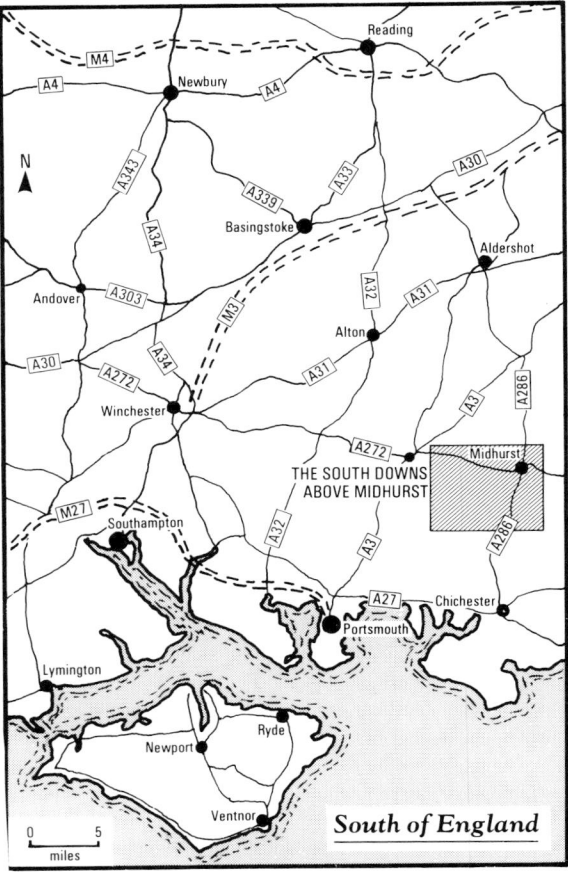

Less well known than the section of the South Downs behind Brighton or Beachy Head, the western end is, however, freer of the plough which spoilt so much of the beautiful springy turf once covering all the downland in the South of England.

Officially the South Downs start to the south of Petersfield and their dramatic outliers are Old Winchester Hill and Butser Hill. To the south of Midhurst, and in particular the River Rother, the chalky downs take on the distinctive shape of a long straight ridge which tops 700ft in many places. Deep dry valleys and combes cut its sides, and with the general tilt of the land dipping south, the angle of the valleys on that side tends to be gentler than those cleaving the steeper northern scarp.

All but the crest of this section of the downs is covered by forest, both natural and planted. As a

Village pond and church, Burton

The South Downs Way above Treyford

result walking is free from the effects of ploughing, and whilst views can sometimes be restricted, there is still a great feeling of freedom everywhere.

The South Downs Way follows, as far as is possible, the spine of the downs and uses ancient tracks. These tracks are also bridleways, and so it is possible for riders as well as walkers to cover this the longest continual stretch of high ground in the south-east.

Neolithic people settled the downs and from the relics they left behind, it would appear that a complex and highly intelligent society flourished 4,000 years ago. Flints, which abound in chalk, were mined for use as tools and weapons and later as a building material. Forts, earthworks, burial mounds and cultivation terraces were so well constructed that they are easily identifiable today, and make interesting diversions when walking along the downs.

The whole of this part of southern England was settled by prosperous Roman families, and no doubt Britons who had accepted the Pax Romana. Remains of luxurious villas, such as the one at Bignor, tell us a lot about their life; details abound such as the fact that they were partial to oysters!

Agriculture has long been an important feature of the area and many old buildings and crafts have been brought together, to make a skilfully preserved working display in the Downland Museum at Singleton.

PLACES OF INTEREST
Singleton Downland Museum
Cowdray park   (Polo)
Petworth House and Deer Park
Bignor Roman Villa   (GR988147).
Fishbourne Roman Palace
Midhurst Common

WALKS IN THE AREA
The route of the South Downs Way makes an excellent link when used in conjunction with paths radiating from the villages along the foot of the downs. The following are a selection of some of the possibilities.
Beacon Hill from South Harting
Cross Dykes and Graffham Down from Cocking or Graffham
Bignor Hill and Houghton Forest from Bignor or West Burton
Levin Down and North Down from Singleton
Linch Down and Didling from Bepton

HAMBLEDON AND BROADHALFPENNY DOWN

Hampshire

OS Map: 1:50,000 Sheet Nos 185 and 196

Location

Hambledon is on the B2150 about half-way between Waterlooville and Droxford (on the A32) in the Meon Valley. Broadhalfpenny Down lies to the north-east of Hambledon above the Clanfield road.

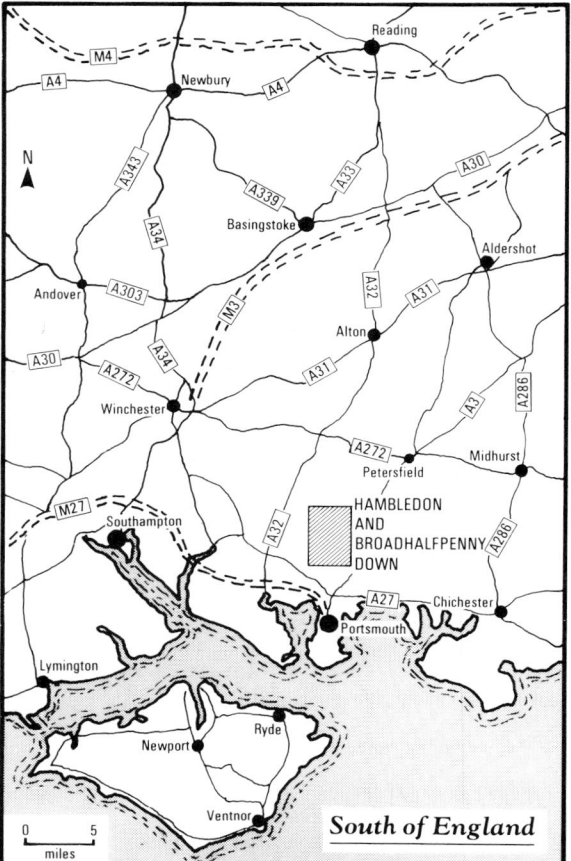

South of England

Broadhalfpenny Down is said to be the birthplace of cricket, that typically English sport. At least that is what the monument opposite the Bat and Ball Inn states. To be factual, the game has medieval origins, but it was polished and organised by the men of nearby Hambledon, and certainly they can claim to be the fathers of the modern version of crickett (the final 't' was dropped later). The history surrounding the development of the game is that the Hambledon men decided, in the mid-eighteenth century, to form what would today be roughly equivalent to a cricket league; and the Bat and Ball Inn rightfully claims to be the oldest cricketing pavilion in the game.

The Hambledon version would be barely recognisable as modern cricket, not the least due to the fact that they only used two stumps instead of three, and the bat was more like a hockeystick. However, the popularity of their game soon increased with the third stump being added in 1778. The reason for this was to eliminate any possible doubts of balls passing unseen between the stumps! In 1788 the newly formed MCC took over the game and it is now, of course, played world-wide.

The area around Hambledon is a quiet haven in the Hampshire countryside, a mere five or six miles from the industrial conurbations of Southampton and Portsmouth. Vineyards were established in Roman times on the warm, easily-drained southern slopes of the downs, and produced many excellent wines. These vintages were produced in the Middle Ages and even later, but with easier transport, cheaper wine from the continent made the local product uneconomic. Since the end of the last war, determined local growers have been slowly but surely developing English vintages. While still expensive, they are becoming acceptable

Hambledon

alternatives to other wines produced in Northern Europe.

The Bat and Ball Inn, Broadhalfpenny Down

PLACES OF INTEREST
Hambledon Vineyards
Portsmouth Harbour *HMS Victory*, the *Mary Rose* Tudor warship.
Gosport Submarine Museum
Fishbourne Roman Palace Chichester.
The Solent Coastline

WALKS IN THE AREA
Broadhalfpenny Down Climb the steep road opposite the church on the south side of Hambledon's main street. At a fork in the road at the top of the hill, turn left for a field path which climbs up to Glidden. Follow the lane north-east from here and across Broadhalfpenny Down, reaching Clanfield road by the Bat and Ball. Walk north from the pub and in a quarter of a mile turn left on a field path towards Chidden Holt Woods. Walk through the woods and down to Hambledon by way of Park House Farm.

Windmill Down This lies behind the vineyard and can be reached by a footpath which starts to the north, opposite the church.

Pithill A pleasant stroll along lanes can be enjoyed by walking to Pithill by a side road south-east from Hambledon. Return either by the road via Rushmere Farm, or turn left and follow the lanes through Glidden and left again for Hambledon.

THE NEW FOREST

Hampshire

OS Map: 1:50,000 Sheet Nos 195 and 196

Location

From the north and east, by the A33 to Winchester; A3090 to Romsey then A31 and A337 to Lyndhurst. From the west, from Salisbury take the A338 to reach the western section of the Forest. From Bournemouth or further west, the A31 reaches the forest boundary beyond Ringwood.

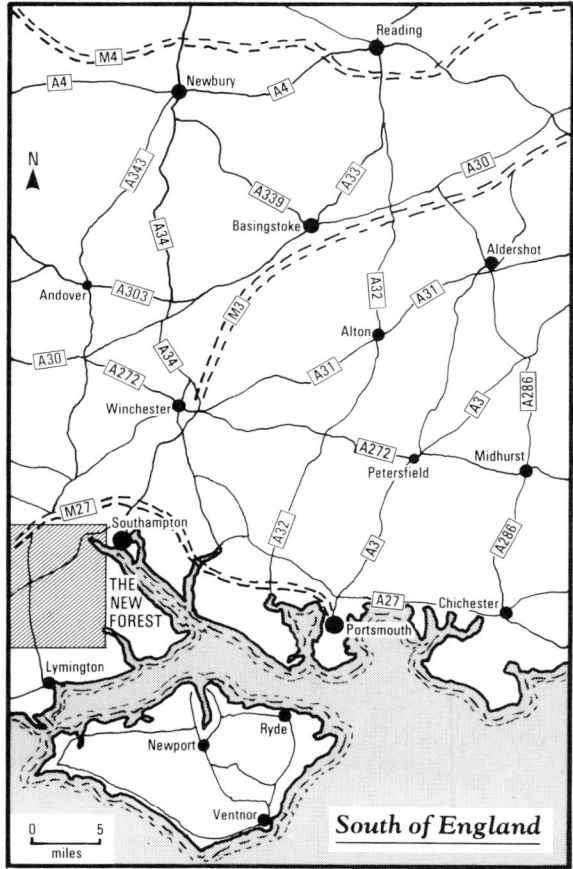

The New Forest was new when William the Conqueror designated it a royal hunting ground. This is where his son, William II, better known as William Rufus, was killed, some say accidentally, by an arrow fired by Walter Tyrell. The strange thing about this story is that Tyrell was a crack shot and claimed that the sun got in his eye. Briefly, records tell us that Tyrell and the King had quarrelled the previous night, and the next morning the Abbot of Gloucester spoke of a dream in which a new king was crowned. Ignoring this warning the king set out to hunt in the forest — a ride which was to be his last. How accidental the killing was is unknown, but suspicion must remain with Tyrell who fled the country soon afterwards.

Visitors from the uplands of Northern Britain are often surprised to find moorland so far south — locals call it heath. Heather and yellow broom grow in profusion on enclaves of sandy ground surrounded by the chalklands of Southern England; careful preservation of ancient rights and privileges have prevented any large developments over the years.

Wild New Forest ponies have freedom to roam the heaths until roundup time, when they are sold at traditional sales grounds such as Beaulieu Road. Decisions on common rights are sorted out at Lyndhurst, the 'capital' of the New Forest.

This is open country and unless you know the area, or are good with a compass as well as a map, take great care when wandering around some of the quieter reaches of the forest. Walking on the unenclosed heaths can be confusing to strangers to the forest. Footpaths are often only lines on the map, difficult to relate to the actual terrain. Mists are a frequent hazard in autumn and winter. The way to appreciate the forest is to explore it in short

The New Forest near Lyndhurst

The Beaulieu River at Bucklers Hard

stages rather than to attempt long excursions, especially at first.

PLACES OF INTEREST
Ornamental Drive (GR250070). Rhododendrons and woodland.
Rhinefield House (GR265037). Gothic-style house near the Ornamental Drive. Restaurant.
Beaulieu Abbey (GR388026).
Bucklers Hard (GR409999). Maritime museum.
Palace House, Beaulieu (GR387024). Stately home of Lord Montague. Vintage car museum.
Rufus Stone (GR270125).
Broadlands (Romsey). Home of the late Lord Mountbatten.

WALKS IN THE AREA
Brockenhurst and the Queen Bower A six-mile stroll through typical New Forest scenery. From North Weirs on the western outskirts of Brockenhurst follow the path across the heath to Ober House and then north, crossing a minor road to Queen Bower and its ancient oak trees. Return by Bolderfold Bridge and turn right before the A337 to join a track to Brockenhurst.
Emery Down (Near Lyndhurst). A walk through ancient forest glades. At White Moor, 1¾ miles west of Lyndhurst a series of paths wander through forest glades and open heath by way of Warwick Slade, Brinken Wood and Allum Green.
Rufus Stone The site of this ancient mystery is signposted from the A31, 1½ miles west of Cadnam. Set deep in a forest glade, the stone can be the focal point of an easy walk by way of Bignall Wood (north-east), Cauterton (west), where the Walter Tyrell inn offers refreshements as well as an interesting mural depicting the death of William Rufus.

THE ISLE OF WIGHT

Isle of Wight

OS Map: 1:50,000 Sheet No 196

Location

Ferries run from Portsmouth, Southampton and Lymington. The service is fast and frequent and if it is a really speedy crossing you are after, then there are hydrofoil and hovercraft ferries from Southampton or hovercraft from Portsmouth.

To most people the Isle of Wight is mainly looked on as a holiday island where its permanent residents, if not looking after holidaymakers, are perhaps engaged in one of the island's specialised engineering industries or in growing some of the more exotic fruit and vegetables. It is also well-known that the island's waters are famous amongst sailing devotees. What is not perhaps so well known is that the Isle of Wight has some excellent and extremely varied walking, which can vary from coastal pottering to striding out on some of

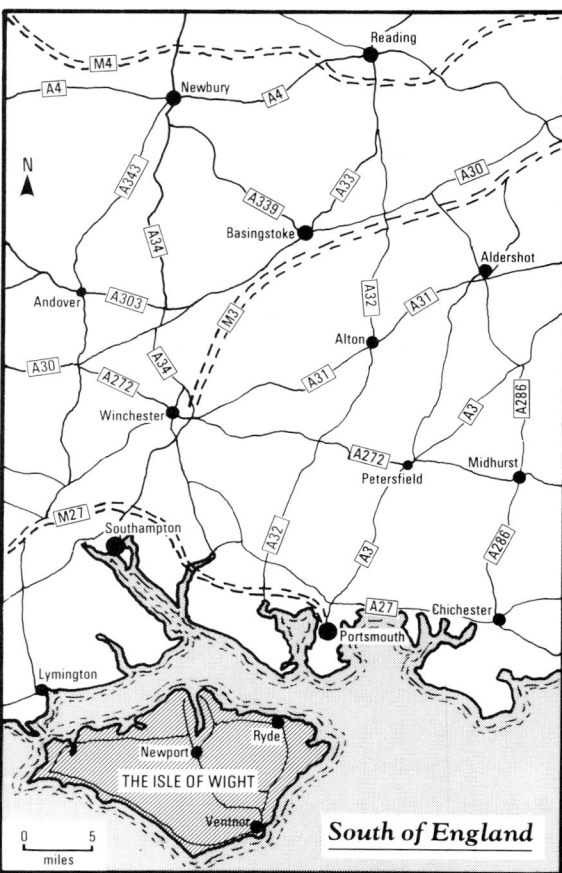

South of England

The Landslip, Bonchurch

the last downland in the south of England to escape the plough.

The island is an amazing mixture of geological features, such as the dramatic Needles to the west, or the multicoloured sands in the cliffs above Alum Bay. Wet underlying strata between Shanklin and Ventnor has caused a landslip where the walker can wander in an almost fairyland-like glade from Luccombe Chine to Bonchurch. The island rises steeply from north to south with deeply indented waterways, the one at Freshwater almost severing its western tip.

The Isle of Wight had always been sought after for its mild climate. The Romans first settled here and built their palatial villas, safely protected by the sea from the warlike people further north.

Freshwater Bay and Tennyson Down ▷

This was the first place in England to be truly settled.

When England courted with the idea of becoming a republic, King Charles was held prisoner in Carisbrooke castle while Parliament debated over what to do with him. Much later Queen Victoria, shunning the world in mourning for her consort, lived out the last of her days at Osborne House. The house, incidentally, was designed by her husband, Prince Albert.

Railways once spread all over the island, but now the only one is that which meets the ferry at Ryde pier. Strangely enough these trains are the same design as those running on the London Underground.

In contrast to authorities in other parts of the country, the local county council has adopted an outward looking policy towards footpaths and walking in general. They must be commended for this, especially their work in mapping out so many long distance trails across the island. Details of these routes are published on a comprehensive set of leaflets which are available from the County Offices, Newport, Isle of Wight.

PLACES OF INTEREST
Carisbrooke Castle
Alum Bay
Blackgang Chine
Godshill village
Newtown Nature Reserve Trail
Roman Villas
Shipping in the Solent
Tall Ships Race

WALKING IN THE AREA
Quiet walking can be found more or less anywhere on the Isle of Wight away from centres of population. The following are suggestions of areas where the most enjoyable walking may be found.
Coastal:
Ventnor (The Landslip and St Boniface Down).
Blackgang Chine to St Catherine's Point.
Chilton Chine to Brook Bay.
The Medina estuary to Newport.
Tennyson Down above Freshwater Bay.
Inland:
Brighstone Forest on either side of the Calbourne – Brighstone road.
St Catherine's Hill above Niton.
St Martin's Down above Ventnor.

Dorset

CRANBORNE CHASE

Dorset

OS Map: 1.50,000 Sheet No 195

Location

Knowlton is on the B3078 between Cranborne and Wimborne Minster. The A354 Salisbury to Blandford Forum road parallels the B3078 here. The A31 trunk road comes west from Ringwood over the border from Hampshire through Wimborne Minster to continue to Dorchester. This area is seventeen miles south of Salisbury.

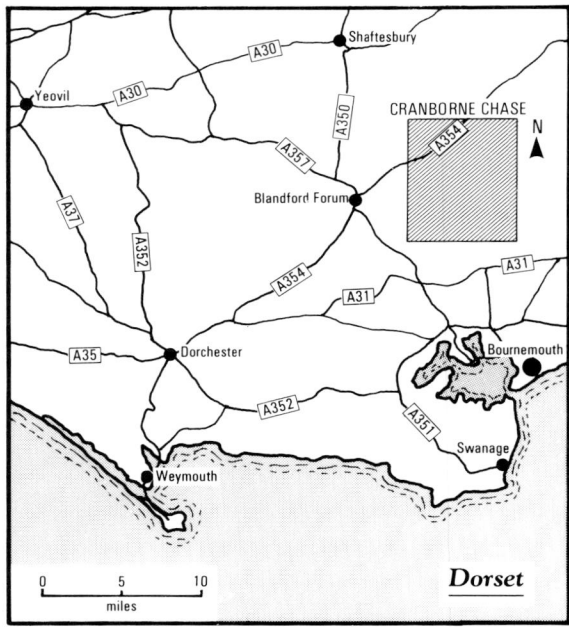

This is an area of transition; the country changes from the heathlands to the east and the little valleys of the chalk downs to the west. Here the slopes are gentle. All around is the mystery of ages gone by. Not far away are the traces of ancient settlements: a great Roman road came down this way from Salisbury; the Saxon invaders came this way, and Bokerley Dyke, a few miles north, was erected by the Romano-British as a defence in the sixth century.

Here where the downs begin, and the main roads have not yet arrived (and, it is hoped, never will), one must tread carefully. The peace and solitude of these open downs stir the soul.

Cranborne Chase, west of the A354, is an excellent place to walk. A chase was a hunting ground owned by a non-royal; a royal hunting ground was called a forest.

Alongside the B3078 is the River Allen. It rises swiftly from the chalk with one major source near Monkton-Up-Wimborne, and another near the A354. The latter stream flows through Gussage St Michael and Gussage All Saints before the two join near Knowlton Circles.

Knowlton is a strange and timeless place. There was a medieval village here which has now completely disappeared. There are still the remains of a bronze age henge, however. It is interesting to speculate on the forces at work which caused the

Knowlton Church within a prehistoric henge

Cranborne Chase near Tollard Royal ▷

invading Normans to build a church in the centre of the henge; and caused the settlement to become depopulated and the church to fall into disuse. The ruin, in its atmospheric setting, keeps its secrets.

The River Allen flows gently on its way before joining the River Stour just south of the cathedral-like Wimborne Minster. The Great Minster stands on a Saxon site. Inside is an 800-year-old font and a chained library.

PLACES OF INTEREST
Chettle House   House and gardens.
Wimborne Minster   Minster. St Margaret's Hospital chapel. Priest's House Museum. Merley Tropical Bird Gardens.
Cranborne   Twelfth-century church. Picturesque village.
Knowlton Circles
Shaftesbury   Abbey ruins. Mediveval church. Local history museum. Craft and Art Gallery.
Blandford Forum   Georgian market town. Royal Signals Museum at Blandford Camp.

WALKS IN THE AREA
Walk 1   Park a quarter of a mile east towards Ringwood from the junction of the A354 and the B3081. The earthwork is the Roman road. Go southwards, cross a minor road. (At the next junction turn left for a shorter walk.) At the next road turn left to Gussage All Saints. The road bends left then right. Where the road goes right keep straight on. Ignore two side turnings, take the next fork right and soon rejoin the shorter walk. At the next road go right then left on a track to Squirrel's Corner. At the B3081 go left back to the car.
Walk 2   From Chettle near the church head south-west. At a track junction turn left. Go round three sides of a field to a barn then almost south. At the next crossing track go left to return to Chettle.
Walk 3   Park at Badbury Rings. Walk northeast on the Roman road. A half-mile past King Down Farm turn right and then next right. At the road (B3082) take the footpath past Lodge Farm and over the fields to the start.

THE VALLEYS OF THE CERNE AND PIDDLE

Dorset

OS Map: 1:50,000 Sheet No 194

Location

The A35 runs from Bournemouth to Dorchester. North of Dorchester the A352 goes to Sherbourne which is on the A30 between Shaftsbury and Yeovil. From Dorchester the B3143 almost parallels the A352 and the A37 to the west, heads northerly to Yeovil.

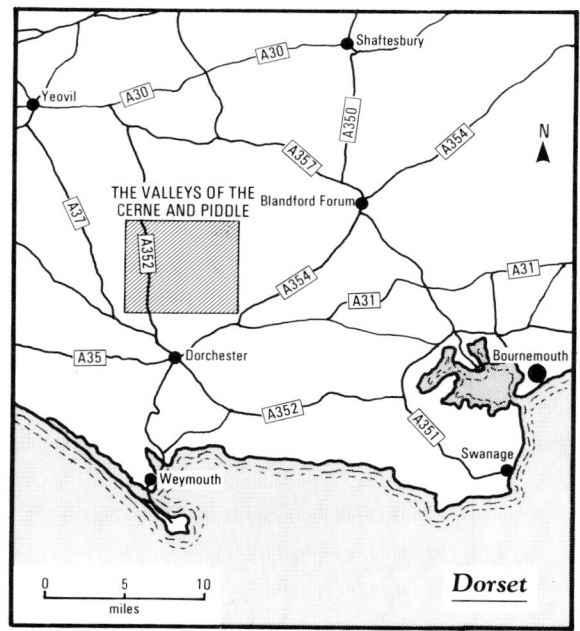

From Dorchester take the B3143 north up the valley of the River Piddle. This is a lovely scenic drive through the tiny hamlets and the villages, some of which have changed little through the years. Branch off on to the B3146 to go through Glanville Wootton passing the great hillfort at Dungeon Hill on the way. The B3146 joins the A352, turn left for Minterne Magna and Cerne - Abbas, following the course of the River Cerne back to Dorchester.

This is an area of tranquil byways and minor roads, small manor houses and small farms. Buzzards soaring gently, riding the air currents, match a mood that can often be felt in this part of Dorset. A mixture of awe at the ancient past, stretching into prehistory that shaped the land and brought about the present beauty that so inspired the more recent poets and authors.

'Dorset grows on you in quite a mystical way' wrote Norman Wymer in 1984. This happens to many people. It is amazing how peaceful and quiet it can be on these byways and footpaths, when one considers that not far away main roads traverse the county taking holidaymakers further south or west. However these two valleys, and the footpaths around are a haven of peace and tranquillity. In the various walks around this area one is unlikely to meet many people, once away from the roads.

Stocks at Cerne Abbas

Start of footpath to Giant's Hill, Cerne Abbas

PLACES OF INTEREST

Purse Caundle Manor House Fifteenth-century house with original great hall, period furniture.

Sherborne Old and new castles. Abbey. Small museum.

Lullington Silk Farm Butterflies in natural surroundings, breeding rooms, silk processing.

Cerne Abbas Church of St Mary. Remains of ninth-century Benedictine Abbey. Fourteenth-century abbey house (gardens only). Gardens at Minterne Magna.

Wolfeton House At Charminster. A fourteenth-century moated manor house.

Athelhampton House Near Puddletown.

Dorchester

  Military Museum Exhibits from the Dorset regiments.

  County Museum

  Town Trail 3½ miles, three hours.

  Old Crown Court Scene of the Tolpuddle Martyrs' trial.

  Maiden Castle and Maumbury Rings Pre-historic hillfort and circle.

WALKS IN THE AREA

East Hill Ridge North of Minterne Magna turn left for Telegraph Hill. Park near the highest point and walk south on the ridge of East Hill. After one mile the bridleway swings west to descend to a track near some ponds. Turn right and go up the valley to the road near the start.

Dorsetshire Gap Just clear of the last buildings north of Alton Pancras a track goes east up the hill. In a quarter-mile take a left fork, then right, follow a bridleway to Armswell Farm. Cross the road and carry on south-east to the Dorsetshire Gap. Here turn left to return to the minor road at The Folly. Return over Ball Hill and Church Hill to the start.

Crete Hill From Godmanstone take the bridle-way westerly 100m south of Smith's Arms. Climb to the highest point overlooking the next valley. Turn left, south to Crete Hill (189m). Continue to a double fork, turn left and left at the next junction down the road. Cross over to Higher Forston Farm. Go north past the farm, soon uphill. At a junction go left down to the river and a footbridge back to the Smith's Arms.

ISLE OF PURBECK

Dorset

OS Map: 1:50,000 Sheet No 195

Location

The Isle of Purbeck must be reached through Wareham, which is a few miles south of the A31. It is across the bay from Bournemouth and the A351 runs from Swanage, on the coast, to join the A35 just north of Poole harbour.

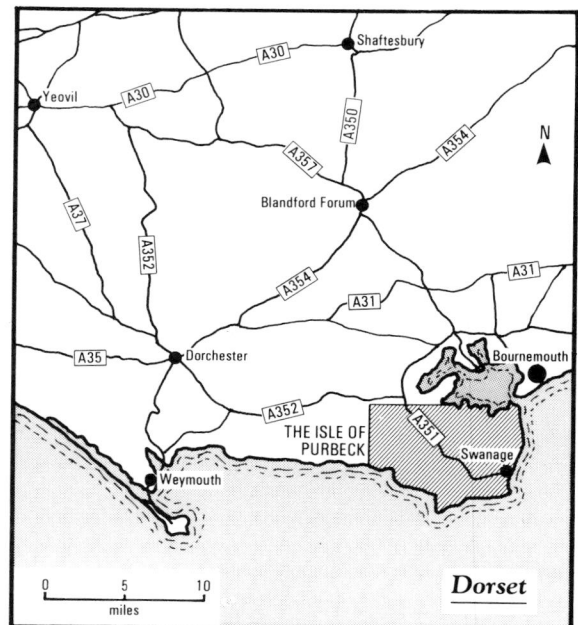

The Isle of Purbeck is a fascinating place. The only sensible modern route is via Wareham. Of course there is the ferry across the mouth of Poole Harbour from Sandbanks and there are a couple of minor roads to the west; it is possible to work out a route with a detailed map.

It is called an Isle because in the past, it probably was, to all intents and purposes, an island for most of the year. The River Frome is less than six miles from the coast near Lulworth and just beyond that there is a large marshy area near Moreton Heath. Even when the River Frome was crossed and the heath and bog beyond negotiated, a second major barrier loomed; the Purbeck Hills.

The first record of habitation at Corfe goes back to 978 when Elfrida, widow of King Edgar, had a hunting lodge there. The castle was begun in 1080 and it was a royal castle until sold by Queen Elizabeth I.

Corfe Castle though in ruins is still imposing. It was never taken by storm but by treachery. In 1646 Parliament voted to destroy the castle and its present state is due to the blasting in that attempt.

A magnificent ridge walk is possible from Ballard Point to Grange Arch. In such a small area there is a great variety: the cliff paths forming part of the Dorset Coast Path; the ridge walk; the heaths to the north of the hills. Again, north of the hills is Poole Harbour, the largest natural harbour in the world.

Though busy in summer — often the main road, the A351, is very congested — it is quite possible to get away from the crowds. Once more than a few hundred yards from the car park, there are few enough people about. Walk along the cliffs to Chapmans Pools and you may well be alone.

Corfe Castle

A path in Wareham Forest

PLACES OF INTEREST

Corfe Castle Open daily.

Smedmore House An eighteenth-century house near Kimmeridge.

Swanage Steam trains at the old railway station. Sandy beach. Diving school.

Wareham The chapel on the wall with the tomb of Lawrence of Arabia. The old town walls. Art gallery. Old church and priory.

Durlston Country Park Swanage.

Nature Trails At Studland, Arne Heath, and Wareham Forest.

Blue Pool Near Corfe Castle.

WALKS IN THE AREA

Ridge Walk (25 miles) From Swanage take the coast path westerly to Kimmeridge Bay. Head inland over the first ridge to the road near Steeple. Take the road uphill, north-west. Turn right on a track up to the second ridge. At the ridge go east to pass Grange Arch and Corfe Castle, here take the minor road under the old railway bridge. Take a path ahead, left off the road. Continue high on the ridge to Ballard Down, crossing another minor road.

Rempstone Heath Just off the B3351 is a minor road to Bushey. Park carefully on the minor road and take the track over Rempstone Heath towards Ower. There are three possible turnings to the right depending on how far you wish to walk. Return over Newton Heath.

Studland From Studland near the coastguard station take the coast path north. From South Haven Point use the road for just over a mile to return. Turn sharp right on a track to Greenland, here start to swing round left just short of the wood and head straight for Studland.

Note Stay on the paths over the heaths. If you reach the water's edge round Poole Harbour *never* venture on to the mud flats, they are extremely dangerous.

Devon & Cornwall

HARTLAND POINT

Devon

OS Map: 1:50,000 Sheet No 190

Location

In its north-western corner Devon provides two
high barriers to the sea — Baggy Point to the north
of the Taw estuary and Hartland Point to the west
of Bideford, around the holiday town of Clovelly.

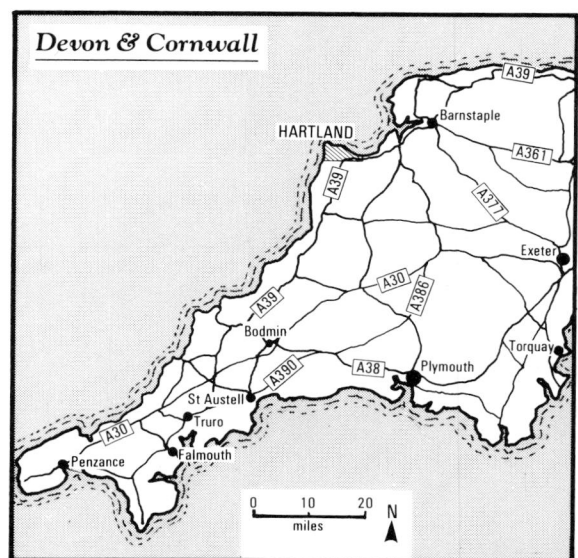

Devon & Cornwall

Apart from places where arbitrary bureaucratic
decisions have robbed it of the distinction, the
River Tamar divides Cornwall from Devon from its
source to its mouth. The river source is about 4
miles inland and instead of following the line of
the river to the sea up around Clovelly, the
boundary-maker turned seaward, following Hars-
land water to the Atlantic. At a stroke the high-
cliff 'Cornish' seascape was transferred to Devon.
Those who associate the seascapes of Devon with
the sandy beaches of Slapton, and the holiday
towns to its north, are sometimes surprised by the
rugged, majestic coastline around Hartland Point,
particulary the spectacular section that lies south
of the lighthouse-crowned headland. Neither is
the country inland from the Point so much in
demand by the tourist trade that the cliff-line is
overburdened with people. En route to the Point
the visitor passes an RAF station, a 'prohibited
area in the meaning of the act', well sited in this
secret corner.

Considering that this is off the beaten track, and
has been deliberately sought out as a remote place,
it seems strange to include in the section a
'honeypot' like Clovelly. A walker does not
always visit an area in high summer, however. On a
still, fine winter's day the cliffs at Hartland are just
as spectacular, and on that day Clovelly is revealed
as a charming pretty village, so unexpected not
only in this part of the county, but in Britain today,
a village without cars. And how could anyone
resist a solitary local piece of roadway called
Hobby Drive, named because its construction
really was the hobby of one lord of the manor.

Clovelly

◁ *Bodmin Moor near Minions*

Bole Hill Quarry, Peak District

The Upper Dove Valley, Peak District

White Moor near Lyndhurst, in the New Forest

Freshwater Bay, Isle of Wight

Old lime kiln, Clovelly Harbour

PLACES OF INTEREST

Clovelly Dykes South of the village; a large (20 acre), Iron Age hillfort also used by the Romans. It would be interesting to know how the Roman soldiery, used to the tideless Mediterranean, viewed the Atlantic rollers crashing into Hartland Point.

Hartland Point The lighthouse attracts many interested visitors impressed not least by the curious cement slope beside the gates. It was, until quite recently, used as a rainwater catcher, the lighthouse-keeper's only source of water.

Hartland Quay South of the Point, with a hotel. The quay was originally built by monks from the Abbey, but was destroyed by the fury of the ocean many years ago. The Abbey itself stood a little way north-east of Stoke village. A more modern mansion incorporates what remains of the Augustinian building and is occasionally open to the public.

Stoke A village worthy of note. Its church, with an interesting dedication to St Nectan, is quite lovely, its 130ft tower being the highest in the county.

WALKS IN THE AREA

Clovelly to Longpeak From Clovelly to Longpeak are 12 miles of marked coastal path along which walks of any duration can be made. At any time the coast has something to offer in terms of seascape and elemental forces. The cliffs themselves are a wonderful sight, tortured grey strata, slabs and pinnacles, the vegetated flat tops, at the right time, ablaze with nature's colours. Near Clovelly, the first section west of the village, the Coastal Path really does go past the 'No Right of Way' sign, on a permissive path through the Clovelly Court Estate. A little further on here is Gallantry Bowers, named not for the gallants of century's past, but from col-an-veor, great ridge in Cornish. The Cornish connection reigns supreme here in Devon.

Inland, the best walking is in the valley of the Abbey River from Stoke to Hartland village and in the wooded approach to Clovelly near National Trust land to the west of the village.

THE LAND OF THE TWO RIVERS

Devon

OS Map: 1:50,000 Sheet No 180

Location

The area is bounded by the Torridge and the Taw, themselves followed by the A386 and A377 respectively, and lies about 4 miles south-east of Great Torrington.

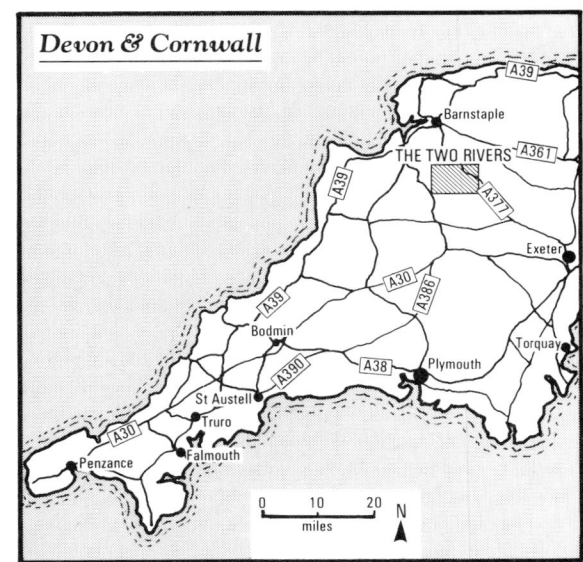

It has been commented that the village of Ashreigney lies in poor and unvisited country to the north of Okehampton. Poor and unvisited it may be, but it is also delightful.

The 'two rivers' are the Torridge and the Taw, famous angling rivers. They are also, sadly, famous as otter-hunting rivers, the Taw being the Gentleman's River, because the inns along it were sited for the hunt's lunches, unlike those on the Torridge. In this country Henry Williamson set *Tarka the Otter*, naming his hero with the prefix

Rolle Aqueduct over the River Torridge, near Torrington

Ashreigney church

Ta, as the two rivers have, and as also have the Tamar and Teign and other rivers in this area. Ta is the ancient word for river hereabouts. It was the waters of the Taw that closed over the heads of Tarka and Deadlock as they fought their last battle.

Between the two rivers the North Devon farmland is bleaker than the lower land of cream teas to the south and west; near Beaford and Roborough it even shows a touch of moorland. But the wooded Torridge valley and the sheltered Mully Brook that drains down to the Taw are excellent, perhaps not as spectacularly beautiful as other Devon rivers, but secluded and unspoilt. The land is heavily farmed and long walks have to be constructed with care, but the lanes that cross the countryside are wide and quiet and can be used to link footpaths.

PLACES OF INTEREST

Great Torrington An excellent centre for the visitor. It is set high on the Torridge valley side and from Castle Hill there are fine views to the river. The town has fairs in May. Within the town is the Dartington Glass Factory, while nearby is Rosemoor with its ornamental gardens.

Beaford A well-kept village above the Torridge, home to an Arts Centre with theatre, music and poetry concerts. The concert season is in summer, so most visitors can take advantage of the centre.

Ashreigney and Burrington Two villages set on the high plateau between the' two rivers', windswept, but with views towards Exmoor and Dartmoor.

There is excellent fishing on both rivers.

WALKS IN THE AREA

Sadly the banks of either of the rivers are rarely followed by footpaths, though the valleys are crossed and visited by many quiet lanes that make a driving visit enjoyable. A notable exception to the lack of footpaths is a section of the Torridge south of Beaford bridge, reached by a pathway from north of, that is above, Beaford Mill. From here a fine circular path continues via Harepath, Beaford itself and the hotel at Abbot's Hill.

An equally fine water-walk follows the Mully Brook by footpath and lane down to the Taw near Hansford Barton. If a return by lanes to the south of the brook is made, then the village of Ashreigney can be used as a starting or ending point.

Elsewhere there are fine pathways across the open farmland (a very good one crosses Beaford Moor), that link minor roads and villages.

TEIGN VALLEY

Devon

OS Map: 1:50,000 Sheet No 191

Location

To the east of the River Bovey and the A382 is Mardon Down, an outlier of the Dartmoor Forest, to the north of which flows the River Teign. The valley described here is from Drewsteignton to Dunsford, a couple of miles north of Moreton-hampstead.

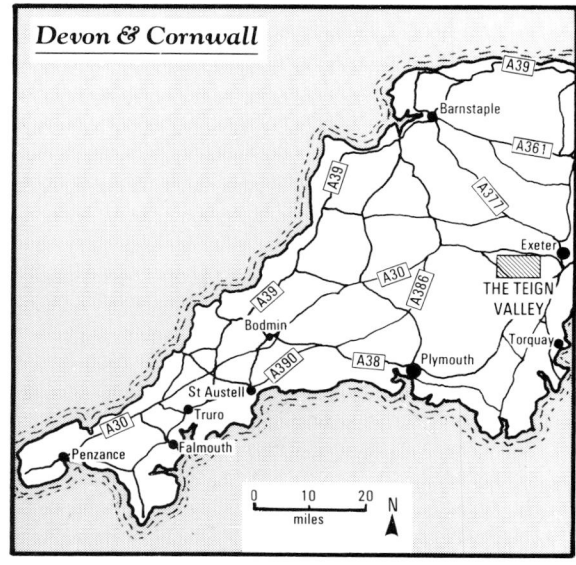

Ask anyone to name the most beautiful river in Devon and the likelihood is they will say the Dart, extolling the virtues of Dartmeet, Dittisham and Dartmouth. Ask if they know the Teign, and most are dismissive. Apart from perhaps knowing that Stokeinteignhead has the longest single-word placename in England (or, at least, shares the distinction with another Devon village, Wool-fardisworthy), or knowing of the less-aesthetic pleasures of Teignmouth, the river passes unnoticed. And yet from its rise, on Dartmoor near Quintin's Man, it cuts a beautiful valley towards the sea, and nowhere more so than in the deeply wooded cleft that takes the river around the final eastern bastion of Dartmoor, Mardon Down.

In the wooded valley are the occasional remains of mills, evidence of the river's old use as a source of power in local industry, but industry has long gone and now the trees grow right down to the water's edge. The whole valley in this section is now natural, a protected haven for wildlife. The protection even extends, in imagination at least, to the twin hillforts that stand on each bank of the river above Fingle Bridge.

In sharp contrast to this wooded splendour is the barren moor of Mardon Down. Perhaps moor is too strong a description, because this is not the bleak, boggy moor of the popular image of Dartmoor, but a lower, softer, grass downland, more akin to the Quantocks further north. It is also a fine place to see the 'real' Dartmoor, the view from the southern edge of the Down, above

Castle Drogo

Moretonhampstead, being excellent. But drivers beware; after the views the penalty is exacted, the roads down to the town being narrow and verge-less, with high turf and stone walls.

PLACES OF INTEREST

Castle Drogo Built by Sir Edwin Luytens in 1930, of local granite. Its angular form is either loved or hated by the visitor. It is owned by the National Trust and open in the summer months.
Fingle Bridge Where the river valley is at its prettiest. The bridge is a packhorse bridge from the sixteenth century.
Prestonbury Castle A towering mass, while the more easily reached **Cranbrook Castle** is to the south. Both castles are Iron Age hillforts.
Clifford Bridge An elegant structure, beyond which there are nature trails in Bridford Wood.
Dunsford A show-piece of thatched cottages — real Devonshire. Do not miss the Fulford monument in the church, to members of the family who lived at Great Fulford, a mansion, not open to the public, a little way north-west.
Headless Cross On Mardon Down, is just what its name implies. Four centuries ago such crosses, at crossroads and at the top of steep climbs, were common, but the wave of Puritanism that swept England took many away. In the case of Mardon Down only the cross was removed, the shaft remaining.
Moretonhampstead Below the Down, once capital of Dartmoor, now a small quiet town. Be sure to visit the almhouses with their granite-pillared frontage.

WALKS IN THE AREA

From the hotel at the Teign Bridge on the A382, a pathway leads off eastward on the left bank of the river. This follows the river to Fingle Bridge which it crosses, following the right bank to Clifford Bridge. Here take the lane for Dunsford and leave this to again follow the left riverbank to the B3212 near the village. The whole of the valley has been followed and the visitor need look no further for the finest walk in the area.

On the Downs above the valley there are fine walks at Cranbrook Castle, Butterdon Hill, and on Mardon Down.

BODMIN MOOR

Cornwall

OS Map: 1:50,000 Sheet No 201

Location

This section of the moor is on the extreme eastern edge, bounded by the minor road following the Fowey river to the west, and the A30 to the north.

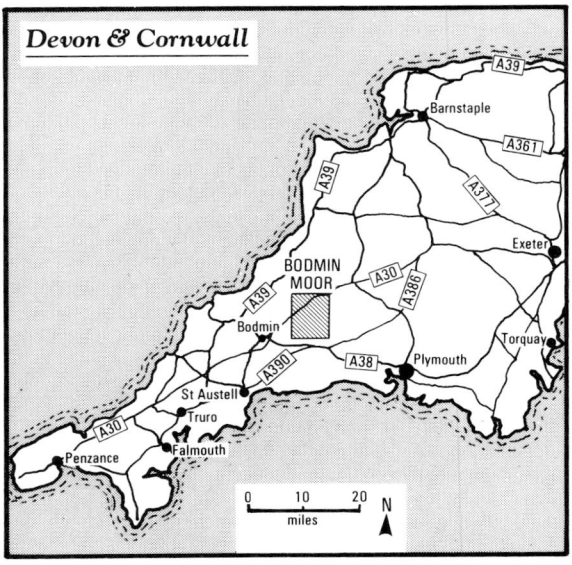

Though Bodmin Moor is both smaller and lower than Dartmoor, it is by no means the poor relation of its big brother across the Devon border to the east. It too can boast the weather-worn tors, and wonderful barren, wild quality that characterises granite moorland. It can also equal Dartmoor in the quality of its mix of legend and reality. There are several sites associated with King Arthur — his Hall and his Bed — as well as the megaliths that are so frequently associated with the uplands of Cornwall.

The River Fowey springs from the high plateau north-east of Brown Willy, the high point of the Moor, to the north of the area. For the record, the name Brown Willy, that gives rise to everything from mirth to mystification, is derived from *Bron Hwilla*, high point. As it flows down its shadowy valley to the sea, the Fowey civilises the moorland, its presence softening the landscape, its clear waters, bubbling over small, boulder waterfalls,

adding a touch of levity to the harsh moor. As the river leaves the moor, entering a delightful wooded valley section, it tumbles over the Golitha Falls, a beautiful spot and a haven for river birds.

To the east of the Fowey is an expanse of wild moorland, not large enough or featureless enough to frighten off the walker, but covering sufficient territory to give the central region a really solitary air. The southern part of the moor is dominated by the TV aerial on Caradon Hill, a useful landmark for the walker, and by the weird rock geometry of

The Hurlers stone circle, with the ruins of a tin mine in the distance

Cheesewring

Cheesewring. The quarries here supplied stone for Westminster Bridge. Leaving the minor road at Minions the walker can follow the Withey Brook into the centre of the moor, past the hollow skeletons of the tin industry.

PLACES OF INTEREST

Dozmary Pool Just west of the Fowey river, is a lonely moorland pond steeped in myth. Part of the reason for its mysterious reputation is the absence of any stream feeding it, a fact viewed by ancient Cornishmen as evidence of the supernatural.

Jamaica Inn North of Dozmary Pool at Bolventor, used as the subject and title of Daphne Du Maurier's book on smugglers.

St Cleer Near the village just off the southern edge of the moor are two famous historical sites. To the north-west is **King Doniert's Stone,** in fact a pair of stones, both incised with geometric patterns, one with a Latin inscription to a Cornish king drowned in 875 AD. North-east of the village is **Trevethy Quoit,** a fine cromlech.

Golitha Falls To the west of St Cleer.

Near **Minions** is a series of three stone circles and a pair of standing stones. The circles are called **The Hurlers** from the legend that they are a group of men turned to stone for daring to hurl a ball on the Sabbath. The two stones are **The Pipers,** two men who played as the game progressed. From the nearby **Cheesewring** the views are breathtaking taking in both the Atlantic and the Channel.

WALKS IN THE AREA

The open nature of the moorland means that the walker can wander at will. The finest walk is from Minions taking in The Hurlers, the Cheesewring and then following Withey Brook to Twelve Men's Moor or Trewartha Tor. The walk along the Fowey river is excellent, and a fine series of footpaths links the sites near, and village of, St Cleer.

ROCHE

Cornwall

OS Map: 1:50,000 Sheet No 200

Location
Situated astride the A30 about 6 miles south-west of Bodmin, bordered by the A39 through St Columb Major to the west.

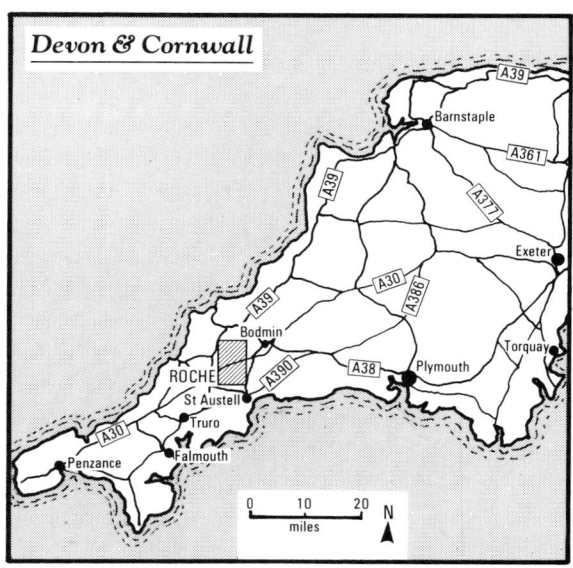

William Cookworthy, a Quaker from Kingsbridge, Devon, came to land around Hensbarrow many years ago, and realised the potential for industry in the kaolinised granite that underlay the poor soil. The local tin-mining was in decline and Cookworthy found no shortage of eager hands to help him found the Cornish china clay industry, still a major employer in the county. Cookworthy made the first genuine English porcelain at his Plymouth factory in 1768. Today the spoil from the clay mines stand, perfect cones of white rock debris grouped around green pools, the water-filled remains of ancient pits. Now, it may not seem that a landscape dominated by industrial spoil heaps would appeal to the walking visitor seeking seclusion and nature in the wild. That is a narrow view: climb to the top of Hensbarrow Down, a mountain creeping all of 27 ft past the 1,000 ft contour, and look out in any direction. The pyramids here may not have been artistically conceived, like those of Egypt, but they do have a wild and desolate majesty.

If the landscape has an alien feel it is, perhaps, not surprising; it is a strange area. In 1664 at nearby St Dennis it rained blood, large drops the size of shilling-pieces, to foretell the Great Plague and the Great Fire of London. Why it should be necessary to rain blood in Cornwall for a fire in London is not clear: another version of the story has it that at that moment in France St Dennis was murdered in Paris.

The area is divided by the A30, and to the north of that the countryside is different, though still dominated by the white pyramids. The change to the Cornish moorland that forms the backbone of the county starts south of the main road, though the boggy mass of Goss Moor is not accessible by footpaths. St Breock's Down in the far north of the area is a beautiful, windswept moor, a mother of Cornish rivers, with occasional curious concrete huts, doorless and windowless (but excellent

China clay waste heaps from Roche Chapel

windbreaks for picnic stoves). At its heart is Mene Gurta, the Stone of Waiting, a bronze age standing stone, and from its northern edges are superb views to the northern coast around Padstow Bay.

Off the down, to the south-east, is a quiet area of farmland grouped around the villages of St Wenn and Withiel, small and windswept, and the romantically named Tregonetha.

WALKS IN THE AREA

There are walks in all sections of the area. That to Hensbarrow Down in excellent, as is the circular path around Castle-an-Dinas. On St Breock Down there is good walking with little hindrance and fine views, while those with a map can link the villages in the farmland to the south-east.

◁ *Roche Rock and its ruined chapel*

PLACES OF INTEREST

Roche Rock   Just south of Roche village, with remains of a chapel sculpted out of, and built upon, its craggy outcrop. The visitor can climb the iron ladders and polished rock to the cell-like chapel, following in the footsteps of John Tregeagle, pursued here by the Devil. Tregeagle was a real seventeenth-century Cornishman, a nobleman's steward, hated by his tenants, who has become mixed up with myths surrounding Dozmary Pool to the west. Tregeagle, for his wickedness, was made to empty the pool with a limpet shell and fled here for sanctuary. The chapel dates from the fifteenth century.

Holy Well   North of Roche, by the station. Here lunatics were immersed as a cure for their madness, and a thrown pebble will reveal, in the bubbles that rise after it, the future of the thrower.

Castle-an-Dinas   An Iron Age hillfort, a fine site believed in legend to be King Arthur's hunting lodge.

PENWITH

Cornwall

OS Map: 1:50,000 Sheet No 203

Location

Situated at the north-west of Cornwall's foot, an area bounded by the sea to the north-west, and the A30 to the south-east, between St Just and St Ives.

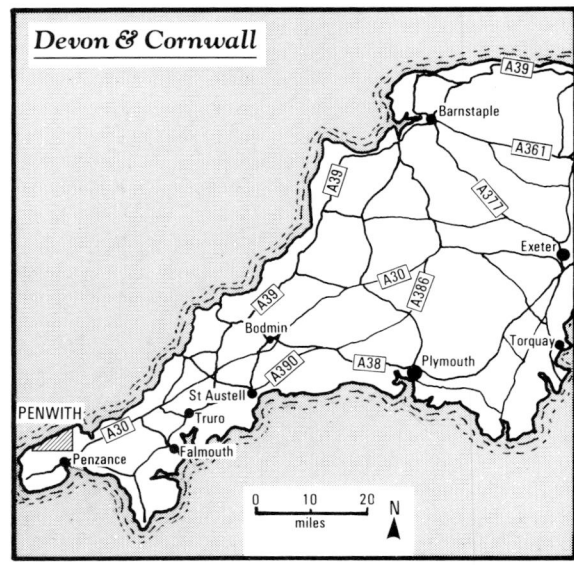

With the expertise at fragmentation that cost their forefathers control of Britain, the inhabitants of the foot of Cornwall maintain that you are not really Cornish unless you come from west of Hayle river. So we go west of Hayle river, but not to the crowded cliff-scapes of the tip of Cornwall, or the area next to Penzance, but to the more secluded northern coast. The seascapes here are as good as those to the south, and inland is some of the most mysterious scenery in Britain, littered with prehistoric stones, amazing not only for their number but for their beauty.

Zennor Head and Gurnard's Head are excellent points from which to view the granite cliffs, each thrusting further out into the Atlantic than the local coast. The Cornish Coastal Path comes this way, but it is still possible, usually easily so, to have a stretch of high cliff to yourself. Go when the wind and tide is bringing the sea in, to catch the best of Cornwall's sea scenery, thudding white water, and lungfuls of salty air. In calmer moments the caves offer excellent spots to picnic and watch the gulls or, perhaps, the rockclimbers on the Great Zawn at Bosigran. How would the old miners who worked tin from below the engines that still stand gauntly near Bosigran view those who sweat with Cornish granite beneath their hands and feet for pleasure?

Lanyon Quoit

*Building a traditional
Cornish stone wall*

Inland from the coast the country is wild and ancient. Penwith District's policy of restricting building and immigration has left the landscape as depopulated as it may have been in Neolithic times, the perfect backdrop for the cromlechs, here called quoits, the standing stones and stone circles. But there are places of light relief, as well as refreshment — Morvah and Treen, and Zennor village where grazing was so scarce that cows ate the bell rope. Or so the story goes!

WALKS IN THE AREA
The whole of the coastline of Penwith forms part of the Coastal Path, and is waymarked. No one area stands out, the whole is excellent; but the most expansive views are from the headlands, as mentioned above.

Inland the country is threaded with footpaths linking roads to the major historical sites. There is good walking on the hill spur and in the valley south-east of Zennor, and a very fine walk circles Madron Moor visiting Ding Dong mine, the Nine Maidens stone circle, Men Scryfa, Men-an-Tol and Lanyon Quoit with superb views to St Michael's Mount to the south.

PLACES OF INTEREST
Zennor village A fascinating museum housed in an old mill, with exhibits of bygone Cornwall, both mining and farming.

The prehistoric sites are almost beyond number, to mention them all would fill a chapter. The best are the quoits of **Zennor** and **Lanyon; Men Scryfa,** a standing stone inscribed with Ogham script; and the **Nine Maidens** stone circle near the wonderfully named **Ding Dong** mine near Boskednan. But best of all is **Men-an-Tol,** three stones in a row, the middle one with an almost perfect circle bored through it. Precisely what it is no one knows, but legend has it that it will cure sick children who crawl through it. From a later time, **Chun Castle** is an Iron Age hillfort.

St Ives Just outside this area should not be dismissed as just another seaside resort. Barbara Hepworth's influence has made it an excellent centre for local artists.

North Wales

NEWBOROUGH WARREN AND MALLTRAETH SANDS

Anglesey

OS Map: 1:50,000 Sheet Nos 114 and 115

Location

The area is best approached along the A4080, turning off in the centre of Newborough and following the minor road into the Forestry Commission enclosure and car parks.

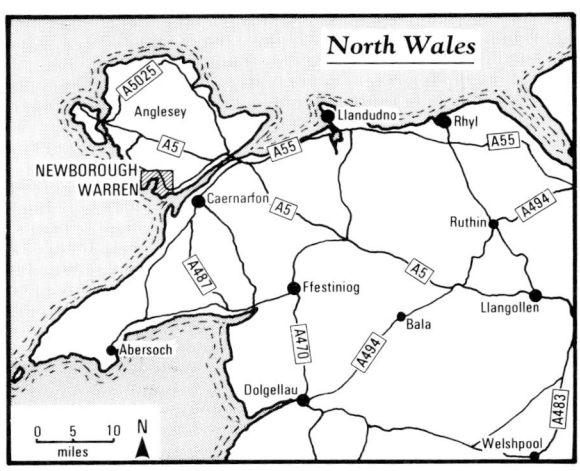

A day on the beach sometime during a holiday, particularly if you have children, can be a pleasant experience. For those used to wild and quiet hills, the southern corner of Anglesey can provide a pleasant substitute. In a magnificent setting, overlooking the Menai Straits and the mountains of Snowdonia is the Newborough Warren — Ynys Llanddwyn Nature Reserve. Approached from the town of Newborough (Niwbwrch) the vast area to the south was at one time an area of sand dunes, shifting constantly in the winds. Since 1948 the Forestry Commission has transformed and stabilised much of the dune area with a light covering of conifers, mostly Corsican Pine. It is now all part of a vast nature reserve the main interest of which is marsh, dunes and forest areas. The beach of fine silver sand follows the curve of Caernarfon Bay for many miles from Malltraeth Sands in the north to Abermenai Spit in the south, reaching almost across to the coast of Arfon. It is a wild and wonderful place.

In the thirteenth and fourteenth centuries, the area to the south of the forest had been fine agriculatural land and a favoured anchorage point at the western end of the Menai Straits. Storms gradually shifted the sands, burying the fields and blocking the access creating a vast area of dunes. The marram grasses which took root provided the nearby villages with a limited income in the manufacture of baskets, mats and ropes. Until the ravages of the myxomatosis 80,000 rabbits are said to have been caught here each year. With the depleted rabbit population, the marram grasses are spreading again stopping much of the drifting sands.

The forest area forms a large part of the reserve but perhaps one of the most interesting sections is Ynys Llanddwyn, a rocky premontory stretching almost a mile into Caernarfon Bay. Formed of Pre-

Ynys Llanddwyn Visitor Centre

Cambrian rocks, which at 600 million years old are some of the oldest in Britain, it is all but an island. An idyllic spot, one can understand why it was the refuge of St Dwynen, patron saint of Welsh lovers. A sixteenth-century ruined church stands on the site of the original chapel and several modern crosses commemorate her presence there.

The 'island' is now a nature reserve, with marked footpaths amongst the rocks. Points of interest are labelled, and the views are marvellous. The old pilots' cottages below the lighthouse have been tastefully converted to form a display of flora and fauna to be found, and a Victorian fisherman's cottage has been recreated.

Across the small bay can be seen the old slipway and walls of a lifeboat station carved deeply into the ancient rocks.

North of Ynys Llanddwyn, the seemingly endless sands stretch to the Gefni estuary and

Malltraeth Pool, a bird sanctuary. The associated area of salt marshes is known for sea plants and grasses, forming altogether a fascinating area covering many acres. The wide beaches are south facing and safe for bathing. A highly recommended place to visit that everyone will enjoy.

PLACES OF INTEREST

Newborough Warren — Ynys Llanddwyn Nature Reserve Adequate parking. The information centre provides a leaflet describing the attractions in the forestry and nature reserve.

Malltraeth Pool At northern tip of reserve close to A4080. Bird sanctuary.

Bryn Celli Ddu Well preserved burial mound, with huge stones and passage. One and a half miles north of A4080 between the A5 and Newborough.

Plas Newydd On the edge of the Menai Straits, home of the Marquess of Anglesey with many fine pictures and set in beautiful grounds. Off the A4080, two miles from Llanfair PG.

WALKS IN THE AREA

Access to the area is by a single track road through the forest. It is best visited when the weather is warm to take maximum advantage of the beach.

There are marked trails through the forest, but do bear in mind that it is a National Nature Reserve and stick to the path. Information is available on the Hendai Forest Trail from the Forestry Commission. The trail with marked stations crosses the area where traditionally it is held that the old village of Rhosyr lies buried beneath the dunes.

Newborough Warren extends beyond the forest with several footpaths around its perimeter to the nearby Llyn Rhosddu. There are also access routes to the salt marshes, sand dunes and the Abermenai Spit which stretches almost a mile into the Menai Straits.

The sands themselves can provide many happy hours of easy walking, or just relaxing, but the walk across them to Ynys Llanddwyn is a must for all visitors.

Once on the island the paths are easy to follow with most features of note marked or pointed out. The views are superb and the cliffs though small give an opportunity to see many of the different sea birds that inhabit this coastline and to study the ancient and colourful rock formations.

The walks are obviously very different to a hard day in the hills but there should be time to visit and enjoy this delightful stretch of Welsh coastline.

THE GWYDYR FOREST

Gwynedd

OS Map: 1:50,000 Sheet No 115
1:25,000 Snowdonia National Park,
Conwy Valley

Location
North of Betws-y-Coed and on the western side of
the Conwy Valley.

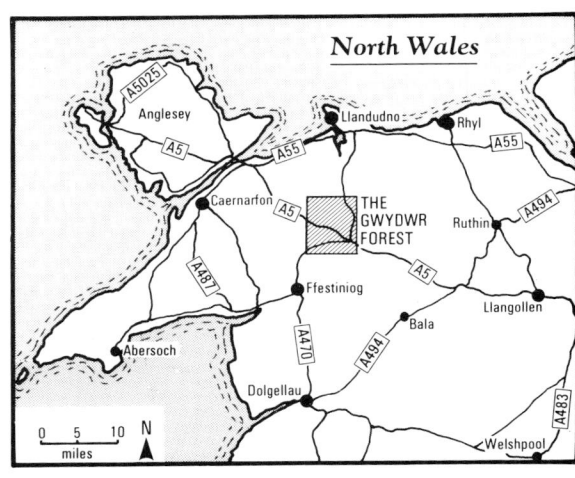

The great beauty of Snowdonia is that it is a land of
contrasts; the unexpected can always be found.
Some views are all mountains and scree, others are
delicately balanced by a small mountain lake
appearing out of the morning mist; trees can add
colour to an otherwise barren hillside.

Similarly it is often near the busy centre that
some of the most overlooked scenery in the park
can be found. Take for example the popular
Harlech coastline and the neglected Rhinogs, or
the busy little town of Bala and the rarely trodden
Arans. Close to Betws-y-Coed is just such an area;
enclosed by the valleys of the Afons Llugwy and
Conwy, it is perhaps scenically one of the most
delightful areas in Northern Snowdonia.

Approached by steep, narrow single-track
roads, or by foot from the valleys, is a forest land
of hidden lakes, hills and secret valleys. There are
places to sit, forest walks, and most memorable
superb views across the forest lakes and mountains.

An area of high plateaux and steep hillsides, it
was once renowned for its natural oak. Denuded
over the centuries for boatbuilding and further
devastated as a result of the nineteenth-century
copper mines it was acquired, in 1921, by the
Forestry Commission. Through the years they
have gradually planted many of the hills and
valleys with a wide range of coniferous trees.

Known as the Gwydyr Forest after the nearby
estate and castle, it covers an extensive area from
the very edge of the Conwy Valley to the slopes of
Greigiau Gleision at 1,600 ft above sea level.

If any corner of Wales can be called a lake
district it is this, with about a dozen lakes within
the Forest Park and the larger Llyn Cowlyd, Llyn
Eigiau and Coety further to the north. Many are
now reservoirs supplying water to the nearby
valley towns.

Within the forest Llyn Crafnant is undoubtedly
the most perfect; approached by a steep road that

follows the river from Treffriw, visually it has
everything: tree-clad slopes, wild moorlands and
peace. To the south just over the hill is Llyn
Geirionydd, equally picturesque but perhaps
marred a little by the waste from the adjacent
copper mines and the noise from the power boats
and waterskiers playing there in summer. It is
approached by a daunting road from Llanrwst
which climbs steeply throught the forest but does
offer some superb views on route.

Other smaller lakes are dotted throughout the
forest. All can be reached by the many footpaths
and miners' tracks that meander uphill.

The landscape has, on the whole, been treated
sympathetically by the Forestry Commission with
a range of coniferous trees planted for variety.
These include Scots Pine, Douglas Fir, Sitka
Spruce and various larches. The native hardwoods
of oak, ash, birch have all been retained to balance
colour where necessary. It is a unique area which
has been enhanced by the forest growth; much is
done to encourage and educate visitors for leisure
and pleasure in the forest.

To the north, the larger lakes of Cowlyd and
Eigiau are a stark contrast in high bleak cwms;
both are now reservoirs serving townships in the
Conwy Valley. The latter lake, somnolent and
almost surrounded by high steep crags, burst its
wall in 1923 causing a torrent of water and
boulders to crash down to Dolgarrog, killing 16
people and destroying much property.

It is fine walking country with a varied range of
mountain scenery dominated by the Carnedds to
the north.

PLACES OF INTEREST
Conwy Valley Railway Museum Adjacent to Betws-y-Coed station, railway memorabilia.
Swallow Falls Superb tumbling cataract on the Afon Llugwy upriver from Betws-y-Coed.
LLyn Crafnant Boats for hire in summer.
Gwydyr Castle One mile west of Llanrwst, fine Tudor building, home of the Wynne family. Open occasionally in summer.
Forest Information Centre and Exhibition Centre On B5106 almost opposite Gwydyr Castle.

WALKS IN THE AREA
The emphasis that the Forestry Commission have put on leisure activities within the Gwydyr Forest has already been mentioned. They have produced a number of leaflets giving details of most of the walks or suggestions for outings within the forest.

Many of these are specific and demonstrate various aspects of forestry and workings within; they include an arboretum. There are planned trails for the elderly and the disabled, all within easy reach of Betws-y-Coed. Leaflets are available for most from the Forestry Commission, Gwydyr Uchaf, Llanrwst.

All the major lakes are in their own cwms; all have entirely different characters. Llyn Geirionydd, the southernmost, is fairly easily accessible with adequate parking. A footpath crosses the ridge to the beautiful Llyn Crafnant and thence north to Llyn Cowlyd and Llyn Eigiau.

From Trefriw a narrow picturesque road leads uphill to Crafnant. Turn right at the lake and follow a forest road around the northern bank. Take the higher track at each junction and gradually ascend Greigiau Gleision (Blue Rocks). From the highest point of the road the southerly views are superb. Cross the shoulder of the hill and descend via Llyn Cowlyd and back to Trefriw.

There is much in this small area to cater for all walking activities, ages and tastes.

The Swallow Falls

RHOSYDD QUARRY

Gwynedd

OS Map: 1:50,000 Sheet Nos 115 and 124
Outdoor Leisure Map Snowdonia
National Park, Harlech

Location

Cradled in the Moelwyns at GR665463, most
easily reached from Tan-Y-Grisiau close to Blaenau
Ffestiniog.

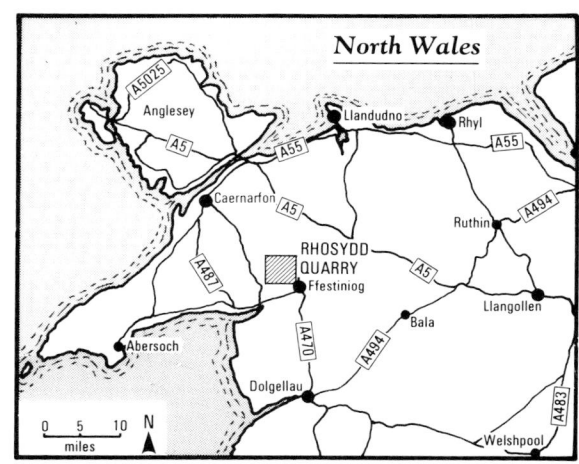

Throughout North Wales and Snowdonia there is
much scarring of the hillsides and other evidence
of mining. In the limestone areas in the east can be
seen the old engine houses of the Victorian lead
mines, while high on the hillside around Snowdon
are shafts of the almost fruitless copper mines
with piles of ochre waste. By far the most
prolific of all mining or quarrying operations,
however, which everyone connects with North
Wales, is slate.

Many slate towns exist in the valleys, amongst
them Bethesda near Bangor, Llanberis in the pass
of the same name, and furthest west of the great
Cwm of Nantlle. Few valleys in northern Snowdonia
are without the great piles of grey waste or the huge
redundant face.

Blaeneau Ffestiniog was the king of them all, as
evidenced by the mountains of slate. The waste
tips descend to the very backs of the rows of
terraced cottages. Now developing into a major
tourist centre based upon one of the hardest trades
of all, it had some of the largest mines in the
country. One can visit several of the mines in the
vicinity for a guided tour of the caverns. With all
the associated commercialism it is difficult to
appreciate just how hard a quarryman's life was.

High above Blaneau Ffestiniog, tucked away in a
plateau between Cnicht and Moelwyn Mawr in an
almost idyllic situation is the old quarry of
Rhosydd. The old barracks, the sites of the old
machine shops, the tramways and lower down,
even the old chapel can still be seen, as can the adits
at different levels and the vast holes carved out of
the hillsides.

It is a place to conjure up just the picture of the
life in a quarry: the long Sunday evening or
Monday morning walk to work, the cold, the
bleakness — it takes little to imagine the hardships
of a winter up here.

Rhosydd Slate Quarry was one of the highest and most productive in the Blaneau Ffestiniog area. It operated from 1850 to 1950, with varying levels of productivity. Perched on the high plateau of Bwlch Yr Rhosydd between the mountains the workings cover an area roughly a mile square. The main buildings and workshops are at 1,487 ft whilst the highest workings are at 1,900 ft.

The quarry is a combination of opencast and mining. The earliest extractions were from what remains as an enormous hole — the West Twll — about 120 ft deep and at the highest level. When it became uneconomic to move the slate from this and the nearby East Twll mining began in earnest, horizontal adits were driven in at several levels. These extracted the slate from underground in huge chambers up to 40 ft high, following the line of cleavage. Some of these worked through to the West Twll and more was taken from there.

The entrances to many of the shafts can be seen as you follow the line of old winding gear uphill. The longest shaft, which emerges close to the barracks and has access to the West Twll, is approximately 1,000 yd. Without expert guides it is obviously not advisable to explore, as many of the shafts have suffered rockfalls. Above ground there is much to see: many of the old buildings, reservoirs, sites of machine sheds, power stores and even the old toilets can be found with a little time and patience.

The line of the old tramways which took the cut slates to the coast heads off towards the West and down the steepest incline in Wales to the Croesor valley and Porthmadog.

There is much to see and much scope for the imagination.

PLACES OF INTEREST
Festiniog Railway Scenic trips from Porthmadog.
Ffestiniog
Ffestiniog Power Station Hydro-electric scheme and the first pumped storage generator in Britain.
Llechwedd Slate Cavern and Glodfa Ganol Two slate mines offering trips inside to see the workings.

WALKS IN THE AREA
Rhosydd formed a community of its own during the working week, and being in the centre of a mountain range it attracted workers from all the nearby villages. Footpaths and trackways approach it from all directions; much of the enjoyment of the place can be found in discovering these routes from the map and exploring the surrounding area. It is a wonderful and complex area of mountains, hills and lakes.

Only two possibilities are therefore suggested. Starting from Croesor, ascend Cnicht and follow the superb northern ridge over and down to a small cairn at its lowest point. Turn south-east and a not very well defined footpath leads close to a reservoir (for the quarry) before descending down to Bwlch Yr Rhosyddd. From there either head south over the col and back via Croesor quarry to the village, or return via the tramway. Other alternatives, depending on fitness, are over Moelwyn Fawr or via a terraced footpath to the south and Bwlch Stwlan or Moelwy Mawr and thence return. Llyn Stwlan, which is contoured is the top reservoir of the CEGB pump storage scheme.

A second superb day can, if desired, be combined with a trip on the Festiniog Railway from Porthmadog to Tan-y-Grisiau, taking the wide track behind the station into Cwmorthin and its quarry workings, past the lakeside chapel and up to Rhosydd. Follow the footpaths from beside the main adit uphill to the Twlls, and continue over the col. Again pick up the wonderful terrace trackway to above Llyn Stwlan and down the road from the dam back to the rail head.

◁ *Cnicht, above Pont Croesor*

CWM PENNANT
AND CWMYSTRADLLYN

Gwynedd

OS Map: 1:50,000 Sheet Nos 115 and 124

Location

Both cwms lie to the north of Tremadog off the A487 Caernarfon road. There are several access points, all signposted, between Dolbenmaen and Penmorfa.

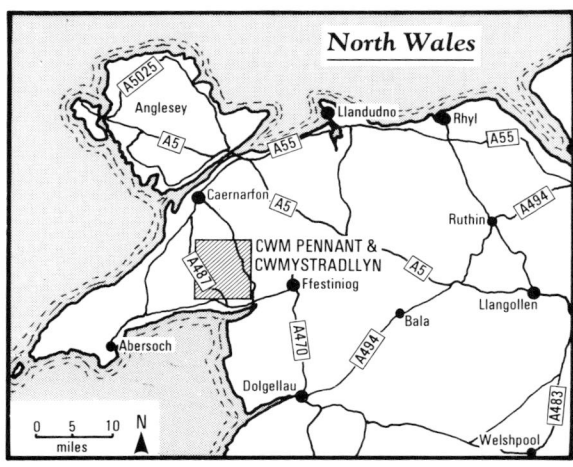

Cwm Pennant, immortalised in Eifion Wyn's poem of the same name, perhaps retains more of the real flavour of Wales than many of the surrounding hills and valleys of Snowdonia. It is a deep valley penetrating far into the hills, which form a perfect cirque around it. The hills, though only around the 2,500ft mark, appear much higher from the depth of the valley, sombre and brooding above the quiet fields below.

It is approached along a single track road that leads far away from the hustle and bustle of the coastal plain and beaches. It winds slowly inland over humped bridges, crossing and re-crossing the tiny Afon Dwyfor, with many spots which tempt you to stop. The road rises slowly; one is never more than 400ft above sea level, and the valley is unveiled as it rises.

Isolated farms dot the hillsides, blending easily into the grey-green slopes; ancient stone walls rub shoulders with their more recent counterparts, showing that man has farmed here from time immemorial. It is quieter now that the Prince of Wales Slate Mine at the head of the valley has closed, the inevitable waste heaps blending slowly into the landscape.

High up to the west is Cwm Ciprwrth with its now-defunct copper mine; only the open shafts and rusting machinery remind us of the lengths to which man will go in search of profit. Much of the machinery was imported from Cornwall, carried high up on to the mountain in the 1850s and rebuilt. Now all is quiet, the mines are closed, and for the time being the industrial revolution is over in that part of Wales.

Moel Hebog to the east is, at 2,568ft, the highest peak in the great circle that surrounds the cwm, but the mountains to the west seem to dominate it. Joined by a narrow tumbling ridge that forms a barrier across the head of the valley, they give an impression of enormous bulk. Gently rounded on this side, they are steep and craggy on their northern flanks forming an unbroken chain for the full length of the valley, known as Nantlle Ridge. They provide a splendid day's walking.

Parallel to Cwm Pennant and separated by Moel Hebog is Cwmystradllyn. The two valleys are entirely different in character, the only similarity being an equally winding approach road. The cwm is higher and much more open, with no overwhelming peaks to close it in. It too has the ubiquitous slate quarry at the head of the valley. In its bottom is a small lake, now dammed to form a reservoir and a playground for trout fishermen. There is ample parking here.

Cwmystradllyn does not give the impression of age or habitation, though the map tells us otherwise. It does have a feeling of spaciousness lacking in its neighbour, even though it is smaller.

Ruined slate mill, Cwmystradllyn

Old quarry track, Llyn Cwmystradllyn

PLACES OF INTEREST

Maritime Museum Porthmadog. Sailing ketch moored on quay authentic vessel and setting.
Tyn Llan Pottery Penmorfa. Welsh crafts and pottery with teas available, picnic spot.
Brynkir Woollen Mills Dolbenmaen, close to Cwm Pennant. Traditional Welsh patterns.
Criccieth Castle Criccieth, one of Edward I's 'ring of steel', now very picturesque.

WALKS IN THE AREA

There is a wide variety of walking in each cwm, from relatively easy high-level routes to more gentle strolls in the valley. The dismantled railways, which once carried the dressed slates from the old quarries to the quays in Porthmadog, now make excellent footpaths from which to explore each cwm.

In Cwm Pennant the old railway traverses the head of the valley, about 500 ft above the road on the eastern side, for its full length. It can be joined at many points and, linked with other footpaths, makes a fine low-level walk.

The quarry in Cwmystradllyn is much more obvious, and the old railway easier to reach; it simply continues where the road turns sharply right to the reservoir. It is a wide track, and a very pleasant walk well within the scope of all ages, leading first past a ruined house (presumably the old quarry manager's) before reaching a magnificent retaining wall which must rank as one of the wonders of quarry engineering. The layout of the quarry and its buildings can be easily seen, but do take care. A rather indistinct path returns on the opposite side of the reservoir to the dam.

The ascent of Moel Hebog from Cwmystradllyn is one of the easier and more pleasant expeditions in the area. It is a steady but not too strenuous climb, rewarded with magnificent views over the cwms and the valleys radiating from Beddgelert as well as the whole of the Snowdon Massif. Start climbing just after the second gate along the tramway and just keep climbing; there are stiles over the walls.

There is a range of footpaths in the area which can be easily linked to give a thorough exploration of each cwm. For the more experienced, the complete traverse of the horseshoe around Cwm Pennant or just the Nantlle ridge to the west of that valley, gives a full and excellent day's walking.

THE LLŶN PENINSULA
AND BARDSEY ISLAND

Gwynedd

OS Map: 1:50,000 Sheet No 123

Location

Either from Caernarfon and along A499 and then
B4417 or from Criccieth along the A497.

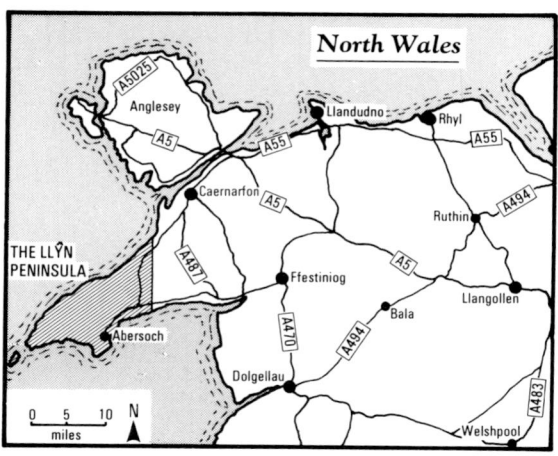

The great mountains of Snowdonia almost sever
the long arm of the Llŷn Peninsula from the rest of
Wales. As you leave them behind, the countryside
becomes almost at once lower and more rural, the
sky brighter and the atmosphere less brooding.

Heading west it is the great bulk and perfection
of Yr Eifl with its three peaks which catch the eye.
Crouched midway along northern coastline they
exude an air of mystery, and despite their lack of
height (the highest is only 1,850 ft), they give an
impression of tremendous bulk.

A vast influx of visitors in the summer swells the
population of the hills and coastal hills and
villages, and converts almost every coastal field
into a tented town. Few of today's visitors, racing
to the sea, realise that they are following closely
route used by pilgrims of a different kind for over a
thousand years.

The object of their veneration was Bardsey
Island, off the westernmost tip of this lovely
peninsula. Known as Ynys Enlli by the Welsh,
('Island of Currents'), it 'floats' approximately 2
miles out to sea. Bardsey, a Norse name, was also
known as the Island of Saints, as 20,000 are
reputed to be buried there. From the sixth century
onwards the island and chapels were a place of
pilgrimage almost on a par with Rome.

The first church was founded on the island by St
Cadfan from Brittany in 429. A later abbey, St
Mary's, built in the twelfth century, had a
monastic community until the dissolution in the
sixteenth century and attracted pilgrims for most
of that period. Now little evidence remains of the

*Prehistoric burial chamber
on the slopes of Carn Fadryn*

religious occupation, just the site and churchyard of the abbey containing the remains of some 20,000 saints. The island is now a nature reserve with one of the nineteenth-century farmhouses converted to a bird observatory.

The small size of the island limited its ability to support a resident and pilgrim population. So in monastic fashion, enclaves and farmhouses were established on the mainland. Much of the land around Aberdaron and towards the end of the Peninsula served this purpose. Some of the isolated farmsteads still bear the names of the old religious hamlets, Anelog, Cwrt and Bodermid. It is probably for this reason that this land is so peaceful and almost medieval in appearance. Here you are far away from the hurly-burly of such places as Abersoch and Nefyn.

The tiny village of Aberdaron was the last contact most pilgrims had with the mainland. The white painted cottages, now mostly souvenir shops, provided their victuals for the crossing while the sea-shore church looked after their spiritual needs. Heading south-west from the village by road, one gets a real feeling of heading towards the end of a land. The countryside is low and rolling, the sea never far away, with occasional views across to Bardsey. What a thrill it must have been for a pilgrim to get such a glimpse.

This headland is everything a Land's End should be, windswept with crashing waves and screeching gulls.

PLACES OF INTEREST

There are many fine beaches all around the peninsula most are ideal for boating and bathing. Those towards the southern tip tend to be quieter.

Penarth Fawr Interesting fifteenth-century manor house, signposted about 1 mile south of Butlins.

Tre'r Ceiri Iron Age ruined town perched on a hilltop on Yr Eifl. Remains of walls and hut circles, worth seeing but please leave it as you found it. Footpath off B4417 between Llithfaen and Llanaelhaearn north of Nefyn.

Nant Gwytheyrn Old quarry villages, renovated as centre for Welsh studies. Idyllic setting must be approached on foot. Turn off in centre of Llithfaen on B4417 to car park.

WALKS IN THE AREA

Bardsey Island is now owned by a Trust which guarantees to protect the beauty, wildlife and historical interest of this ancient island. They also intend to maintain access to the public, so visitors are permitted.

Across the sand from Bardsey the headland is more easily accessible. The two outstanding points, Pen-y-Cil the southern headland, and Braich y Pwll to the north-west, are joined by a meandering path above cliffs. The latter was a embarkation point for pilgrims, and there is a holy well and the foundations of a chapel. High above, up a steep flight of steps, a coastguard lookout on the very edge of Mynydd Mawr gives splendid views across the wide blue sea and along the length of the Llŷn.

A series of small hills continue north from Braich y Pwll, riddled with paths which are worthy of exploration.

There is much to see on the Llŷn; most walks are short but very rewarding. It is not easy to escape man's imprint upon this landscape. For that reason it would perhaps be best to suggest a number of destinations.

Mynydd Rhiw (GR230290). Above Porth Neigwl, Hells Mouth, a storm-tossed beach of old. Plas-y-Rhiw and stone axe factory on slopes. Fine views and short walks.

Carn Fadryn (GR280350). Cone-shaped hill in centre of Llŷn surmounted by Iron Age hillfort; marvellous views.

Nant Gwythern (GR350450). Old quarrying village on the very edge of cliffs, now a centre for Welsh studies. Steep descent, accessible on foot, down Vortigern's Valley, recommended.

Yr Eifl (GR375440). Wonderful range of hills, accessible and invigorating. Known as 'The Rivals' which is a misnomer; translated, the Welsh means 'The Forks'.

Tre'r Ceiri (GR375445). Iron age town on summit of Yr Eifl. Well preserved with ramparts, parapets and approximately fifty hut circles. Visibly deteriorating through lack of care.

Along the northern coast many fine cliff and bay walks can be enjoyed, particularly around Porth Oer (Whistling Sands) and Porth Colmon. Off the beaten track the Llŷn Peninsula is well worth exploring; it retains a unique atmosphere of its own.

THE RHINOGS

Gwynedd

OS Map: 1:50,000 Sheet No 124
1:25,000 Outdoor Leisure Map,
Harlech

Location

The area is surrounded by major roads but crossed by none; to the east is the A470 Maentwrog – Dolgellau road, to the west, following the curve of Cardigan Bay through Harlech, is the A496 to Barmouth.

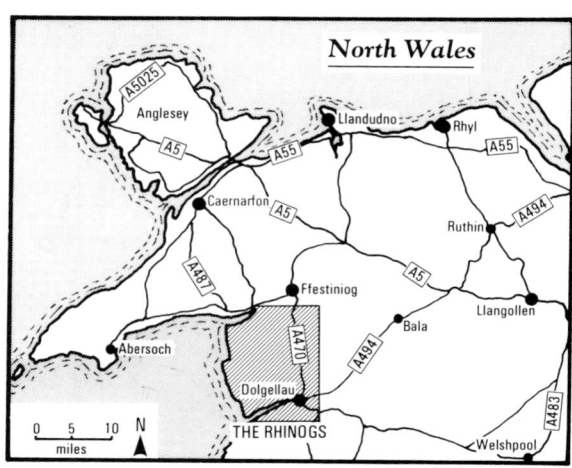

Geologists refer to this area as the Harlech Dome. It is roughly in the centre of the great upthrust that also formed Snowdon in the north and Cader Idris to the south. Nowadays it is a rough craggy landscape formed of hard Cambrian grits giving short sharp cliffs and large rocky pavements. The Rhinogs are unusual mountains, not at all like the more popular ranges of Snowdonia, with few footpaths to guide the visitor. Should visitors wish to penetrate these hills they must plan it themselves, with the aid of a map.

The complete traverse of the Rhinog Range from Maentwrog to Barmouth is both a challenging and exhilarating day's walking, needing stamina, as it is perhaps one of the toughest mountain walks in Wales. The casual walker or visitor can enjoy these hills, either from the coast or from inland, though few roads penetrate these mountains.

The whole area is fascinating. In addition to the unusual scenery and the ancient rocks, it is criss-crossed by ancient trackways and dotted with prehistoric remains, particularly on the seaward side. Many of the old trackways lead directly from the coast, for in the past this was the main access point for trade with the Bronze Age people from Ireland and other visitors, friendly and otherwise. There are old drove roads where sheep and Welsh Black cattle were walked to markets in England. Miners' tracks and packhorse trails can be traced through to the borders, their origins lost in the mists of time. Many have standing stones alongside to mark the routes, old hut circles where these people lived and cromlechs where they were buried. For the observant, these points can add much interest to any day out, but please do not touch or move any of the ancient stones.
From the A496 at Cilfor a minor road is

perhaps the best introduction to the area. It winds its narrow way half-way between the sea and the hills, with magnificent views of the coast and the Llyn Peninsula. Traversing above and along the northern half of the bay there are several places to park and explore further. At the highest point, almost directly behind Harlech, is an Iron Age hillfort and some ancient hut circles. To prove the antiquity of this road, huge standing stones mark the ancient route to and from the coast.

Two further roads penetrate this magnificent range of hills; both leave the coast at Llanbedr. The most popular leads up to the idyllic Cwm Bychan and the Roman Steps. To the south, another minor road leads to the head of Cwm Nantcol at the very foot of Rhinog Fawr, and Rhinog Fach; from there the pass Bwlch Drws Ardudwy, dividing the two mountains, is accessible on foot. One of the most impresssive and desolate passes in Wales, it was as its name implies ' the doorway to Ardudwy' for those approaching this ancient land from the east.

PLACES OF INTEREST
Harlech Castle   This fine castle ,which dominates the coastline, is in superb condition.
Shell Island   Sand dunes with wide beaches and lots of room for children to play. Approached by causeway from A496 in Llanbedr.
Maes Artro   Craft village just off A496 south of Llanbedr. Aquarium showing local sea life, cafe and playgrounds.
Coed-y-Brenin Forest and Visitor Centre
Off A470 north of Ganllwyd. Remnants of nearby gold mines and   displays of forestry machinery and methods.

Bryn Cader Faner stone circle

WALKS IN THE AREA

The most popular excursion is probably up to Cwm Bychan and the Roman Steps. The Steps are unlikely to be Roman, but though the route may well have been in use even earlier, they were probably laid in the Middle Ages for a packhorse trail. It is undoubtedly a beautiful spot and can be busy but, approached from Llanbedr, it gives easy access to the two main summits in the range, Rhinog Fach and Rhinog Fawr. There is a lake and picnic area at the road end in Cwm Bychan.

Further to the south at Dyffryn Ardudwy, several interesting old tracks lead to the hills; one, an old coach road between Harlech and London, can be followed easily up to the bridge at Pont Scethin, then over the shoulder of Llawlech (1,750ft) before descending to join the A496 at Bontdu.

The best introduction to the character of these hills however is in the northern ranges. A lane rises steeply beside the Maes-y-Neuadd Hotel above Eisingrug. The second gate is as far as you can go by car, and a well-made track continues inland. It can be followed right into the mountains, past some of the most unusual rock scenery in Snowdonia, to the top of a pass and a small lake. From there to the north is Moel Ysgyfarnogod, an interesting scramble. An alternative is to leave this track earlier at a sharp right-hand bend and follow an ancient trackway that wanders easily across the moors past stone circles to Bryn Cader Faner, an old burial mound in a magnificent setting. Other easy tracks lead round the hill and back to the top of the lane.

On the inland side of the Rhinogs is the Coed-y-Brenin Forest with the Maesgwm Visitor Centre close to Pont Dolgefeiliau with an exhibition of silver mining equipment. Leaflets are available covering the walks in and through the forests. There are fifty miles of waymarked walks within the forest including the popular walk to Pystyll Cain and the old gold mine.

AFON DYFI AND THE ARANS

Gwynedd

OS Map: 1:50,000 Sheet No 125

Location

The area lies between the A494 south of Bala and the A470 north of Mallwyd.

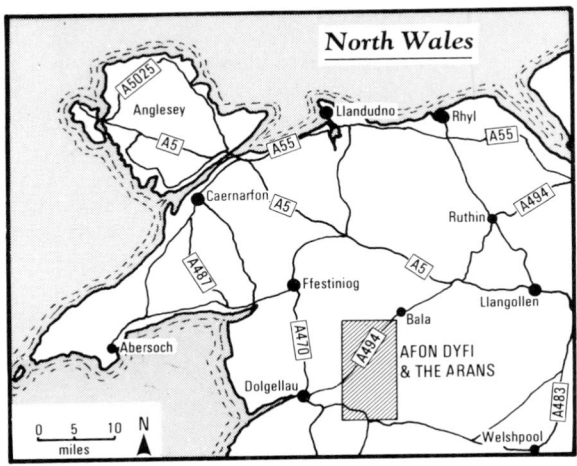

One of the most interesting aspects of George Borrow's book *Wild Wales*, relating his epic journey through the Principality in the 1850s, is the comparisons one can make with the scenery and surroundings then and now. If one were to follow his footsteps south from Bala over the Bwlch-y-Groes and along the banks of the Afon Dyfi to Dinas Mawddwy one would find little change. His host in Bala warned him as he left for that day's journey 'that the greater part of it was over hills and mountains which constituted upon the whole the wildest part of Wales'. This is surely true today.

The valleys have perhaps mellowed a little but the mountains and hill scenery are still as wild. At the top of the Bwlch-y-Groes the dark foreboding peat bogs give a sense of utter desolation, while to the north shines the steely surface of Llyn Tegid (Bala Lake). An information board at the top of the pass, the highest in Wales, tells us that here peat was dug and sledged down to the valleys for fuel; some traces can still be seen of this old trade. Amongst eroded peat bogs are the occasional remains of tree stumps from primeval forests. Above all tower the peaks of Aran Benllyn and Aran Fawddwy. Looking almost a mirror image of each other, they dominate the view for most of southern Snowdonia.

Descending from the Bwlch-y-Groes through the Glen of Rhiwlech to the valley of the Afon Dyfi down one of the steepest passes in the country can be hair raising with the cliffs overhanging on one side and with almost vertical slopes on the other. All around are steep grey-green hills divided by deep cut streams and hidden valleys.

The Dyfi can be seen at the head of the valley off to the west, tumbling through the deep rocky pools at Pennant. The Welsh name Graigllyn Dyfi tells all about the source of this beautiful river, a small lake set below the crags of Aran Fawddwy. One can understand why it is sometimes known as the Royal Dyfi, for it is a king amongst rivers,

passing through some of the most beautiful scenery in Wales.

The valley is a delightful contrast to the hills, lush and peaceful it winds south through Llanymawddwy between the high steep slopes. Peaceful now, it was once the hunting ground of a band of red-haired brigands. They terrorised the area stealing sheep and cattle and pillaging and looting the countryside; nothing and nobody was safe. Eventually rounded up they were condemned to death in 1555, but their fearsome reputation still lingers.

It is possible to identify clearly many of the buildings Borrow saw en route; only the characters have changed. He describes the valley most aptly: 'Scenery of the wildest and most picturesque description was rife and plentiful to a degree'. It still is.

Cwm Cywarch, which joins the main valley from the west, leads to the very base of the Arans. This deep cwm seems to be even wilder with the steep grassy slopes rising high above the road.

PLACES OF INTEREST

Dinas Mawddwy   Holiday and fishing village in a beautiful setting at southern end of Dyfi.
Lake Vyrnwy   Narrow lake 4 miles long in beautiful wooded setting, now supplies Liverpool with water. Can be approached by exciting road from top of Bwlch-y-Groes.
Bwlch-y-Groes   North of Dinas Mawddwy, at 1,790 ft it is the highest road in Wales. Can be a hair-raising drive for the nervous. Good parking for view of beautiful scenery.

Bwlch-y-Groes pass ▷

WALKS IN THE AREA

The Afon Dyfi valley is fringed by steep green hills, the slopes climbing evenly for what seems forever are a daunting prospect. The narrow streams tumble steeply down deep incised valleys. Behind the village of Llanymawddwy is Pistyll Gwyn. About a mile west on the Afon Pumryd, it falls sharply into a dark amphitheatre of rock and scree. A path climbs to it from close to the church giving a fine introduction to this valley.

At Blaen Pennant, the head of the valley, the Dyfi emerges from Llaethnant, Milk Valley, in a succession of cataracts and rocky pools with the dark peak of Aran Mawddwy brooding behind. The Afon Dyfi can be followed to its source at Graiglyn Dyfi, at the very base of the cliffs below the mountains. Start at the sharp bend at the bottom of the Bwlch-y-Groes. A little footpath follows the fence going uphill to the west. It soon reaches the superb rocky pools below Ogof Ddu. Many will find this far enough. In an idyllic situation high above the valley the pools are deep enough for bathing if you can stand the cold, or perfect for a picnic on a warm sunny day. The path continues above to climb steadily up Llaethnant to the small lake below the cliffs.

For those wishing to reach the summits of the Arans, the head of Cwm Cywarch is the best starting point. First ascend the steep path to Hengwm to the north-east and thence to Dyrysgol.

The summit ridge is a superb walk, the mountain falling away easily to the west but steeply to the east. Aran Mawddwy at 2,970ft is the highest mountain south of Snowdon. With its twin, Aran Benllyn at 2,901ft, it offers one of the finest views in the whole country, hills and mountains all around. The descent can be made by continuing along the wide ridge to Llanuwchllyn at the southern end of Llyn Tegid or by a roundabout route back to Cwm Cywarch.

The ascent of the Arans from Llyn Tegid in the north makes a fine alternative, climbing easier slopes with fine views all around.

THE BERWYNS

Clwyd

OS Map: 1:50,000 Sheet No 125

Location

The area can be approached from almost any
direction though most of the roads are single track
and care must be taken. Arriving from England the
best introduction is on the B4500 which follows
the River Ceiriog from the A5 at Chirk.

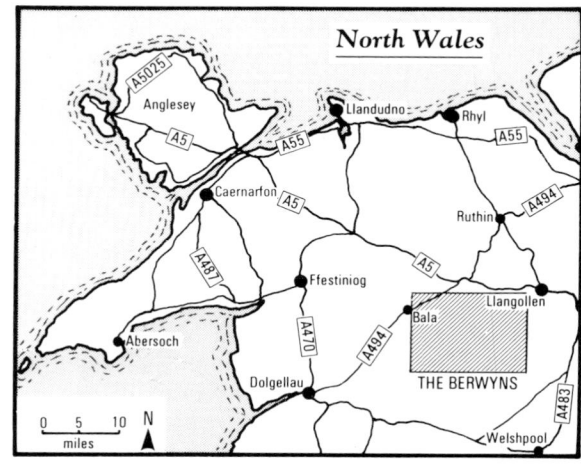

The County of Clwyd, tucked away in the north-
east corner of Wales, has a wide range of
attractions for visitors. There are the brash coastal
resorts in the north, the ancient towns of Denbigh
and Ruthin and the beautiful Vale of Dee and
Llangollen.

To the south, and enclosed by the river valleys
of the Dee and Tanad and the border with
England, lies probably one of the most surprising
and beautiful areas in the county. Generally
known as the Berwyns after the range of hills
forming the western boundary, it is a land of deep
hidden valleys and rounded hills. Fortunately still
relatively free from the usual trappings of tourism,
it is a marvellous area to wander in both on foot
and by car. The hills provide some excellent
walking in relative isolation and the switchback
roads some surprising views around each bend.

There are few easy approaches; the only main
road enters along the banks of the River Ceiriog by
way of Chirk. As you follow the winding river to
Glyn Ceiriog the tree clad slopes seem to get closer
and steeper. Other approaches are more daunting;
from Llangollen in the north a switchback road
gives some idea of things in store.

The heart of the area is the little village
Llanarmon Dyffryn-Ceiriog, a collection of stonebuilt houses, a church and two excellent inns set in
a beautiful fold of hills. The Berwyn range leans
away to the west with few access points and no
vehicular crossing points. From the village the
road climbs south to some magnificent viewpoints
and superb country lanes before descending
steeply to Llanrhaeadr-Ym-Mochnant. This was
once the home of Dr William Morgan, who in
1572 came here as vicar and painstakingly trans-

Pistyll Rhaeadr

lated the Bible into Welsh thus perpetuating the Welsh language. The village is now mainly visited for the waterfall, Pistyll Rhaeadr, four miles to the west. The highest in Wales with a drop of 240ft, it falls through a natural arch, between steep wooded slopes in a magnificent setting. It is said to be one of the wonders of Wales and can easily be visited on foot. Nearby is a small car park, and the nineteenth-century Swiss-style pavilion now sells teas and other refreshments.

The scenery of the whole area is full of surprises; the valleys are steep sided, generally wooded with a stream running along the bottom. The mountains, always dominating the scenery, stand aloof, impenetrable to all but those prepared for some effort.

The long spine of the hills from which the area takes its name, the Berwyns, are to the west with the highest summit in the county, Moel Sych, at 2,713ft. They are crossed by several ancient trackways which provide some excellent walking for those who enjoy a quiet or vigorous day on the hills. The heather-covered slopes make pleasant walking but there are few trackways so do go prepared.

There is much to enjoy in this area which has retained its peace and tranquillity.

PLACES OF INTEREST
Llangollen
Plas Newydd   Once home of two spinisters, lovely house and setting.
Canal Exhibition Centre   Offers trips on barges.
Railway Society   In old station yard.
Valle Crucis Abbey   A superb setting.
Chirk Castle   Interesting variety of styles in the house. Large park and section of Offa's Dyke.
Llanrhaeadr-yn-Mochnant   Home of Bishop Morgan.
Pistyll Rhaeadr   Highest waterfall in Wales in splendid setting.

WALKS IN THE AREA
The Berwyn range is perhaps one of the less-frequented ranges of hills in North Wales, the walking is excellent and not too strenuous. For those whose interest is in following ancient trackways there are several superb walks east – west (or vice versa) across the range. Obviously a map is an essential item so route details are brief.

One excellent east – west and return traverse is from Llanarmon Dyffryn Ceiriog west along the minor road that follows the Afon Ceiriog; at first metalled, it soon becomes a trackway which climbs easily to the pass marked by a memorial stone. An old drovers' road and the route traditionally held to be the one attempted by Henry II in 1169 en route to attack Owain Gwynedd, it descends pleasantly towards the Dee Valley. Return by a similar ancient roadway from the junction of the two minor lanes. A superbly situated stone circle gives an excuse to rest before climbing up to the pass between Cadair Bronwen and Cadair Berwyn marked by a prehistoric standing stone and the final descent towards the Afon Ceiriog.

An excellent north to south traverse of the range can be made following the ridge easily all the way; it makes a superb high level walk, though a vehicle at each end is desirable. Start at Glyndyfrdwy on the Dee and take the minor road south towards the first summit, Moel Fferna, then keeping to the high ground head south taking in all the summits to meet the B4391 at Milltir Gerrig.

For those who prefer an easier day, there are many footpaths and trackways in the area at a lower level. It is usually best to ask locally for a recommended route, and much depends on the time you have available. Many trails are marked and give easy walking, such as the disused tramway at Glyn Ceiriog that ambles easily alongside the river. Leading in the past to an old quarry, it is now owned by the National Trust.

Stone circle high above Llandrillo

South & Mid-Wales

DYLIFE AND THE FFRWD FAWR FALLS

Powys

OS Map: 1:50,000 Sheet No 136

Location

South of Machynlleth, a range of hills divided by deep valleys, bounded on the north by the A470 to Llanbrynmair, and the B4518 to Llanidloes to the east.

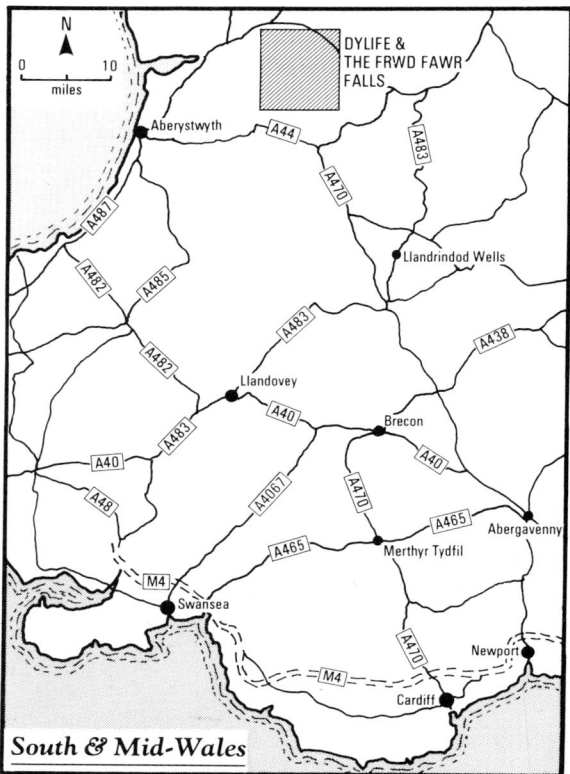

South & Mid-Wales

It is sometimes the quiet lanes and minor roads, leading to some of the more isolated villages, that give the most surprising views. In this area they lead to high moorlands and can provide many starting points for the walker and a revelation round each corner for every traveller.

Such a road leaves the main street in Machynlleth to wander south over the hills to join the B4518 just north of Staylittle. Signposted Dylife, it climbs, first through the less attractive side of the town before reaching open wooded valleys, and then climbs along wide ridges to reach high moorlands. These are the northern foothills of Plynlimon. There are several signposted walks starting from the road with a small lake, Glaslyn, and a minor Roman fortlet at Penycrocben to visit.

Plynlimon, which lies just a few miles to the south of this small mountain road, is considered one of the major mountains of Wales despite its apparent lack of height, 2,427ft. It is surrounded by mists and water, and is the source of no less than five rivers: the Dulas, Rheidol, Llynfnant, Wye and perhaps most famous of all, the Severn. Notorious for its bogs, a round of the mountain summits and sources can provide an interesting and formidable day's walking for those with a reserve of energy.

After reaching its highest point at 1,671ft, the road begins to descend to the old mining community of Dylife, where a scattering of cottages and farms is all that is left of a once thriving village. A pleasant little pub, The Star, shelters from the prevailing westerlies behind a line of conifers. Close by, waste tips from the old lead mines are gradually weathering into the surrounding landscape, but it will always by a bleak spot.

Descending east from Dylife, the road crosses a cattle grid and soon comes to a large lay-by on the

left-hand side. Along the fence is a rickety stile which must be climbed with care; the steep path descends to a small plateau overhanging a magnificent valley. To the left is one of the most spectacular waterfalls in the country, the Ffrwd Fawr Falls. Deep in a natural amphitheatre of vertical rock, the Afon Twymyn falls magnificently to the broken rocks below. The river then tumbles through a series of cataracts between the steep scree-covered hillsides, before emerging in the quiet valley beyond.

Unfortunately the steepness of the descent from the road to the waterfall precludes any further exploration from this point. Most people will be content to admire on one hand the superb setting of the waterfall, and the contrasting panorama of peace and tranquillity, to the north.

PLACES OF INTEREST
Hafren Forest   Off the B4518 west of Llanidloes. Seventeen square miles of forest on the eastern slopes of Plynlimon. Several waymarked trails.
Clywedog Dam   Off the B4518. Built in 1968, regulates the flow of the River Severn. Picnic sites.

Newborough Warren, Anglesey

The Berwyns in winter, North Wales

Eyemouth Harbour, Scottish Borders

The Cuillin Hills, Isle of Skye

Bryntail Lead Mines   Old lead mines now an industrial monument. Path leaves close to Clywedog Dam.

Llanidloes   Old Market Hall, half-timbered and the only one of its kind in Wales. Museum of Local History — emphasis on textiles, lead mining and chartist riots of which the town was the centre.

WALKS IN THE AREA

A pleasant walk can be taken from Dylife which gives a fine introduction to the area and also outstanding views of the falls and river on the return trip.

Start close to The Star, and take the metalled road past it to a gate by an old chapel. Go through the gate and cross to the far side of the fields where an obvious trackway is picked up. This climbs over the hills to descend steeply to a small stream, which joins the Afon Twymyn after a short distance. A minor footpath follows the river along the valley to some farm buildings, where a roadway is met which returns up the valley to Pennant. A series of tracks and footpaths lead up the wooded hillside, with splendid views of Ffrwd Fawr, to the mountain road below Dylife. The walk uphill gives further opportunity to enjoy the panorama and see the remains of the old mining activities.

To the south is Llyn Clywedog and the Hafren Forest, for those who prefer a more relaxing day or shorter walk.

After leaving the Dylife road to join the B4518 a second minor road heads east at Staylittle towards the lower slopes of Plynlimon. It soon divides, one branch climbing up and through the forest, the other meandering gently around the reservoir. On both routes there are several picnic sites and opportunities for short walks. Two leaflets are available from Tourist Information Centres locally. 'Hafren Forest Walks', detailing several walks, short or long, through the forest to points of interest.

The other leaflet, 'Llyn Clywedog Scenic Trail', describes a circuit from the dam at the southern end of the reservoir which wanders close to the shoreline. A footpath also leaves from there to the Bryntail Lead Mine, a monument to Wales's industrial past.

Castle Rock and the Clywedog Valley

THE BLACK MOUNTAINS

Powys

OS Map: 1:50,000 Sheet No 161
1:25,000 Brecon Beacons National
Park, Eastern Region

Location

An area of hills on the English border between Hay
on Wye and Abergavenny.

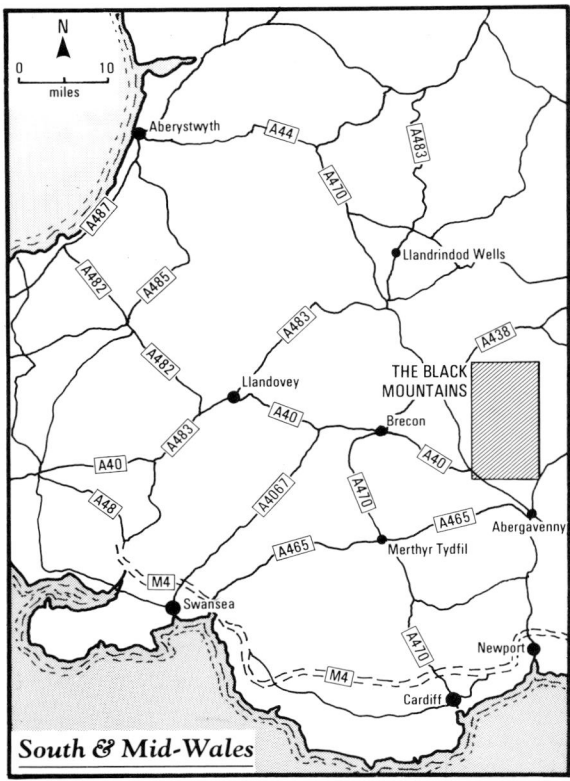

South & Mid-Wales

The Black Mountains, straddling the English/Welsh
border, are eastern outliers of the Brecon Beacons
National Park. Formed of the same Old Red
Sandstone, they form an area of high moorland
divided by deep lush valleys. The area is shaped
roughly like a trident, with three ridges running
north to south, and an adjoining main ridge
overlooking the Wye Valley along the top.
Characterised by the sharp north-westerly scarps
and relatively level tops, the mountains can
provide much satisfaction for the walker who
gains most from the scenery.

Three south-flowing river valleys divide the
ridges. With fifteen separate summits over 2,000ft,
and such a variety of scenery and terrain, there is
much to occupy the visitor prepared for a short or
long day on the hills. There is no shortage of
paths which criss-cross hill and dale.

Separated from the main mass by the Vale of
Ewyas is the longest and most easterly ridge. It
marks the border with England, and stretches
from Hattersal Hill to Hay Bluff in the north.
Offa's Dyke, the long distance footpath which
follows the Welsh border, joins the ridge for a
good stretch. Like most of the hills in the group,
the walking is generally moderate but offers
superb views towards Hereford and the Golden
Valley.

The Vale of Ewyas with the Afon Honddu has
several interesting religious connections. The
most important is the Llanthony Priory, founded
in the twelfth century for an Augustinian order. It
is easy to see why they chose this vale, which is so
peaceful and tranquil. Dissolved in 1538, the
priory has had a chequered history since then,
with various additions to the ruins in recent
centuries. It contained at one time a shooting
lodge, enlarged to a house and now converted to a
small hotel. Amongst the magnificent backdrop
of hills it is an almost idyllic situation. In the

nineteenth century, Joseph Leycester Lyne, known
as Father Ignatius tried to purchase and revive the
Priory as a religious community. When his efforts
failed, he moved north in the valley to Capel-y-
Ffin, and started building from scratch there.
Unfortunately the 'new' monastery only survived
until 1908. The roofless church is all that is left.

Continuing north, the narrow road climbs over
the Gospel Pass to a magnificent viewpoint before
descending to the Wye Valley.

The two eastern valleys are quieter and more
secluded, retaining a pastoral quality rarely found
nowadays. Entirely different in character, they are
divided by the highest mountains in the range Pen-
y-Gader Fawr (2,625ft) and Waun Fach (2,660ft).
The Grwyne Fawr valley, the easterly of the the the
two, is long and deep. Heavily afforested, it leads
far into the hills and has a high reservoir at its head.

Overlooking the entrance to the shorter Grwyne
Fechan valley is Table Mountain. Not as famous
as its southern counterpart, it is nevertheless well
named. Defined by the Iron Age hillfort of Grug
Hywel, which gives its name to the nearby town,
Crickhowel it makes a splendid introduction or
end to any visit to this fine range of hills.

PLACES OF INTEREST
Vale of Ewyas
Llanthony Priory Eleventh/twelfth century remains of priory church.
Capel-y-Ffin Small but interesting remains of more recent priory.
Cwmyoy Church Leaning church victim of a landslip.
Grug Hywel Iron Age hillfort above Crickhowell surrounding summit of Table Mountain.

WALKS IN THE AREA
The hills and valleys of the Black Mountains are, under normal conditions, an area where one can walk and explore with relative ease. The gentle whaleback ridges are covered by a comprehensive network of footpaths. Once an initial ascent has been made, and the ridges attained, reasonable distances with excellent views can be covered without too much difficulty.

The Gospel Pass is crossed by the B4223, which runs through the Vale of Ewyas. The summit of the Pass makes an ideal starting place for several walks. A short climb to the east will bring you to the ridge leading to Hay Bluff, the northernmost point of these hills, with magnificent views across to Hay on Wye and the Wye Valley. Turning south along the Offa's Dyke path, one can follow the ridge easily for as long as time allows.

West from Gospel Pass, a similar short ascent reaches the summit of Twmpa and the main ridge. A choice of paths can be followed from here, being easy to maintain along the grassy tops.

In the valleys the choice of footpaths is wide-ranging, with several walks around Capel-y-Ffin. To the south behind Llanthony Priory, a way-marked path leads up through some woodland and other places of interest. Opposite the lane to the priory is the start of a longer walk up to the summit of Bal Mawr, worth doing too if only to see the magnificent views.

All the other summits are fairly easily approachable by shorter walks from their nearest points in the valleys. It is, however, worth planning a walk that is a little longer to take in a few summits while you are up high, and then return along a different ridge or along the valley to fully appreciate the whole area.

Gospel Pass and the Vale of Ewyas

Southern Scotland

GULLANE

Lothian

OS Map: 1:50,000 Sheet No 66

Location

Gullane can be reached direct from Edinburgh following the coastal A198. This road also links with the A1 just north of Dunbar. The village is some 40 minutes drive from the centre of Edinburgh; traffic can be heavy in and out of the city in high summer, so allow up to an hour to ensure a relaxed drive.

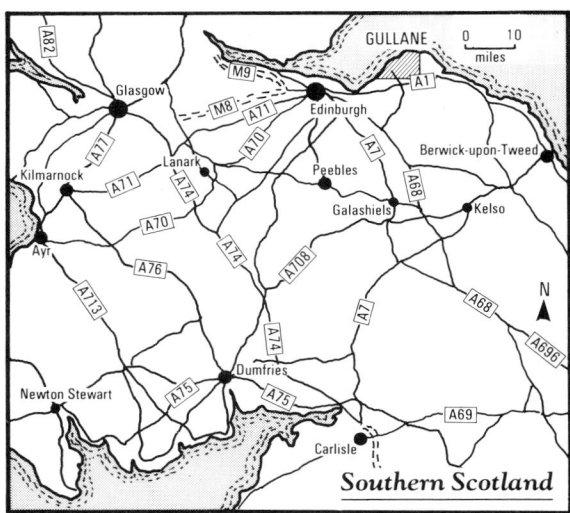

Southern Scotland

A very well known holiday village and golfing centre on the Firth of Forth, some 18 miles from Edinburgh, Gullane was once called the 'Newmarket of Scotland' because of its racecourse. That was in the nineteenth century, when tourists were beginning to discover the scenic delights of the area. Walks along this part of the Lothian coastline show how drifting sands and shoreline reclamation have been turned into an exceptionally fine nature reserve and seascape area. In a rehearsal for the D-Day landing, Allied forces stormed the Gullane beaches during World War II.

Gullane was an important settlement from the twelfth century with its own, now ruined, parish church. Once in the possession of the monks of Dryburgh Abbey, the church was closed in 1631 and the last vicar of Gullane, it is said, was sacked by King James VI for smoking tobacco. Yet, Gullane's troubles were always associated with the sea.

In 1935 the people of Gullane asked the County Council to take over the sand dunes, known as Gullane Bents, but the extensive programme of reclamation was not undertaken until 1956. At that time brushwood fences were erected to hold the sand; thus was a new foredune made and the height of the coastal area raised. Behind this dune marram grass was planted, and its long roots have knitted together to hold the sand. Sea buckthorn was also planted to provide shelter. Today reclamation planting still takes place.

Behind the dunes are hundreds of acres of well-drained turf, useless for farming, but ideal for golf. So, in 1882 Gullane Golf Club was formed, and today the village sports three 18-hole courses. To the east is the world-famous Muirfield Championship Course, the headquarters of the Honourable

Company of Edinburgh Golfers. Today Gullane remains a golfing resort, but preserves its old colour and romance which was so charmingly caught in Robert Louis Stevenson's *Catriona*.

PLACES OF INTEREST
Saltcoates Castle Within the village. This sixteenth-century castle has a tower with an interesting set of fourteen gargoyles. Note the lectern-shaped dovecote.
Nature Reserve Aberlady Bay.
Motor Museum Myreton.
Museum of Flight East Fortune.
Dirleton Castle Thirteenth-century, two miles from Gullane.
Viewpoint on the coastal walk
Luffness Castle One mile east of Aberlady, a sixteenth-century castle with a thirteenth-century keep. Still has its old moat.

WALKS IN THE AREA
Gullane Bay and Cliffs From the car park (reached via Sandy Loan, off the A198) take the cliff path left bordering Gullane Bay; this leads to the cliffs from which there are spectacular views along the Firth of Forth and towards Edinburgh Castle and Arthur's Seat. To the far west are the Pentland Hills, and in the middle of the Firth is the island of Inchkeith. To the south run Gullane links, once the training grounds for racehorses.
Gullane Point and Corby Craigs From the car park, walk down the track to the beach path of Gullane Bay. Follow this path to Gullane Point. Look for the birdlife here, eider ducks, shelduck, cormorants, shags and terns are regular visitors. On the shoreline dunlins, turnstones and oyster-catchers can be seen. To the left, facing the Viewpoint, are Corby Craigs.
Coastal path to Aberlady From the car park take either the cliff, or coastal path. From Gullane Point the path follows the sands of Aberlady Bay to the Nature Reserve, the haunt of botanists and ornithologists. The Nature Reserve is some 2 miles south of Gullane and there are maps of the area available at the entrance.
Coastal path to the Nature Trail at Dirleton From the car park follow the coastal path round by the Black Rocks. Dirleton is on the right and in the distance is North Berwick and its eponymous Law. In the dunes the skylarks and reed buntings mix with a wide range of seabirds which inhabit the islands hereabouts.

Dirleton from the castle

ST ABBS

Borders

OS Map: 1:50,000 Sheet No 67

Location

If travelling down the A1 from Edinburgh, take the A1107 left, south of Cockburnspath and follow the signs for Coldingham. St Abbs is thence reached down the B6438. From the south, leave the A1 at Burnmouth (5 miles north of Berwick-upon-Tweed) and take the A1107 to Coldingham, and on to St Abbs via the B6438.

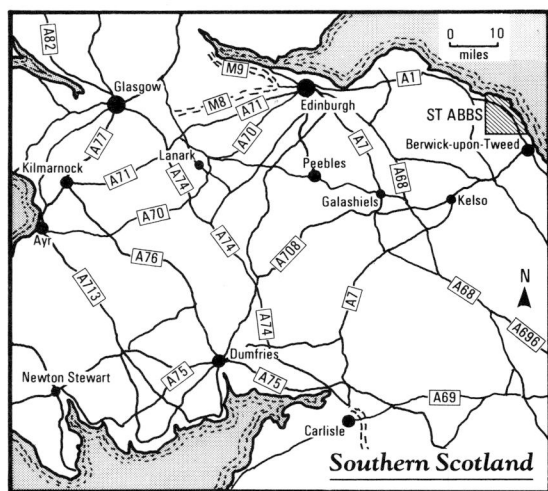

Southern Scotland

The quaint fishing village of St Abbs takes its name from St Ebba, daughter of Ethelfrith, King of Northumbria. She landed hereabouts in 640, and founded an ecclesiastical community over which she set up as abbess. It is believed that the fort on St Abbs Head marks the spot of the first monastery. The steep irregular streets of St Abbs run down to the harbour, which was built by the brewing family of Usher; strange to tell, Andrew Usher, who also built the church, stipulated that there should be no public house in St Abbs.

It is the exciting cliff-bound coastline hereabouts which attracts the visitors, for, to the north towards St Abbs Head, with its lighthouse, the red cliffs rise to over 300ft, forming an impressive headland. From the small inlet of Pettycurwick Bay, the rugged coast with its teeming birdlife is well viewed.

Within the town there is a row of fishermen's cottages with a parallel row of picturesque tiny buildings used by local fishermen to store their gear. The headland is pitted with caves, long the haunt of smugglers, for the fishermen once eked out a difficult trade with fruits from an alternative 'sea harvest'.

Walks in this area offer many contrasts and the ancient burghs of Eyemouth and Coldingham are a bonus. Eyemouth, the busy fishing town and holiday resort on the Eye Water, has long been recognised as one of the most important fishing ports of the east coast and has been a burgh since 1597. The tower nearby the harbour, now used by the Eyemouth Golf Club, dates back to Cromwell's visit of 1650. Smeaton's harbour of 1768 has a charm all its own, while the Hurkar Rocks at the entrance to the bay set tourists' cameras clicking with their perpetual furious breakers. Remnants of the smuggling age can be seen too at Gunsgreen House. Overlooking the harbour, the house has 'secret passages' beneath where booty was hidden from the excisemen.

To arrive at St Abbs, the visitor passes through the delightful village of Coldingham with its ruined priory. Coldingham Bay still has Edwardian beach huts, and is a popular bathing place noted for its coloured pebbles.

Eyemouth Harbour

St Abbs

PLACES OF INTEREST

Coldingham Priory Founded in 1098 by Edgar, King of Scotland for Benedictine monks from Durham, the priory ruins have been renovated and excavated, and the old choir contains the local parish church, deemed one of the oldest in Scotland still open for public worship.

Eyemouth Harbour Famous for its eighteenth-century smuggling trade; the town has a local museum.

Wildlife Reserve Managed jointly by the Wildlife Trust and the National Trust for Scotland, at St Abbs Head.

Fast Castle Four miles north-west of Coldingham, the castle was once the sixteenth-century seat of the Home family. The castle is the 'Wolf's Crag' of Sir Walter Scott's novel *The Bride of Lammermoor*.

WALKS IN THE AREA

Coastal Walk to Eyemouth From the car park at St Abbs, make for the marked coastal path to Coldingham Bay. Follow the path at the top of the cliffs and descend to Coldingham Bay Sands. Cross the sands and pick up the path again. Follow

this past Yellow Craig, Linkim Shore and Callercove Point and join the tarred footpath round the coastguard station and caravan park and descend into Eyemouth. On the headland are the remains of a sixteenth-century fortress which was garrisoned by French troops.

Along the shore look for the geologist's wonderland of greywackes and shales of this volcanic coastline. Sea pinks, sea bindweed and vipers' buglass are common on the coastline path, while the shore sports sea milkwort and sea campion.

St Abbs to Coldingham Follow the signs from St Abbs for the Wildlife Reserve. The headland is of considerable botanical and archaeological interest, and the sea offshore is designated a voluntary marine nature reserve in recognition of its rich underwater life. Hereabouts are to be seen guillemots, kittiwakes, razorbills, shags, fulmars and herring gulls.

Coldingham Loch From Coldingham take the A1107 north-west and follow the signs for the loch. Around the loch are the remains of Iron Age Settlements.

Clyde Valley at Lanark

Strathclyde

OS Map: 1:50,000 Sheet No 71

Location

Reached by the A74 from Glasgow (north), or Carlisle (south), then the A744 – A72 from Kirkmuirhill following the signs for Lanark.

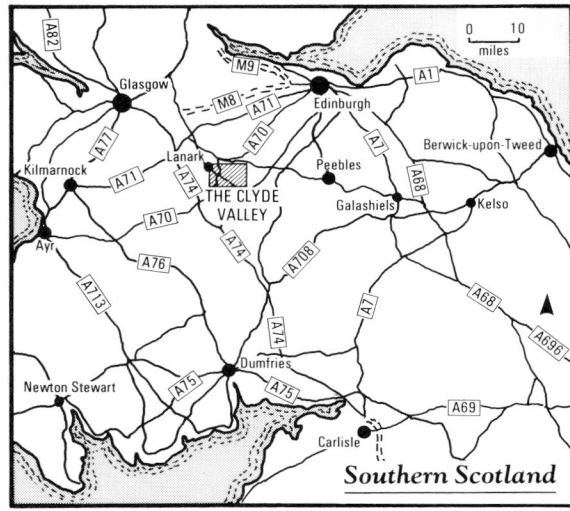

Southern Scotland

The Valley of the Clyde is still hailed as 'one of Scotland's best-kept secrets'. The whole length of the River Clyde offers visitors a set of fast-changing scenes, from the great industrial areas of the north, through the pleasing orchard country to pastoral Clydesdale, which gives way in turn to the purple hills and moorland in southern Scotland. The area chosen for these walks has been designed to give the visitor a taste of the timeless villages, the country parks and picnic sites.

Lanark, a Royal Burgh since 1140, stands elevated above the banks of the River Clyde, some 25 miles from Glasgow. The parish church of St Nicholas dates from 1774 and nearby is the statue (1822) to the Scottish patriot William Wallace (1270-1305). On the edge of town are the ruins of the twelfth-century St Kentigern's church, which the parish church replaced. Look too, in Broomgate, for the seventeenth-century Hyndford House, the town house of the Earls of Hyndford.

A mile or so south of Lanark is New Lanark, situated in a deep and magnificent wooded gorge of the River Clyde. The river itself was the main reason for the building of the textile mills here during the Industrial Revolution and the creation of the workers' 'model village'. This was a part of an experiment in community living which was started in the 1780s. Today the name of the pioneer socialist Robert Owen (1771-1858) is most associated with New Lanark, which has been developed as Scotland's showplace of industrial archaeology.

Whuppity Scoorie and *Lanimer Week:* If the visitor is in Lanark in March, the childrens' festival of 'Whuppity Scoorie' can be witnessed. Of nineteenth-century origin, children gather at the Cross for the customary swinging around their

River Clyde at Thankerton, near Biggar

New Lanark ▷

heads of paper balls on lengths of string. This is to celebrate the recommencing of the ringing of the town bells which have remained silent over the winter.

During the mid-weeks of June, Lanark holds its 'Lanimer' festival, a relic of the old 'Riding of the Marches' ceremonial.

PLACES OF INTEREST

Cartland Bridge From Lanark take the A73 (Glasgow) road north. A mile or so out of the town is Cartland Bridge, which carries the road over a 130ft gorge of the River Mouse (pronounced 'moose'). The bridge was constructed in 1822 by Thomas Telford (1757-1834), the Scottish stone-mason turned engineer; it is one of the highest road bridges in Scotland.

Craignethan Castle This sixteenth-century castle lies some 4½ miles north-west of Lanark, and is a Tower House defended by considerable walls. Begun by Sir James Hamilton of Finnart, it is reputedly the 'Tillietudlem Castle' of Sir Walter Scott's *Old Mortality*. The castle is administered by the Department of the Enviroment and is open during normal tourist times.

WALKS IN THE AREA

A Lanark Town Walk For a representative view of the town of Lanark park by Castlebank park (the site of Lanark Castle) and walk into Broomgate; turn right into High Street and at the junction walk down South Vennel, and right again into Wellgate and left into Castlegate and back to the car park.

New Lanark From Lanark follow the signs for New Lanark and descend sharply into the Clyde Gorge. The village is freely accessible to the public (except the mills) and is about one mile from Lanark. Guided tours are available at set times, and an exhibition is open daily in summer months. A 'New Lanark Heritage Trail' booklet is available on site.

Corra Linn – Bonnington Linn The Falls of Clyde were 'discovered' by eighteenth-century artists and writers. Half a mile upstream of New Lanark is Bonnington Power Station (built in 1927, it was the first hydro-electric scheme in Scotland); pass this and climb to the viewpoint of Corra Linn, which plunges 90ft. Continue another half mile along the gorge to Bonnington Linn, which drops 30ft. The small island between the falls is connected to the river bank by an early nineteenth-century cast-iron bridge; on the island there are the remains of a seventeenth-century dovecote, converted into a summerhouse. The weir gives access to the opposite side of the river and the nature trails.

PEEBLES

Borders

OS Map: 1:50,000 Sheet No 73

Location
Peebles lies at the junction of two main Border highways, the A703 to Edinburgh (23 miles away) and the A72 to Galashiels (19 miles away).

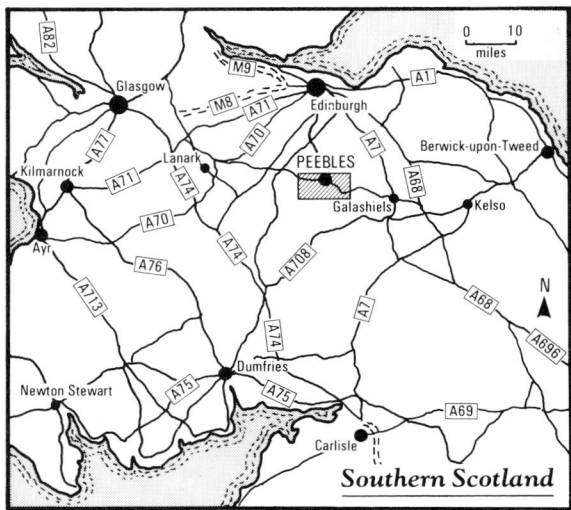

Southern Scotland

Once, the early Scottish kings came to the green hills of Tweeddale, which surround Peebles, to hunt and relax from the toils of monarchy. Today, tourists are attracted to this ancient Royal Burgh because of its walks and angling facilities. The River Tweed flows through Peebles, and Scotland's most famous angling river is the playground of rich anglers. Yet, by the town's car park, salmon fishing is reasonably priced and trout fishing is still free during the season.

The old castle of Peebles has now vanished, but those interested in old Border fortications should make for Neidpath Castle some 1¼ miles along the banks of the Tweed. This newly furbished castle was built as a tower house in the fourteenth century, and was besieged in 1650 by Cromwellian troops. It was the home of the first Duke of Queensberry, whose successor, the notorious eccentric rake 'Old Q', felled the fine woods on the estate.

Three bridges are worthy of note. The town bridge was originally built in 1467. The Old Manor Bridge, spanning the Manor water, was built in 1883 to replace the eighteenth-century bridge. The third is the Railway Bridge of 1864 on the line of the old Caledonian Railway, closed to passenger traffic in 1950; each of the bridge's eight arches is built on a skew to make the line curve across the Tweed.

Peebles has had many famous inhabitants from Robert Louis Stevenson to explorer Mungo Park; the celebrated novelist John Buchan and his sister (O. Douglas) lived at Bank House.

Peebles parish church was built in 1784, and the town has a series of inns famous in Border history. The seventeenth-century Cross Keys is the Cleikum Inn of Walter Scott's *St Ronan's Well*: and the Tontine dates from 1808.

Those visiting Peebles in June may be able to catch the Border Riding, within which is incorporated the crowning of the 'Beltane Queen'. In medieval times Peebles' rural games were famous all over Scotland; today the horse parade and festivities date from the resuscitation of 1897.

Peebles

Neidpath Castle

PLACES OF INTEREST

Traquair House Said by some to be the oldest continuously-inhabited house in Scotland, Tranquair dates from the tenth century and is eight miles east-south-east of Peebles. Open during the tourist season, it sports an eighteenth-century brewhouse, woodland walks and craft workshops.

Chambers Institution Museum Donated by the famous publisher William Chambers, in 1859, this museum in Peebles High Street houses many items of local history.

Cross Kirk The remains of this Trinitarian Friary, open free on collection of the key from the custodian's house, is situated in North Gate, Peebles.

Dawyck House Gardens Eight miles south-west of Peebles, the house is the home of Lt Col A.N. Balfour, whose gardens (open daily during the tourist season) display many rose trees, shrubs and delightful woodland walks.

Tinnis Castle The home of the head of the clan Tweedies, this sixteenth-century ruin is 9 miles south-west of Peebles and is reached along a sheepwalk.

WALKS IN THE AREA

To the meeting of the waters There is a car park by the junction of Eddleston Water and the Tweed. Make for the riverside path and walk forward to, and through, Hay Lodge Park. Continue past Neidpath Castle and cross the stile. You now pass under the railway viaduct and follow the riverside walk to Manor Bridge at the meeting of the Manor Water and the River Tweed.

To Manor Sware From St Andrew's Church, walk left over the River Tweed Bridge and go down to the riverside park, right. Walk forward along the path, past the footbridge, and take the grassy track left by the waymarker; soon you will cross the field to the road. Turn right and follow the road round the dog-leg and make for viewpoint. To extend the walk you can retrace your steps and turn left by the rough track which leads by South Park Wood, with Manor Sware rising on the left, to Manor Bridge.

The Glentress Forest Trail Just over two miles from Peebles along the A72 (to Galashiels) is the turn off (left) for the delightful and well-established forest walks sponsored by the Forestry Commission. Herein are picnic sites and a Forest Office for information on this woodland which was purchased from Haystoun Estate in 1920.

Cardrona Walks Take the B7062 out of Peebles for another set of Forestry Commission woodland trails, across the Tweed from Glentress.

EILDON

Borders

OS Map: 1:50,000 Sheet No 73

Location

The Eildon hills are skirted to the north by the
A6091 out of Galashiels, via Melrose. The walks
herein begin in Melrose where there is parking by
the ruined abbey and at the old railway station off
the B6359.

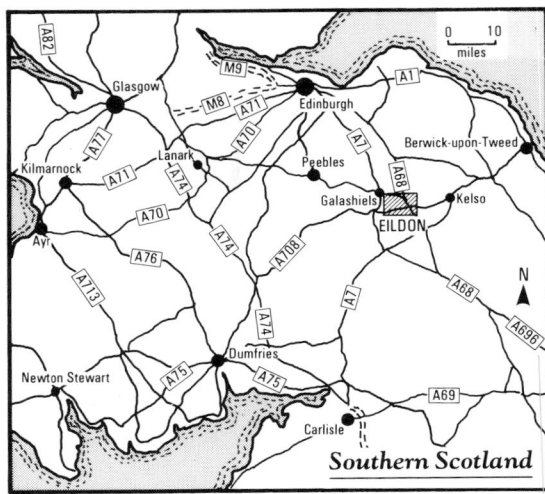

Southern Scotland

The magic of Eildon hills was shaped in the Ice Age
when the glaciers sculpted the steep scree slopes.
Today the moorland, the bell heather, parsley fern
and blueberries mantle the slopes where red
grouse breed and roe deer graze. On the summit of
Eildon the Roman legions had a signal station and
the Picts — those small dark folk who covered
themselves with tattoos of rank and devotion to
long-forgotten gods — set up earthworks around
their 300 hut home which can still be seen.

Sir Walter Scott fell in love with this land and
painted it in literary anecdote. It was Sir Walter
who retailed the legend of how the single cone of
Eildon was split one night by the machinations of a
demon at the behest of the local wizard Michael
Scott. At the foot of Eildon, the old ballads recall,
lies King Arthur and his Knights, sleeping until the
trumpet calls them to battle in the defence of their
realm.

The 'capital' of Eildon is Melrose, nestling at its
foot and girt by the River Tweed. This little border
town still sports many of its old houses and the
Cross of 1642 carries the arms of Scotland.

The tower of the old church dates from 1810,
but the jewel in the ecclesiastical crown is
undoubtedly the ruined Cistercian abbey of St
Mary, founded in 1136. During the fourteenth
and sixteenth centuries the abbey suffered badly at
the hands of the raiding English; but, the building
was restored in part by the Duke of Buccleuch in
1822 and was gifted to the nation in 1919. Beneath
the chancel once lay the heart of the Scottish
patriot King Robert I, the Bruce.

The small village of Newstead — which housed
the masons who built the abbey — is to be seen a
short distance to the east. The village is deemed to
be the oldest inhabited place in Scotland with a
2,000 year history. Just beyond Newstead lies the
site of the major Roman fort of *Trimontium* ('the
three hills' — after Eildon's summits), set on the
line of the Roman trunk road of Dere Street.

The Eildon Hills

PLACES OF INTEREST

Abbotsford House Built 1817-22, this beautiful mansion set near the River Tweed was the home of Sir Walter Scott until his death in 1832. Open during the tourist season the house contains a fascinating collection of relics amassed by Sir Walter as well as his 9,000 volume library.

Dryburgh Abbey Founded in the reign of David I by Hugh de Morville, this twelfth-century house of Premonstratensian Canons contains the tombs of Sir Walter Scott and Earl Haig amongst its tranquil ruins. The abbey is in the care of the Department of Environment.

Scott's View Lying on the B6356, 7 miles east-south-east of Galashiels, this breathtaking view of the Scottish Borderland was once beloved by Sir Walter Scott. Local legend has it that the horses (from his own stables) taking his remains to Dryburgh for burial, stopped here as they had so often done in his lifetime.

Priorwood Garden Adjacent to Melrose Abbey. Owned by the National Trust for Scotland, this garden has flowers suitable for drying, and a visitor and tourist information centre.

WALKS IN THE AREA

Eildon Hill Leave Melrose Square via the B6359. Follow the signs for Eildon Walk; at the first sign turn left down the steps, cross the bridge and climb towards the stile. The path now follows the right edge of the field. If the path to the summit proves too much, another path veers left along the foot of the hill to link with the A6091 and return to Melrose. Or, to cross the A6091 to walk down to Newstead and the footpath left back to the abbey. On a clear day the sight from Eildon can be spectacular, along the course of the River Tweed into the distant haze of the North Sea (thirty miles away). Away to the north-east can be seen the battlements of Hume Castle.

The Roman Camps From Melrose Square (by the National Trust for Scotland Shop) follow the road past the abbey and make for Newstead. Take the road left above the Tweed. Look out for the marker stones which show the site of the Roman fort layout (across the fields to the right).

River Tweed and The Battery From the Square turn down Abbey Street, pass St Mary's Road and join the riverside path. The path leads all the way round to Newstead past the embankment called The Battery. It is safe to walk along The Battery, but after heavy rain it can be slippery.

Melrose Abbey

KELSO

Borders

OS Map: 1:50,000 Sheet No 74

Location

Kelso is located at the junction of three major highways; the A6089 from Edinburgh; the A698 Berwick-upon-Tweed – Hawick route; and, the A699 from Selkirk. Kelso is 43 miles from Edinburgh.

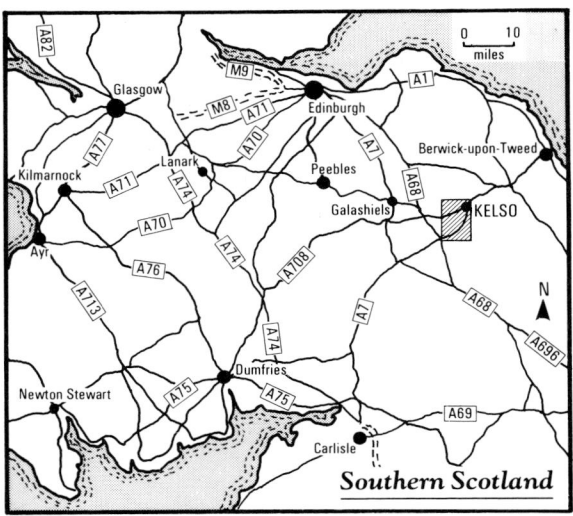

Southern Scotland

Kelso remains a busy agricultural town in a very attractive setting by the junction of the rivers Teviot and Tweed. The Tweed is crossed by a fine five-arched bridge which was built by the famous civil engineer John Rennie (1761-1821): his bridge of 1803 replaced one destroyed by the floods of 1797. On the bridge are two lamp standards from the demolished Old Waterloo Bridge, London, which Rennie built in 1811; at the mid-point are fine views of Floors Castle (the Scottish rendering of the French *Fleurs*), the rivers' junction and the abbey.

Open all year round, Kelso Abbey is but a shadow of its former self. It was one of the largest of the Border abbeys, and was founded in 1128 for the monks of the Order of Tiron in Picardy. When the Earl of Hertford visited Kelso in 1545, the abbey was armed as a fortress, and was besieged to be almost entirely razed. The garrison of 100 men and twelve monks were all slaughtered, and, today, only the tower and fragmentary nave are original. South of the abbey is a modern Romanesque cloister to the memory of the eighth Duke and Duchess of Roxburghe.

In Kelso's pleasant square stands the Court House of 1816; one famous lawyer with Kelso connections was Sir Walter Scott, who was educated at the former grammar-school, and stayed at Garden Cottage (now Waverley Lodge). The town still sports some interesting architecture, such as the nineteenth-century Wooden House, and the Ednam House Hotel which dates from 1761, and from whose garden spectacular sunset views of the river are seen.

Across the river, and now covered by farmland, are the foundations of the lost burgh of Roxburgh which was the precursor of Kelso. The modern village of Roxburgh is some three miles away to the south.

Set on one of the main medieval routes out of Scotland, Kelso had many royal visitors. Mary Queen of Scots came here in 1566, and in 1745 Prince Charles Edward Stuart stayed for two nights on his northward retreat.

PLACES OF INTEREST

James Thomson Obelisk   At Ferniehill, 2 miles north-east of Kelso. Set up to celebrate the poet James Thomson (1700-48) who was born at Ednam. He wrote the words for 'Rule Britannia', and composed 'The Seasons'.

Lyte Plaque   At Ednam bridge is situated the memorial plaque to the hymnologist Henry Francis Lyte (1793-1847), the composer of *Abide With Me*.

Floors Castle   The home of the Dukes of Roxburghe, this very impressive mansion was built by William Adam in 1721, with additions by William Playfair of the 1840s. The mansion and gardens are open the public, May – September. The parkland contains a holly tree said to mark the spot where James II was killed by the bursting of a cannon during the siege of Roxburgh Castle, 1460.

Roxburgh Castle   The ruin, with its elevated earthworks, was once a mighty twelfth-century castle which was destroyed by the Scots in the fifteenth century. It is located one mile south-west of Kelso on the A699.

Kelso ▷

WALKS IN THE AREA

Riverside to Roxburgh   There is limited parking in the square at Kelso, so alternatively park behind the abbey where there are also toilet facilities. From whichever starting point, enter Bridge Street and cross the Tweed via Kelso Bridge. Turn right at the end of the bridge and follow the A699 round by the river and cross the Teviot Bridge. Now take the path down to the river, follow this path all the way to the village of Roxburgh, past the old ruined castle of the same name on the heights along the river. The road from Roxburgh, via Kersmains, leads to the A699 and returns to Kelso.

Riverside to Kalemouth   Follow the instructions as above to get to Roxburgh. In the village,

follow the signposted track along the River Teviot. Continue under the old railway viaduct. Follow the riverwalk until it leads up on to the old railway track; walk on until this meets the road. Turn left and follow the road past Old Ormiston, Ormiston Mill to Kalemouth. If you wish to return to Kelso via a main road, cross the suspension bridge and walk on to the A698 (left) for Kelso. These two walks give fine views of the Tweed and the Teviot, and their water fowl. Watch too for the salmon jumps during the spring/autumn spawning runs. Along the walks woodpecker, kingfisher and heron are often seen.

Warning: Stay away from the large plant (cannot miss it) which grows along the riverside; this is the gaint hogweed which can cause dermatitis.

ALLOWAY AND AYR

Strathclyde

OS Map: 1:50,000 Sheet No 70

Location

Alloway and Ayr can be reached by the A77 from Glasgow via Kilmarnock, and by the A76 from Dumfries and the south. Ayr is also on the A78 coastal route to Glasgow skirting the Firth of Clyde.

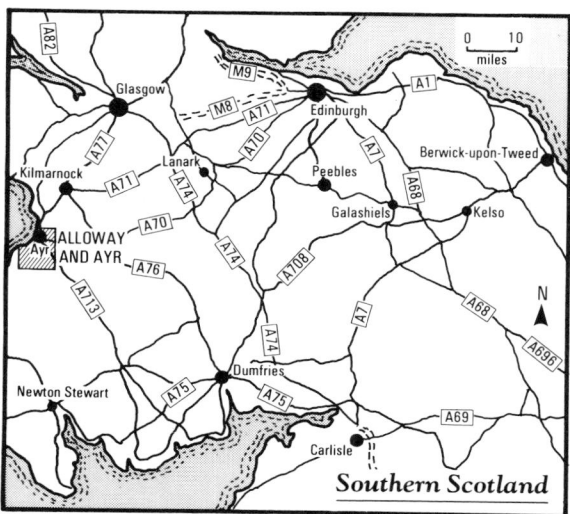

Southern Scotland

Ayr is undoubtedly the most popular holiday resort on Scotland's west coast. Created a Royal Burgh in 1202, there was a community here from the eighth century, and the burgh is now the principal town of the new Kyle and Carrick District. Kyle and Carrick have always relied on the land and what grows from it; the countryside around Ayr is of rich lowland soil and green sheep pastures are the foundations on which everything else rests.

The town is packed with buildings and monuments of interest. A slender spire still surmounts the Town Buildings (1828), and the burgh Academy is a thirteenth-century foundation. In the High Street stands the Wallace tower, a memorial of Gothic proportions set up in 1832 to honour the Scottish patriot Sir William Wallace (1274-1305). The Auld Kirk (Old Church) dates from 1655 and has Crowellian associations. The Fort Castle is the tower of the ancient Church of the Greyfriars, dedicated to St John, in which King Robert I the Bruce's parliament of 1315 met; herein is a perfect viewpoint of the coast and the Isle of Arran. The oldest building in the town is the much restored sixteenth-century Loudoun Hall.

John Macadam, the internationally celebrated roadmaker, was born in Ayr in 1756.

Throughout Ayr are strong links with Scotland's national poet, Robert Burns (1759-96). Particularly famous for its Burns associations are the thatched Tam o'Shanter Inn and the 'Twa Brigs' (Two Bridges) of Ayr, celebrated in Burns's poem of the same name, of which the 'Auld Brig' dates back to the thirteenth century. Near the station is Burns Statue Square.

Burns was born three miles away at Alloway, a place now totally associated with the poet. The cottage in which he was born has been preserved, and adjoining is a museum having both his

Culzean Castle

personal relics and national memorabilia. Further along the A719 lies the roofless 'haunted' Kirk, and across the road is the Burns Monument, another repository of relics. Spanning the River Doon is the much-fabled old bridge, another medieval relic, associated with the poem *Tam o'Shanter*.

Kennedy's Pass, between Girvan and Lendalfoot ▷

PLACES OF INTEREST

Culzean Castle   Twelve miles south-south-west of Ayr, and pronounced 'Culane', this castle is one of the famous creations of architect Robert Adam, and was the home of the Kennedy family. Dating from 1777, the castle has fine ceilings, staircases and public rooms. The property is owned by the National Trust for Scotland.

Electric Brae   Some 9 miles south of Ayr, this optical illusion causes a car to be seen going down hill when it is in fact going up. The hill is also known as Croy Brae.

Crossraguel Abbey   Two miles south-west of Maybole and administered by the Department of the Environment, this Cluniac monastery was built in 1244 by the Earl of Carrick. The extensive remains are of important architectural distinction.

MacLaurin Art Gallery   This gallery, 1½ miles south of Ayr (off the road to Alloway), and is in a part of Roselle House, where exhibitions of fine art and local history are displayed. Open all the year round, the gallery is set within extensive parkland with a nature trail.

WALKS IN THE AREA

Town Walk   From the car park in the vicinity of the Public Library (Main Street) walk along River Street to the Auld Brig. Cross the bridge into High Street; watch for the signs left for the Auld Kirk. Continue along High Street, past the Wallace Tower, and just before the junction of Kyle Street there is the Tam o'Shanter Museum. Walk on into Burns Statue Square and turn down Miller Road (a Tourist Information Bureau is sited here); turn right into Alloway Place and thence into Sandgate and the New Bridge. From this point a harbour walk may be contemplated.

Ayr to Alloway   From Burns Statue Square follow Carrick Road into Monument Road which leads to Burns's cottage, some three miles away.

Brig o'Doon   From the car park at Burns's cottage walk right, along Monument Road, past the end of Shanter Way. Soon Alloway Kirk is reached on the right; Burns's father William Burness (note the original spelling of the surname) is buried here. Take the fork left by the hotel and walk down past the ornate Burns Monument completed in 1823. Turn right over the old Brig o'Doon and walk up the line of the old road to the B7024. Walk back towards the Doon and cross the New Bridge of Doon where the famous 'banks and braes' are seen to their best advantage. The road now leads back to the car park at Alloway. The walk may be extended by walking down Longhill Ave and Earls Way to the sea (turn left before the New Bridge of Doon).

LEADHILLS AND WANLOCKHEAD

Strathclyde

OS Map: 1:50,000 Sheet No 71

Location
These two villages are reached along the B797, from the A74 at Abington; or, from the A76 from Mennock.

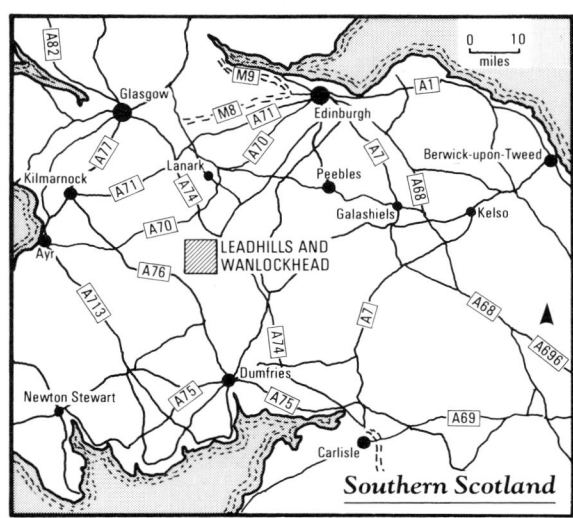

Southern Scotland

Leadhills stands over 1,300ft above sea level in the Lowther hills in southern Lanarkshire; hills clad with heather, thyme and tormentil, disturbed only by the call of grouse, or curlew. Lead was mined in these hills from Roman times and the last shaft in the area was closed in 1959. In the sixteenth and seventeenth centuries, the hills rang with the activities of the gold miners who obtained royal warrants to search for precious metals. A ring of Leadhills gold was presented to the late Queen Mary.

Life was very hard for the miners hereabouts, but they were always known for their hospitality. They had a resthouse in the village for beggars and pedlars who might be in need, and a curfew bell was rung to guide to safety those lost in the hills. Today the Hopetoun Arms inn is the highest in Scotland. The local golf course is said to be the highest in Britain. Apart from the poet Allan Ramsay (1686-1758), another famous son of Leadhills was William Symington (1763-1831), the famous engineer, inventor and pioneer of steam navigation.

The road linking Leadhills and Wanlockhead rises to a height of 1,531ft. Wanlockhead is the highest village in Scotland and, like Leadhills, owes its former prosperity to the mining of gold, silver and lead. Both Leadhills and Wanlockhead are dominated by the rounded Lowther hills to the south-east, of which Green Lowther rises to 2,403ft and Lowther Hill to 2,377ft; from these hills are commanding views as far as Cumberland.

In the late seventeenth century these hills were the refuge of the Covenanters (the signatories of the Scottish National Convenant of 1638 who pledged to uphold the Presbyterian faith against prelacy and popery).

Always deemed a healthy area to live, in the graveyard of Leadhills there is a stone to the memory of John Taylor, who is recorded thereon as having died aged 137.

WALKS IN THE AREA
The newly opened Southern Upland Way has a section which includes Leadhills and Wanlockhead. The Southern Upland Way is Scotland's third long-distance route. It runs from Portpatrick in the west of Dumfries and Galloway region, to Cockburnspath in the east of the Borders region and is 212 miles long. The route is conveniently joined at Wanlockhead where it makes a loop into the hills; look for the waymarkers at Wanlockhead for a circular tour.

There are many walks to be had in the Leadhills – Wanlockhead area, whether you follow old mine tracks or the course of the old railway.
From Wanlockhead you can follow the old mine track past the open air museum to Meadowfoot and follow the Wanlock Water into the hills.
From Wanlockhead cemetery climb the hill (past the beam engine beds) and follow the sheep trails over Wanlock Dod to Leadhills.
From Leadhills, follow the old railway line (it crosses the B7040 out of the village) to the old Viaduct above the Shortcleuch Water.
NB: Do not permit your dog to run wild on the Lowther hills (or indeed, any Scottish hills). If a dog is seen chasing sheep — or ostensibly worrying them — it runs the risk of being shot. Around Leadhills and Wanlockhead too there are sealed mine shafts which should be given a wide berth.

PLACES OF INTEREST

Allan Ramsay Library, Leadhills   This is the lead miners' subscription library, founded in 1741. It contains rare books, mining documents and photographs, and is the oldest subscription library in the British Isles. The library is named after Allan Ramsay, author of *The Gentle Shepherd* who was born in the village in 1686.

Museum of Scottish Lead Mining Industry, Wanlockhead   Run by the Wanlockhead Museum Trust, this cottage museum contains mining and social relics of the area. Nearby is an open-air museum with lead mine beam engines, a smelt and 'butt-and-ben' cottages. Here too is a library with books and records of a Reading Society founded in 1756.

Lowthers Railway Society   Founded in 1984, this Society is active in its construction of a 2ft narrow gauge railway at Leadhills and Wanlockhead on the former Caledonian–LMS trackbed.

Restored mine pumping engine at Wanlockhead

LANGHOLM

Dumfries & Galloway

OS Map: 1:50,000 Sheet No 79

Location

Langholm is situated on the A7 Carlisle – Hawick – Edinburgh road, 21 miles from Carlisle and 76 from Edinburgh.

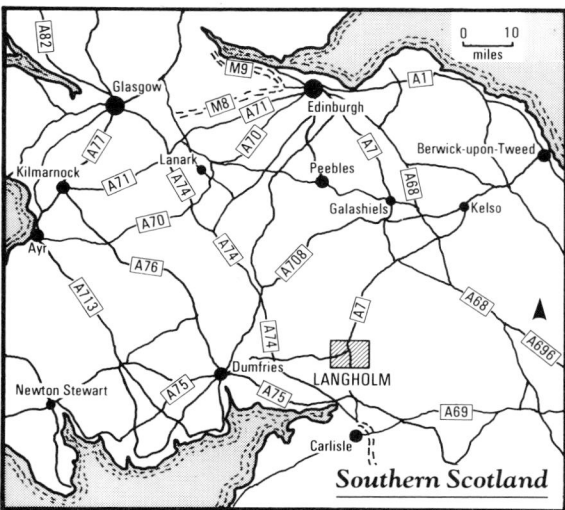

Southern Scotland

Set by the meeting place of three river valleys, and surrounded by hills, Langholm is the 'capital of Eskdale'. Only eight miles from the Scottish – English border, Langholm is in 'The Debatable Lands', that stretch of hills and valleys between the Solway Firth and the Southern Uplands over which the monarchs of the two kingdoms fought for 300 years. This is wild, rugged land, the home of bandits and cattle-thieves, where bloody strife and family feuds were everyday happenings.

Situated on the wooded River Esk, the town is noted for its woollens and is a popular angling resort. The town was built on the site of the battle of Arkenholm (1455), when James II of Scots broke the power of the Douglas family. In the eighteenth century, Langholm was a centre of the cattle trade; by 1788 a cotton mill was founded and the town became an important cloth-making area in 1832, when the manufacture of black-and-white check trousers for shepherds began. In modern times Langholm has been famous for the making of tweed and for rugby football.

Geography made Langholm what it is today, and it is still essentially a Border town, but its former degree of isolation gave it a self-reliance still a part of the local character. The Buccleuch family were major landowners in the area and a former Duke gave the Town Hall. Langholm is the birthplace of Hugh McDiarmid (C.M. Grieve 1892-1978) poet and critic.

Throughout the Borders Region, early June sees the start of the series of festivals known as the Common Ridings. The main purpose of these ridings was to ride around the common lands belonging to the burgh, and establish annually the boundaries; this was particularly important in the days of the 'debatable ownership'. Langholm Common Riding takes place on the last Friday in July and dates from 1816 as a mounted cavalcade led by the chief rider known as 'The Cornet'.

Hermitage Castle

PLACES OF INTEREST

Telford Memorial   Six miles north-west of Langholm lies the memorial to the famous Scottish engineer, canal, dock and bridge builder, Thomas Telford (1757-1834). He was born in the valley of Meggat Water, near Westerkirk.

Scots Dyke   Seven miles south of Langholm are

Bentpath (Westerkirk) in the Esk Valley above Langholm

---

the remains of this wall made of clods of earth and stones; this makes part of the border between Scotland and England.

Hollows Tower Five miles south of Langholm is the sixteenth-century tower, once the home of the Border freebooter (a raider and cattle thief) Johnny Armstrong. With walls 6ft thick, the tower is also known as Holehouse.

Hermitage Castle Sixteen miles east of Langholm is this thirteenth-century castle to which Mary Queen of Scots made her exhausting ride from Jedburgh in 1566, to meet her lover the Earl of Bothwell; the ride nearly cost Mary her life. The well-preserved castle was the grim home of the de Soulis family, and then the Douglases after 1341.

WALKS IN THE AREA

Town Centre to Malcolm Monument A car park is situated on the north side of the town, off the A7 Carlisle – Edinburgh road. This car park is next to Kiln Green, on the banks of the Ewes Water, the haunt of dippers, mallard and wagtails. Across the River Esk, famous for its trout, lies the site of Langholm Castle, a stronghold of the Armstrongs. Make for the town and once in Drove Road turn into Arkenholm Terrace, and walk up left towards the hills. The path leads up to Whita Hill (its well-water was once used in the making of illicit whisky locally) and the monument to Sir John Malcolm, a former Governor of Bombay. The view is one of the best in the Borders, and in clear weather you can see the Isle of Man. The Whita summit is on the route of the Common Riders.

To the site of Wauchope Castle Follow the road forward from the car park and right over Thomas Telford's bridge (1775). Then follow the riverside road to the suspension bridge (1875) and take the road right, up the hill past the old parish church. At the house called Stubholm follow the farm road towards the trees. This leads to Wauchope Water bridge (1794) and the site of the castle. Now signposted 'Gaskill's Walk' unfolds from the bridge along the foot of Warbla Hill. The track leads back to Stubholm and thence the return route to the car park.

GATEHOUSE OF FLEET

Dumfries and Galloway

OS Map: 1:50,000 Sheet No 83

Location

Gatehouse of Fleet lies on the A75 Dumfries – Stranraer route. It is also reached direct from Ayr via the A713 thence the A762 and Loch Ken.

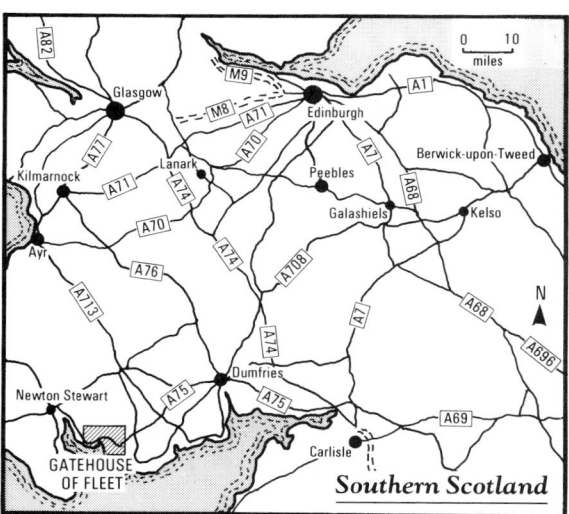

Southern Scotland

This peaceful country town, which stands within some of the finest woods and pastures of Dumfries and Galloway, owes its name to the old military 'gait' or road, laid through Galloway in the seventeenth century. The township is on the river Fleet which was bridged and a 'gait house' was set up to be used as an inn and a tollhouse. Today the 'gait house' is an annexe of the Murray House Hotel. With its own harbour, Gatehouse of Fleet is in the heartland of the old Stewartry of Kirkcudbright, a memory of the days when these lands were held by hereditary royal stewards of the King of Scots. Indeed the word steward led to the naming of the royal house of Stewart (Stuart is the French spelling).

Devotees of Sir Walter Scott will have already met Gatehouse of Fleet as 'Kippletringan' in *Guy Mannering*. Following in the steps of Robert Burns too, writers have visited the town and been inspired. Dorothy L. Sayers (1893-1957) came here in the 1930s and stayed at the Anworth Hotel while writing *The Five Red Herrings*.

Once the wealth of Gatehouse of Fleet was closely dependent on the fortunes of nearby Cally Estate. In 1790 the firm of Birtwhistles established a cotton mill here — with the encouragement of James Murray of Cally — and in time the sleepy hamlet developed into a bustling cotton town. Gatehouse expanded to be a port in 1825 when a linking canal was built to straighten out the Fleet Water; this led to the further 'industrialisation' of Gatehouse with quarrying, tanning and brewing.

During the 1880s and 1890s Gatehouse declined as the town was a long way from markets and supplies (the lonely station was six miles away).

Worthwhile rambles are to be had in the beautiful valleys of the Fleet Water some three miles north-west. Here too, is the sixteenth-century ruined Rusco Castle, the home of the Gordons of Lochinvar. The coastline of Fleet Bay, an inlet of Wigtown Bay, is well worth a visit too.

Rusco Castle

Ardwall, one of the Islands of Fleet, near Fleet Bay

PLACES OF INTEREST
Cardoness Castle This fifteenth-century tower house, on the A75, one mile south-west of Gatehouse, was long the home of the McCullochs of Galloway. It rises to four storeys with a vaulted basement. In the care of the Department of the Environment, it is open at the usual tourist times.

The Murray Arms Hotel Here it is said that the poet Robert Burns (1759-96) wrote his famous poem *Bruce's Address at Bannockburn* in 1793; the poem begins with the emotive words 'Scots! wha hae wi' Wallace bled'. . . . Burns had visited the site of the Battle of Bannockburn (1314) in 1787, and as he walked the hills of Gatehouse the words of this, Scotland's unofficial national anthem, formed in his mind.

WALKS IN THE AREA
Murray Forest Centre A walking highlight at Gatehouse of Fleet is the forest rambles offered by this centre, set ½ mile east of the town. Herein too is a log cabin, with exhibits depicting broadleaf tree species of the Fleet Forest. The centre is open, free, during April – September.

Academy Land and Cally House From the car park beside the Murray Arms Hotel walk right towards the outskirts of town. Walk through the gateway and take the forest path. Soon you will come out of the trees and cross open fields. At the next belt of trees bear right (past the trees) and walk past the Forest Nursery. On the skyline is seen the monument of 1842 set up to Samuel Rutherford, the noted Covenanter. This brings you to the road up to Cally House (now a hotel). Built in 1763 for James Murray by Robert Mylne, the mansion was the first building in Kirkcudbrightshire of this quality to be constructed from local granite.

Bush Bridge and The Temple From the car park walk along the main road. Bear right at the war memorial (note the old mill dam, left) and enter the driveway of the Cally Hotel. Walk past the Forest Centre and bear left down the waymarked road. Walk on the Bush Bridge, once part of the Dumfries – Stranraer turnpike road. On the left is Bush Loch and Park. Follow the forest road (forward all the way) to The Temple, a Gothic-type folly of 1779. The forest paths offer various options on how to return to Gatehouse.

The Scottish Highlands

GAIRLOCH

Highland

OS Map: 1:50,000 Sheet No 19

Location

From the south take the A9 to Inverness then the
A832 to Achnasheen. Turn right and continue
along the A832 to Gairloch.

Gairloch has some of the finest sandy beaches in
Scotland. At low tide, over two miles of firm
silvery sand washed by a turquoise sea make the
breathtaking foreground to the Torridon Peaks in
the south. When the Vikings discovered this
haven, they are said to have dragged their longships
inland to reach nearby Loch Maree. The truth of
this cannot be proven, but Loch Maree was an
important water in olden times. Folklore speaks
of fairies and others inhabiting its many islands,
and one was so special that even when Queen
Victoria visited it, she was expected to leave a coin
in the cracks of an ancient tree as a gift to the wee
folk.

Sea salmon visit the waters of Loch Gairloch on
their way to their spawning grounds, but the
fishing stations along the coast, where anchored
nets were put out from the shore, are no longer
used. Sea fishing is mostly for herring and cod, but
the waters of the Minch are in danger of being

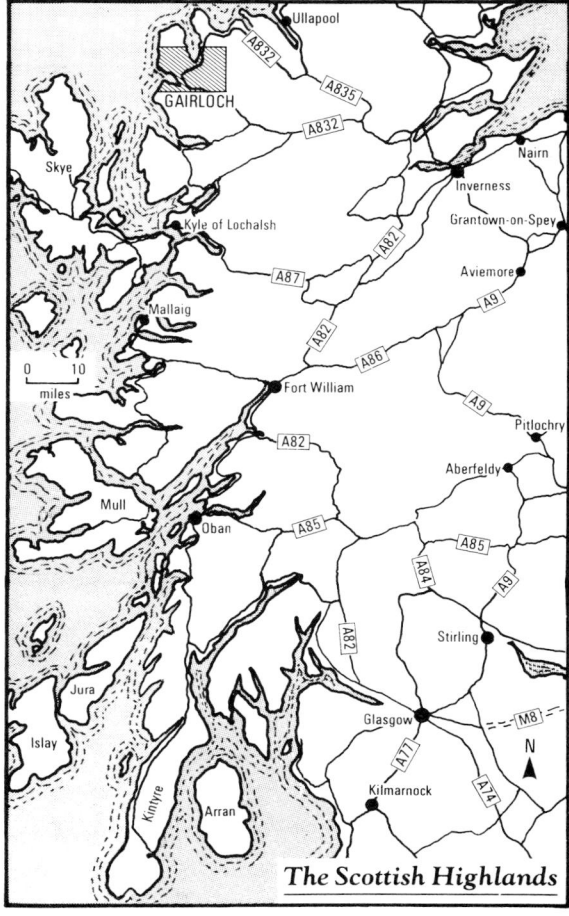

The Scottish Highlands

*The Torridon Hills from
Gairloch Bay*

overfished. East European factory ships take everything that can be caught and unscrupulous fishermen, with no heed to the future, are taking undersized fish for processing.

The Gulf Stream brings all year warmth to this far north-western shore, and visitors from the south are often amazed by the mild winters. Proof of this can be found nearby at the Inverewe Gardens where exotic azaleas and camellias bring a blaze of colour to this otherwise barren coast. The gardens were the dream of Osgood Mackenzie, who in the nineteenth century, employed an army of helpers to carry in loads of seaweed and peat and so make the fertile soil of the present gardens. They are now owned and cared for by the National Trust for Scotland.

PLACES OF INTEREST
Gairloch Beach   Over two miles of unspoilt sands and dunes.
Gairloch Golf Course   Small but tricky course due to strong crosswinds. Views of the sea from every fairway.
Red Point   Remains of salmon fishing stations and secluded beaches.
Inverewe Gardens   Collection of rhododendrons, azaleas, camellias and other colourful plants in a marine setting. National Trust for Scotland.

WALKS IN THE AREA
Tollie to Slattadale   Either use the post bus or arrange transport along the Poolewe – Gairloch road to the Tollie Farm turn off (MR860789), about 1 ¾ miles south of Poolewe. About 150yd west of Tollie Farm road, a well-made footpath crosses rough moorland below Creag Mhor Tollaidh before descending towards Loch Maree. Follow this still well-defined path all the way to Slattadale Forest and join the A832 above the picnic area and car park.

Careful transport arrangements are necessary to avoid a long road walk, but there are post buses along this road to and from Gairloch — check times beforehand.

The view along Loch Maree as you come over the shoulder south of Creag Mhor Tollaidh is one of the finest in Scotland.
Red Point to Craig   Leave the car at the road end near Red Point and follow the footpath (signposted Diabaig), as far as Craig Youth Hostel. Return by the same route.

Look out for feral goats around Craig.
Big Sand   A one-time crofting township which can be reached by footpath along the coast. The path starts about a quarter of a mile beyond the youth hostel of Carn Dearg on the northern side of Loch Gairloch.
Flowerdale   This quiet glen and its waterfall can be reached by a track which starts close by Gairloch harbour at Charlestown and follows the north bank of the stream. Walk past Flowerdale House to the Manse and then beyond along the forest edge to the waterfalls. Beyond are the summits of An Groban and Sitheen Mhor.

Loch Maree and Slioch

TORRIDON

Highland

OS Map: 1:25,000 The Cuillin and Torridon
Hills

Location

From the south take the Inverness – Kyle road
westward as far as Achnasheen and turn right on to
the Gairloch road to Kinlochewe. Turn left into
Glen Torridon. If coming from the north follow
the A832 from Ullapool via Gairloch and turn
right for Glen Torridon.

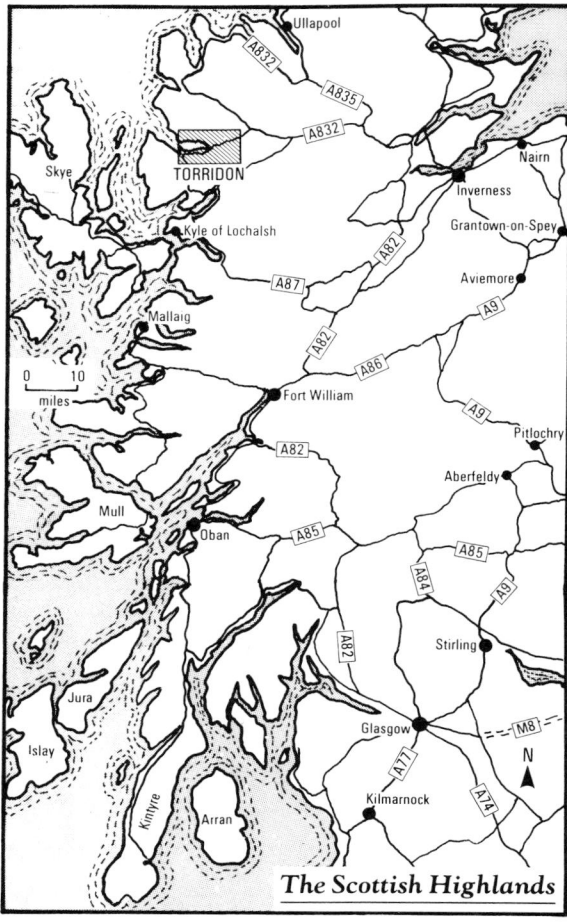

The Scottish Highlands

Scotland is at its best in and around this glen and
sea loch, both taking the grand sounding name of
Torridon. Steep-sided mountains rise from the
sea breaking the 3,000ft barrier in one breathtaking
swoop, ending in narrow ridges broken by rocky
summits. The rocks are almost as old as time itself;
Torridonian Sandstone makes the base of most of
the giants and is the oldest sedimentary rock so far
discovered — so old that it was laid down long
before life was formed on this planet.

Loch Torridon has a fjord-like aspect, its deep
waters cut inland and the 3,000ft giants rise
straight from its waters. Beinn Damph is the
smallest of them all, being only 2,957ft high, but
Beinn Alligin and Liathach are both several
hundred feet taller. Liathach, which means the
'Grey One', is the easiest to remember for its
summit reaches 3,456ft.

Bands of Torridonian Sandstone have built up
the three mountains, but to the east Beinn Eighe
and to a lesser extent Liathach are capped by a
band of shining quartz which is often mistaken for
snow even in summer.

While depopulation and the decline of the
crofting system continues in much of the Western
Highlands, the 'township' of Diabaig, at the
western end of Torridon, has grown with an influx
of young people willing to face the hardships of
crofting life. This rebirth has shown no sign of
abating for at least a decade, and it is to be hoped
that it will continue. Salmon-farming was recently
introduced to the area and gives a steady basic
income to bolster the meagre crofting economy.
Sheildaig, south across the loch, is mostly holiday
or retirement homes, but Torridon village manages
to remain the centre of life for the area.

The glen is now owned by the National Trust for

Scotland. This together with the creation of the
Beinn Eighe Nature Reserve will ensure that the
beauty of the wildlife of this area is preserved in
the future.

While the peaks and ridges are the element of
the mountaineer, walkers can enjoy them in close
proximity by the many easy footpaths of the area.
Most of these paths were made to give access to the
surrounding deer forests and often climb gently to
the remoter parts of the nearby glens and ridges.

PLACES OF INTEREST

**National Trust for Scotland Information
Centre**   Torridon. Permanent exhibition and
film shows explain the lochs and wildlife of the
district. Organised walks to view deer and eagles.
Check for details of the walks and talks with the
National Trust Centre.

Beinn Eighe Nature Trails   Two trails, one
high and the other low level, start from the picnic

Sunset over Upper Loch Diabaig

site between Kinlochewe and Loch Ewe. Information leaflet and detailed plaques.

WALKS IN THE AREA

The start and finishing points of some walks may be several miles apart, but there is a post bus in the area which can be used to reach the beginning of the route and then walk back to a parked car.

The Circuit of Liathach   Leave the car at the car park where the Diabaig road crosses Coire Mhic Nobuill (known locally as the Corrie Bridge Car Park). Take the post bus to Coire Dubh and follow the well marked path up into the corrie, and then across the wilderness of its headwaters into Coire Mhic Nobuill. There is a good path all the way for this 8½ mile walk.

Diabaig from Inveralligin   Follow the coast path through Alligin Shuas and pass the remote croft at Port Laire. Climb past two beautiful lochans full of water lilies in summer, before descending the steep rocky crags above Diabaig. At first glance the route through the crags may look impossible, but the track is good and safe in all but icy conditions.

Catch the post bus back from Diabaig, but wait for it above the harbour in case the postman has no deliveries to make in the lower village.

Ben Damph   This is the easiest mountain to climb in the area. To reach the summit ridge, follow the stalkers' track on the west bank of the stream above Ben Damph House. The track peters out below the col, but the route to the summit, which is to the left of the col, is easy to follow in clear weather.

A short and easier walk is to turn right at the col for Squrr na Bana Mhoraire and its magnificent views across Loch Torridon.

GLEN BRITTLE
AND THE CUILLIN HILLS

Highland

OS Map: 1:50,000 Sheet No 32
1:25,000 The Cullin and
Torridon Hills

Location

A82 and A87 from Inverness to Kyle of Lochalsh.
Take the car ferry to Kyleakin and then the A850
Portree Road to the Sligachan Inn. Turn left on the
A863 to Drynoch and the B8009 as far as Carbost.
Left by the Glen Brittle road over the high moors
of Moineach Mararaulin and Glen Brittle Forest
before descending steeply towards the coast.

Accommodation is available at several cottages
as well as Glen Brittle House and the youth hostel.
Prior booking is recommended. There is a campsite
which can be crowded during the main holiday
season, but unofficial sites for single tents exist
throughout the glen.

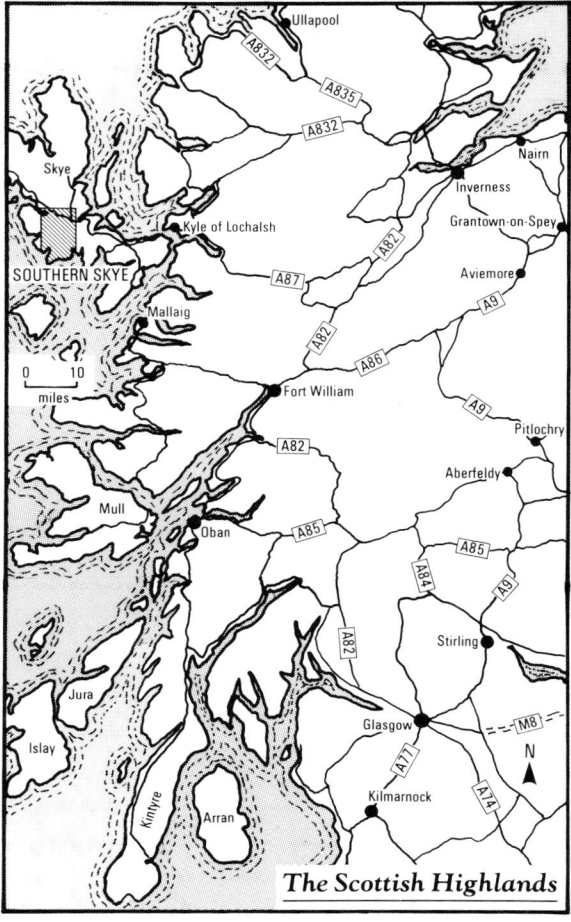

The Scottish Highlands

Glen Brittle has been the mecca of British rock
climbers since the sport became popular in late
Victorian times. Their goal, the Cuillin Hills, is
unique amongst any in Europe, and they are
mostly formed of a special rock known as gabbro.
This rock, a form of basalt, cooled slowly deep
down beneath the earth's crust before being
forced to the surface. Glacial action formed the
fantastically shaped peaks seen from Glen Brittle
or other vantage points. Not only are these sharp
peaks the natural haven of the climber, but the
special hard and rough nature of gabbro makes
climbing a sheer delight. When climbers first
came to the Cuillins, few of the peaks had names,
for there is no grazing on any of them and therefore
the early Highlanders had little or no cause to visit
their remote summits. A few passes were named in
descriptive Gaelic after their shape and colour. As
the Cuillins became better known, some of the
summits, mainly above Glen Brittle, were given
the Gaelic forms of the names of their early
explorers. It was only later, when climbers started
to explore the more difficult faces, that English
crept in. Names like Waterpipe Gulley, Crack of
Doom, West Buttress, all signify the continued
interest in developing more difficult climbs.

The only other English name in the Cuillins
occurs in remote Harta Corrie which feeds down

into Glen Sligachan. This is the Bloody Stone, a
huge boulder used since ancient times as a shelter
bivouac. The name is said to relate to a clan battle
which took place on the spot.

Admittedly the peaks and ridges of the Cuillins
are the preserve of the rock climber and
mountaineer, but adventuresome walkers can
find hours of enjoyment exploring the high corries
and remote glens, or maybe discovering the
remains of ancient habitation in and around Glen
Brittle. A glance at the map will give a clue of how
populated the glen once was. The words 'Hut
Circles' or 'Dun', in Old English lettering, mark
only a few of the visible remains of these long dead
homesteads.

Not only can walking and climbing be enjoyed
around Glen Brittle, but the sea fishing is excellent.
Sea trout can be caught in the river near the
campsite at the right state of the tide.

PLACES OF INTEREST

Ancient village and Dun Glen Brittle Point (east side of Loch Brittle).

Eas Mor Waterfall.

Waterpipe Gully Dramatic gully on the northwest face of Squrr na Fheadain (Peak of the Waterpipe). Seen on the descent by road into Glen Brittle. Rock climbing route.

Bloody Stone Huge boulder capable of sheltering several people. Above Glen Sligachan.

Dunvegan Castle Home of the Clan MacLeod. Open to the public. Fairy flag is supposed to help the clan in times of trouble.

Portree Main town of Skye. Fishing port. Sea trips.

Sligachan Inn A famous climbers' inn.

Talisker Distillery Carbost.

WALKS IN THE AREA

The inexperienced should steer well away from Cuillin summits and ridges, however tempting they may seem. Walkers can reach the following in safety in good weather.

Coire Lagan Via Glen Brittle House.

Eas Mor

Loch an Fhir-bhallaich

Coire na Creiche Along the River Brittle upstream from the road bridge.

Coire a' Bhasteir For close views of Bhasteir Tooth.

Squrr nan Gillean North ridge; from the Sligachan Inn.

Harta Corrie (Bloody Stone) via Glen Sligachan.

Glen Brittle Point The point and its ancient village can be reached by a path along the east side of Loch Brittle.

Sligachan Inn to Glen Brittle An ancient and well-made path follows the stream of Alt Dearg Mor south-west from the Sligachan Inn. Close beneath the northern summits of the Cuillin it crosses the pass of the Bealach a Mhaim before easily descending into Glen Brittle. This is probably the best walk in the area.

A young climber rests above Glen Brittle

KINLOCH HOURN

Highland

OS Map: 1:50,000 Sheet No 33

Location

From the A82 Inverness – Fort William road take
the A87 Kyle of Lochalsh road as far as Loch
Garry to Tomdoun (there is a hotel here). Carry
on above Loch Quoich and then across the
dramatic watershed and descend towards Kinloch
Hourn.

Note   There is only one small campsite at
Kinloch Hourn and a farm with limited accommodation. Pre-booking for the latter is essential.

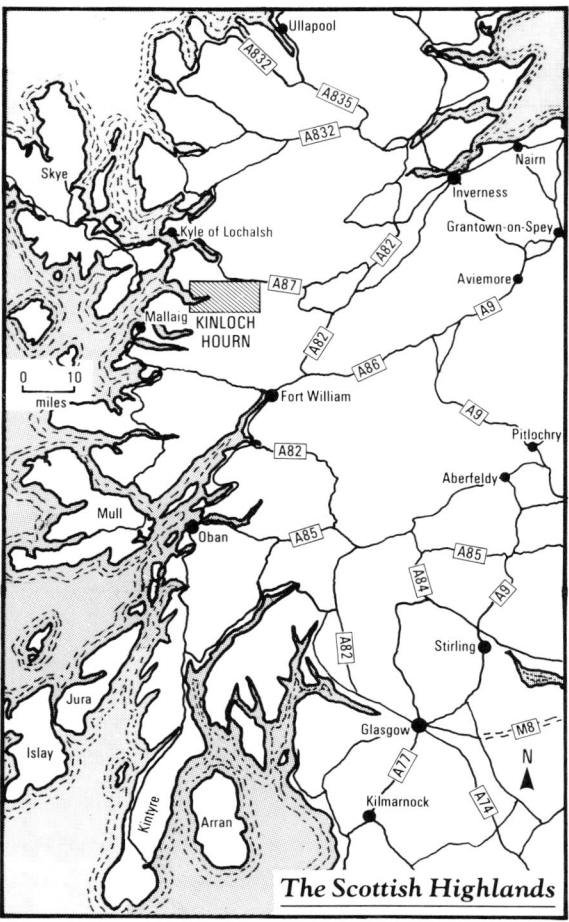

The Scottish Highlands

If any part of the British Isles can claim to be
off the beaten track, it is Kinloch Hourn. Fifteen
miles from the nearest other habitation and
twenty-five miles from any shop, this secluded
spot is an ideal hideaway for anyone seeking quiet
and tranquillity. Nature in all its grandeur is on
either hand; steep mountains rise up from the sea
above narrow Loch Hourn where it cuts deeply
inland. The only bad thing about Kinloch Hourn
is that it has probably the highest rainfall in
Britain, but this is small payment for such
magnificent surroundings.

The mountains rise almost to 3,000ft and are
home for hundreds of deer. Stalkers and their
clients can range these hills in the safe knowledge
that a magnificent stag, or hind depending on the
season, will with care present itself between their
gunsights. The slaughtered animals are then
carried down the hill on the backs of sturdy
highland ponies, known as garrons. These animals
can climb into remote corries along skilfully
engineered paths to await the success or otherwise
of the stalk.

The tracks, which reach so easily beneath the
high ridges and summits, were built in the heyday
of the Kinloch Hourn estate and hunting lodge.
The paths, outside the stalking seasons, can be
used by walkers to reach the high summits.

Garnets, one of Scotland's gemstones, are
found in rocks on the summit ridges of several of
the local peaks and make an interesting diversion
during a day spent amongst the hills. Buidhe
Bheinn has the best examples.

Fishing is another activity — the burns and
lochans are full of delicious trout almost waiting

to give themselves up. The fishing is usually free
but check locally. Sea fishing is also worthwhile,
but a word of caution to any amateur boatman: the
narrows known as Caolas Mor (about two-thirds
of the way between Kinloch Hourn and Barrisdale)
develop a fearsome whirlpool at certain stages of
the tide. Basking sharks are occasionally seen in
the waters beyond Barrisdale, but fortunately they
are harmless.

While the hill walking around Loch Hourn,
especially on the well made stalkers' tracks, is
good and easy, remember that this is a place where
the weather makes sudden and dramatic changes.
Also do not walk in areas where deer stalking is
taking place.

Loch Hourn from the Skiary Ridge ▷

PLACES OF INTEREST

Caolas Mor whirlpool

Garnets on Buidhe Bheinn

Loch Quoich Natural freshwater loch deepened by damming.

Glen Garry Hydro-electric Scheme Salmon ladders.

WALKS IN THE AREA

Kinloch Hourn to Barrisdale Follow the track along the coast past the ruined crofts of Skiary and Runival to the meadowland on the seaward side of Barrisdale Lodge. Return by the same way.

If you are lucky with the tides you should see the whirlpool at Caolas Mor.

Mountain climbs Stalkers' tracks climb easily and high beneath the following summits:

Sgurr Sgiath Airidh (south-west of Kinloch Hourn).

Buidhe Bheinn (north of Kinloch Hourn).

Sron na Brenn Leithin (above Glen Quoich — east of Kinloch Hourn).

Most of these tracks fade away beneath the summit ridges, but they do take the strain out of the steepest sections of the climb.

Arnisdale from Kinloch Hourn An excellent path climbs up above the lodge then crosses rough ground and descends to Glen Arnisdale. This remote hamlet is connected to the outside world at Glen Shiel by road. As the return journey by this route could be lengthy, arrange for waterborne transport back to Kinloch Hourn.

Glen Shiel from Glen Quoich (For experienced walkers only.) Follow the track north up Glen Quoich over the col of Bealach Dubh Leac and down to the Glen Shiel road above Achnagart. This is a hard but straightforward path, often used by backpackers walking north or south between Glen Garry and Glen Shiel.

Many other tracks, the relics of either old drove roads or stalkers' ways, cross this wild but beautiful area.

LOCH MORLICH
AND THE CAIRNGORMS

Highland

OS Map: 1:25,000 High Tops of the Cairngorms
1 in Tourist Map Cairngorms

Location

A9 north as far as Aviemore. Right on to the A951
(Grantown on Spey road) as far as Coylumbridge.
Turn right for the unclassified road to Loch
Morlich; or rail to Aviemore and then bus to Loch
Morlich.

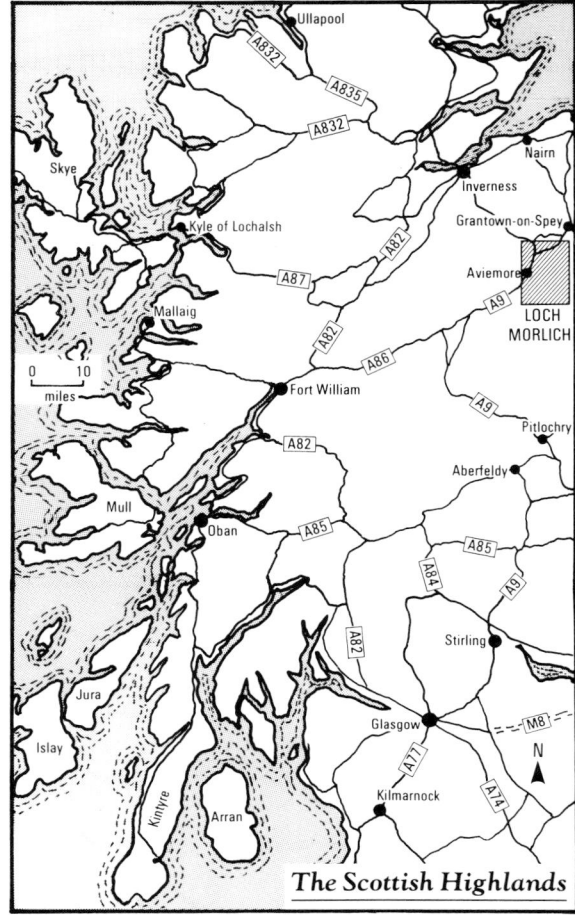

The great basin of Glen More with the backcloth
of the rolling Cairngorm massif has all the
attributes of Scandinavia — vistas of forest and
lakes, and high mountains often retaining patches
of snow throughout the summer. The illusion of
Scandinavia is completed by herds of reindeer
which were reintroduced into the area some years
ago. This successful experiment has brought back
animals which once grazed on the sparse mountain
vegetation of the region.

Glen More, Loch Morlich and the nearby
mountains form a recreation area for lovers of
high remote places. There is every sport available,
from sailing and pony trekking to rock climbing,
in all grades of severity; and of course skiing is very
popular here. It was the development of the

The Scottish Highlands

*Reindeer, reintroduced into
the area from Lapland, are
now making a comeback*

Cairngorm mountain itself, and in particular its north-facing corries as ski slopes, that opened up this area. It has not necessarily been to everyone's taste; access roads and ski slopes have left scars on the mountain sides which will take years to heal; however they have brought good skiing to mainland Britain. Snow, which fills some of the corries well into spring and summer, gives keen skiers almost all the year round sport.

These are mountains where the weather is notoriously fickle, as witness the number of tragedies which have occurred over the years. Anyone proposing to undertake any long distance walks through the interior of the Cairngorm range should take heed of local advice, and certainly leave a detailed note of their planned itinerary. Hill walkers should be competent map and compass readers and also carry suitable survival gear, not least of which should be sufficient high energy food for the journey.

Hill walkers looking for gentler activities are well catered for, and it is possible for the less able to reach the summit of Cairngorm itself in fine weather. The chairlift from the White Lady car park climbs above the 3,000ft contour and strategically placed poles mark the route to the top of the mountain. A restaurant close to the top station of the chairlift completes the most luxurious mountain climb in Scotland. But a word of caution. Remember you will be climbing to over 4,000ft and on the same latitude as Siberia! Dress for the mountain and not Loch Morlich's beach.

PLACES OF INTEREST

Loch Morlich Information Centre   Guided walks.

Speyside Steam Railway   Steam line run by a voluntary society.

Whisky Trail   Follow special road signs.

Reindeer   The keeper will take parties with him when he goes to feed the reindeer. Look out for times listed at the Information Centre.

Cairngorm Chairlift

Loch Garten   GR975183. Nesting Ospreys. Look out for RAC and/or AA road signs.

Craigllachie National Nature Reserve   Nature Trails – Forest Trails.

Pony Trekking   Various local establishments advertise in and around Aviemore Centre.

WALKS IN THE AREA

Although this is a busy area, quieter walking away from the more popular tracks can be found towards the Lairig Ghru. Leave the White Lady car park by way of Creag a Chalamain; or walk into Coire na Ciste from its car park. The track north-east from Glen More Lodge can often be walked without seeing a soul all day.

Glen More Forest, to the south of Loch Morlich, has a lot to offer in the way of easy forest tracks which meander westwards from the ski-lift road. Other tracks climb into remote places around the Cairngorms, but always keep an eye on the time and weather. You can easily be led astray in this wonderful land of mountain scenery.

Loch Morlich

MALLAIG

Highland

OS Map: 1:50,000 Sheet Nos 33 and 40

Location

By road along the A830 north-west from Fort
William, or by rail from Glasgow via Fort William
on the West Highland line, which is probably the
best approach. This line passes through some of
Scotland's best known scenery above Loch Lomond
then crosses the formidable wastes of Rannoch
Moor. From Fort William the line runs north-
west towards the sea past Glenfinnan, where
Bonnie Prince Charlie stepped ashore on his final
and doomed attempt to gain the British Crown.

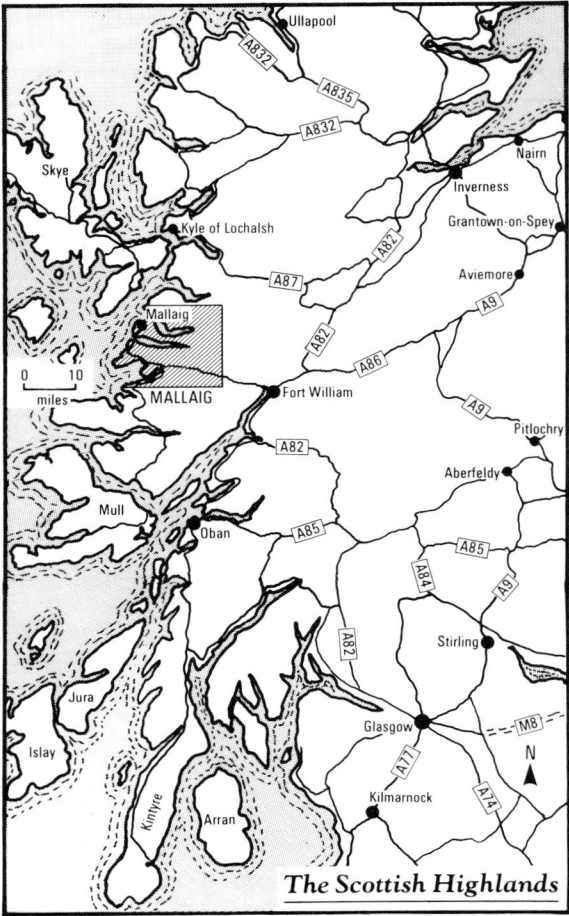

Mallaig to some is a place of journey's end and
journey's beginning. Certainly the fishing town
and rail terminus has that feel and most people
pass through it either to or from the Outer Isles.
The township of Mallaig developed as a port and
railhead so that fish could be rapidly moved south
to market. Skye is less than an hour's sea crossing
away and the fascinating inner islands of Rhum
and Eigg take a little longer. The Outer Hebrides
are connected by regular sailings from this busy
port.

Local herrings, in their season, are converted
into succulent kippers in curing sheds behind the
quay. Crabs and lobsters also make a profitable
cash crop for inshore fishermen.

Arisaig

Mallaig Harbour

The holidaymaker who, rather than using Mallaig as a jumping off point for the inner and outer islands, chooses to spend a few days in and around the village, can enjoy the delights of pure white sandy coves nearby, or perhaps explore the glens and lochs inland from the coast to the south of the village.

Below Mallaig the coast is indented with sandy beaches of such purity and privacy that other visitors can often be a rarity. Such is the space and beauty of this coast.

Inland is Loch Morar, which falls to the sea in a short but dramatic river where salmon can be watched fighting their way to spawning grounds inland. The loch, incidentally, is Europe's deepest lake, only 31 ft above sea level, but more than 900 ft below at its deepest point.

North of Mallaig, the coastline turns eastwards into Loch Nevis. Both Morar and Nevis, one freshwater and the other sea, are worth the attention of the exploring tourist as they offer miles of almost unexplored walking.

PLACES OF INTEREST
Boat Trips To the Inner Isles (Skye, Loch Coruisk, Rhum and Eigg). Local fishing trips to Loch Nevis or further out into the Minch.
Sandy beaches Arisaig, Morar, Loch nan Unmph.
Glenfinnan Monument to Bonnie Prince Charlie and National Trust Information Centre.
Fort William Major town for the north-west Highlands. Shops, hotels, restaurants, museum.

WALKS IN THE AREA
Ancient, but little used footpaths radiate inland from the coast south of Mallaig; some are still well used and maintained, but others have become more indistinct from lack of use. Careful map reading is necessary to follow their routes. A walker along these ancient tracks is hardly likely to see another person all day, but those who are met along the way, whether they be another solitary explorer or a local shepherd, will enliven the day with interesting conversation.

One such route runs inland along the northern shore of Loch Morar, past remote crofts to Tarbert where there is a little used Catholic church. The narrow neck of land is crossed here to join another path which gradually improves along the shore of Loch Nevis all the way to Mallaig. Alternatively, the mail boat which calls at Tarbent on Loch Nevis, may be used for the return journey to Mallaig.

The shoreline between Mallaig and Arisaig, or even further, is the preserve of the beach lover and slow walker alike and few if any paths follow the coast. It is usual to walk down from the road to one of the little coves or bays where, unless the weather is absolutely foul, there will be few who tire of the Mediterranean-like sea scene. Tree lined rocky promontories shelter a turquoise sea beneath which gleams unbelieveably pure white sand in almost all of the bays along this coast.

GLENCOE

Highland

OS Map: 1 inch Tourist Map Ben Nevis and
                    Glencoe

Location

North from the Clyde Valley region through
Dumbarton and by the A82, follow the west shore
of Loch Lomond to Tyndrum. North again across
Rannoch Moor to Glencoe.

   From Inverness, south-west by the A82 through
Spean Bridge and Fort William to Ballachulish.

   From Oban by the A85 to Connel and then
A828 north through Appin to Ballachulish.

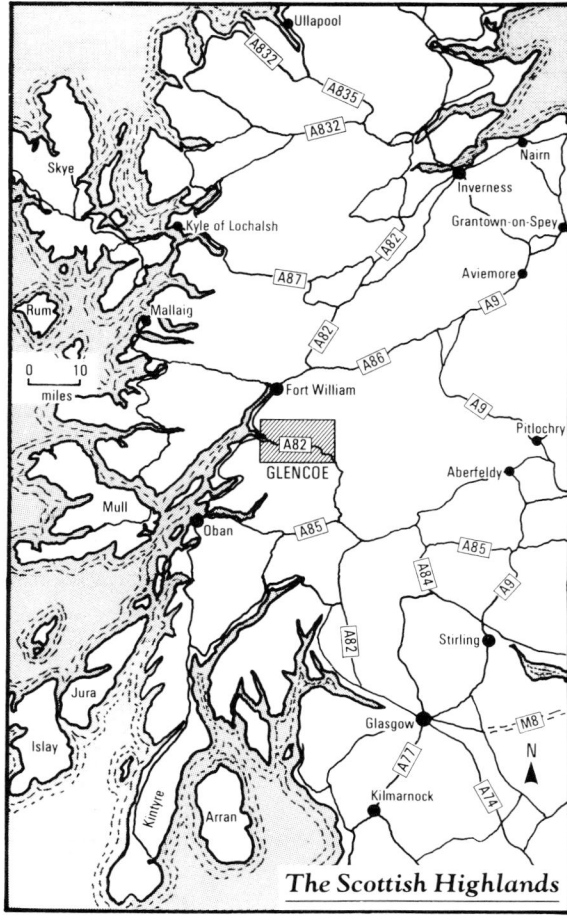

The Scottish Highlands

Whichever way you approach Glencoe, the route
is full of excitement, for this is Highland scenery at
its best. Perhaps the most dramatic, but unfortunately
the busiest, is the A82 over the wilderness of
Rannoch Moor. Beyond the turning for Glen
Etive, the majestic bulk of Buachaille Etive Mor,
the 'Big Shepherd', guards the entrance to Glencoe.
The road continues downhill; to the right is
Aoanch Eagach and on the left are the three north-
east facing ridges of Buachaille Etive Beg (the
'Little Shepherd'). Further to the left is the
complex bulk of Bidean nam Bian, with its
subsidiary ridges radiating in all directions.

   This is climbing country, popular with hill
walkers, rock climbers and snow and ice climbers
alike. Glencoe can offer sport for all levels of
mountain activity. But be warned, the mountains
can be treacherous to the unwary or inexperienced.

   In 1692 one of the most tragic events of Scottish
history occurred in Glencoe, when the Campbells
settled a clan dispute by murdering the local
MacDonalds. This was due to one of the many
quirks of history when one faction takes advantage
of a comparatively innocent event to further their
own ends. In 1692, all the Highland clans were
forced to swear allegiance to the English King
William III. Most of the clans and their various
sub-divisions had fallen into line, but the proud
local chief of the Glencoe MacDonalds was late
getting to Fort William for this purpose. Members
of the Clan Campbell of Glen Lyon, sworn
enemies of the MacDonalds, with very little
prompting from the English commander of Fort
William, took the opportunity to settle old
scores. Under cover of darkness the Campbells

managed to infiltrate the MacDonald settlement
at the lower end of Glencoe (now marked by a
memorial cairn), during the night of 12 February.
At 5.00am next day they set about their grisly task.

   Awakened by the sound of carnage going on all
around them, a few survivors managed to struggle
away into the hills, some to die of cold. Sir John
Dalrymple, the Secretary of State for Scotland,
officially condoned this massacre and as a result,
Scottish loyalty very soon switched to the exiled
King James II. This loyalty was transferred to his
descendants and eventually led to the next tragic
chapter in Scottish history — the heroic but
doomed attempts of the Stuart rebellions of 1715
and 1745.

PLACES OF INTEREST
Site of Massacre   National Trust for Scotland
Information Centre.

*Stob Coire nam Beith from
Loch Achtriochtan*

Ballachulish Slate Quarries   Remains of local industry.

Kinlochleven   Aluminium smelting based on locally produced hydro-electricity.

Fort William   Musem, shops, information centre. Base for ascents of Ben Nevis. Whisky distillery.

White Corries Chairlift   Off A82 near Kingshouse Hotel. Ski lift open on fine days during summer months. Views of Rannoch Moor. High level access to Meall a'Bhuirdh and nearby ridges.

WALKS IN THE AREA
Although this is primarily a mountaineering area, walkers can reach the heart of the peaks by a number of comparatively easy tracks. However, caution must be observed in mist or bad weather of any kind.

Rannoch Moor   Follow the track east of Queenhouse past Black Corries as far as is desired and return the same way.

Kinlochleven by the Devil's Staircase   A military road built by General Wade after the 1745 rebellion; climbs above Altnafeadh Farm at the head of Glencoe.

The Circuit of Buachaille Etive Beg   Take the track south-west along the glen of Allt Lairig Eilde as far as the Glen Etive road where a track north-east along the Lairig Gortain is joined for the return route.

The Lost Valley   Coire Gabhail is an interesting example of a hanging valley formed by a side glacier receding before the one filling the main valley. Access to the Lost Valley is above the Meeting of Three Waters near the head of Glencoe.

LOCH RANNOCH

Tayside

OS Map: 1:50,000 Sheet Nos 42 and 51

Location

From Perth take the A9 as far as Killiecrankie and turn left on the B8019 for Kinloch Rannoch village about 19½ miles further on.

From the Trossachs by the A86 and A827 via Killin as far as Kenmore at the eastern end of Loch Tay. Turn left for the unnumbered road to Keltneyburn and join the B846.

Rob Roy McGregor, folk hero or bandit (depending on ones own point of view), was Scotland's real life Robin Hood. His sphere of influence covered most of the area south of Loch Rannoch, even extending into Argyll. His memory lingers on in the area, with place names such as McGregor's Cave, or McGregor's Leap, cropping up time and time again. It can only be guessed as to how true the connections are, but Rob Roy's memory is certainly still revered.

Links with people of a much earlier era can also be found by studying maps of the area. Ancient stones and cairns reveal that man has lived here for thousands of years. A fine example is the incised cross above Daloist (GR775569), probably even older than its Christian symbolism.

During the years of repression which followed the slaughter of the clans at Culloden in 1745, numerous roads were engineered throughout the Highlands. These were primarily designed for rapid troop deployment and were built by a brilliant young engineer, General Wade. One of his roads, still followed by the B846, enters the Rannoch region from the south by way of Aberfeldy. Hanoverian troops lived in a barracks which can still be seen at the western end of Loch Rannoch.

On a much happier note, Queen Victoria, who did much to popularise the Highlands, thought that the view west along Loch Tummel was one of the most beautiful in all of the British Isles. The view is of the loch with the symmetrical cone of Schiehallion dominating the western peaks of the Grampian Range.

The West Highland railway line crosses Rannoch moor, and Rannoch station is almost at the highest point on the route from Glasgow to Mallaig. When this feat of railway engineering, designed to

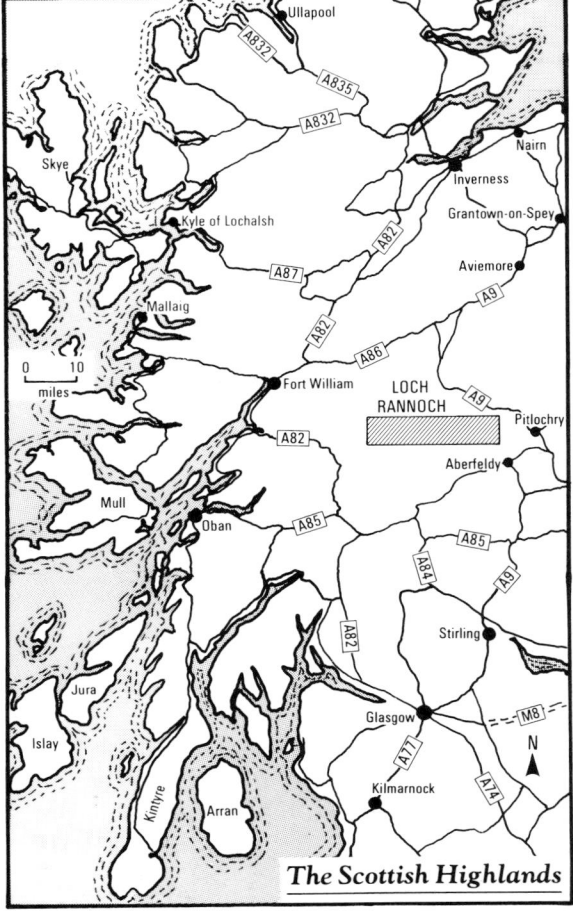

The Scottish Highlands

link the Outer Isles to the Industrial Lowlands, was planned, it was thought to be impossible to cross the bogs of Rannoch Moor. Eventually a route was discovered and the directors, who had almost given up hope of seeing any return on their expenditure, decided to celebrate by following it on foot across the moor. Unfortunately they were overtaken by a snowstorm and were forced to spend several days and nights in a boggy hollow. When rescued they were all safe and sound, still clad in their Victorian frock coats and top hats. No doubt the medicinal use of products of some of Scotland's best distilleries had helped keep out the cold!

View across Lochan na h-Achlaise to the Blackmount ▷

The Byways of Britain

PLACES OF INTEREST

McGregor's Cave GR 711584. In dense woodland south of the B846, 3½ miles east Kinloch Rannoch.

Loch Rannoch Nature Trail and Picnic Site
At Carie on the south side of Loch Rannoch. Waymarked trails and notes available at the picnic site.

Rannoch Barracks Military barracks dating from 1745-6. By Bridge of Gaur, west of Loch Rannoch.

Salmon leaps Kinloch Rannoch river.

Tummel Bridge

Loch Eigeach

Queen's View Above Loch Tummel.

Fishing Salmon and trout. Check locally about permits.

WALKS IN THE AREA

Easy walks can be found along the banks of Loch Rannoch or along tracks in the forest glens.

Schiehallion Usually climbed either from Glen Mor to join the east ridge above Aonach Ban or from the minor road between Kinloch Rannoch and the B846 (Tummel – Keltneyburn road).

The wilds of Rannoch Moor can be viewed from the track which runs south-west from Rannoch Station towards Glencoe. The path alongside Loch Laidon is an ancient route once used by drovers, but now only used by fishermen and shepherds. It is in good condition and will make an excellent all day or evening stroll for as long as you care to make it.

KILLIN

Central Scotland

OS Map: 1:50,000 Sheet No 51

Location

North by the M9 and turn off for Stirling. North-east on A84 via Callander to Lochearnhead and join the A85 as far as Lix, turn right for Killin or via the M90 to Perth and A9 to Ballinluig. Left for the A827 and the Tay Valley.

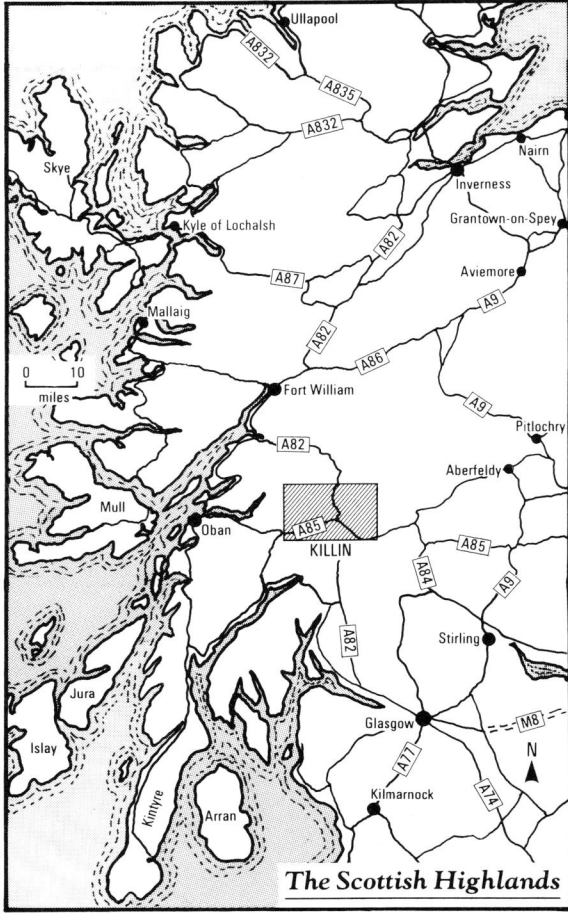

The Scottish Highlands

The mountains north of the Trossachs are not well known, and have become the jealously guarded preserve of those who, rather than rush away to the far north-west, have taken the trouble to explore mid-Scotland.

Three thousand foot summits rise in picturesque grandeur above Loch Tay, amidst scenery much beloved by Victorian tourists who first came to this area. During the enthusiastic expansion of the railway network, one of the most scenic lines in the country was built through this area. The route ran from Perth through the Trossachs and climbed Glen Ogle south of Killin by a steep gradient, before turning west along Glen Dochart to cross the West Highland line at Crainlairich and then on to Oban. Killin, being almost 500ft lower than the main line, was served by a short branch. Plans were once made to continue this track along the Tay Valley but it never went beyond a pier at the western end of Loch Tay. Regrettably, this magnificent approach to Killin is now denied to us.

Hills to the north of the Tay Valley support many rare and unusual alpine flowers; spring gentians bloom in hidden recesses and purple saxifrage can be found on the very summit of Ben Lawers. Such is the special nature of the south face of Ben Lawers and its alpine flowers that it has been designated a Nature Reserve. Visitors are welcome, but all are on trust to respect the delicate beauty of these plants. Do not under any circumstances dig them up or take their flowers, although photographs are permitted. If you dig up an alpine flower it will surely die, and picking their blooms spoils their chances of producing seed. There is good fishing in Loch Tay and local streams, but check locally for permits.

The Falls of Dochart, one of Scotland's most photographed scenes, is almost in the centre of Killin. Beyond the village are the romantic ruins of Finlarig Castle.

Walking in this area, especially on Ben Lawers, is easy, but as with the rest of Scotland, due heed must be given to the weather and caution exercised. Also one must defer to deer stalkers during the season — information of which areas are being stalked will be available at the Ben Lawers Visitor Centre.

PLACES OF INTEREST
Ben Lawers Visitor Centre and Nature Trail An interpretive centre for the flora and fauna of this special region.
Falls of Dochart Famous waterfall within a stone's throw of Killin.
Kenmore Forest Walk Waymarked.
The Trossachs To the south via the A84 and A85.
Pitlochry Shops, restaurants, theatre.

River Dochart above the falls

WALKS IN THE AREA

Ben Lawers A well-defined path climbs the mountain from the Visitor Centre. Not suitable in mist or inclement weather.

Glen Ogle by the old railway track The track is accessible from the Glenoglehead Crossing picnic site and car park.

Glen Lochay North-west from Killin. Turn left about a mile north of Killin on the Aberfeldy road and drive along the glen. Park the car at a suitable spot which will cause no inconvenience to others. Follow the track on foot as far as the ruined croft at Batavaime. Return by reversing the route.

Balquhidder from Glen Dochart From Ledcharrie Farm, 5½ miles west of Killin on the Dalmally road, a hill path climbs the glen of Ledcharrie Burn to Lochan an Eireannaich. Beyond the loch, the track enters a forestry plantation and follows Kirkton Glen downhill to Balquhidder.

Although the crossing of the col between the two glens is marked by Lochan a Eireannaich, the walk must only be undertaken in clear weather. Transport will be necessary for the return journey.

The Island of Arran

Strathclyde

OS Map: 1:50,000 Sheet No 69

Location

By road from the south; M6 to Carlisle, then A74
to Gretna and A76 to Kilmarnock. A71 and A78
to Ardrossan then car ferry to Brodick on Arran.
From the Glasgow area via Paisley and Dalry by
A737 and A78 to Ardrossan and the car ferry.
By rail: Ardrossan station and ferry.
By ferry: advance booking is essential through:
Caledonian MacBrayne Ltd, The Ferry Terminal,
Gourock PA19 1QP. Telephone (0475) 34531/3.

Arran, this small island in the Firth of Clyde, is
Scotland's microcosm. Here is everything that
typifies Scotland and yet at the same time Arran is
a unique island where anyone who visits it and
does not like it, must be hard to please! Baronial
castles, ancient ruins, links with Robert the Bruce
(and his spider); wild glens, soaring peaks and
jagged ridges; forests, heather moors, sandy
beaches and Mediterranean-blue seas delight first
time and regular visitors.

One of the mysteries of this island is that no
matter how crowded the car ferries may be, once
their cargoes of holidaymakers and the small
quantity of commercial traffic have been dis-
embarked, all seem to disappear. Even though
there are few roads on the island (one road goes
right round it, one through its middle and another
across the south-west moors), somehow or other
traffic is always light.

Several caves throughout Scotland lay claim to
being the place where the despairing Robert the
Bruce was persuaded by an industrious spider to
try yet again in his battles with the English Crown.
The Arran cave where he is supposed to have
rested is in a romantic situation above the beach a
mile or so north of Blackwaterfoot on the east of
the island. It is a pleasing thought, therefore, to
suggest that here a momentous event in Scotland's
history took place.

Arran is paradise to most people, not least to
those who can interpret the story of the earth by
looking at its rocks. The geology of Arran is so
complex, again almost Scotland in miniature, that
extensive studies have made it one of the most
accurately mapped geological areas in Britain.

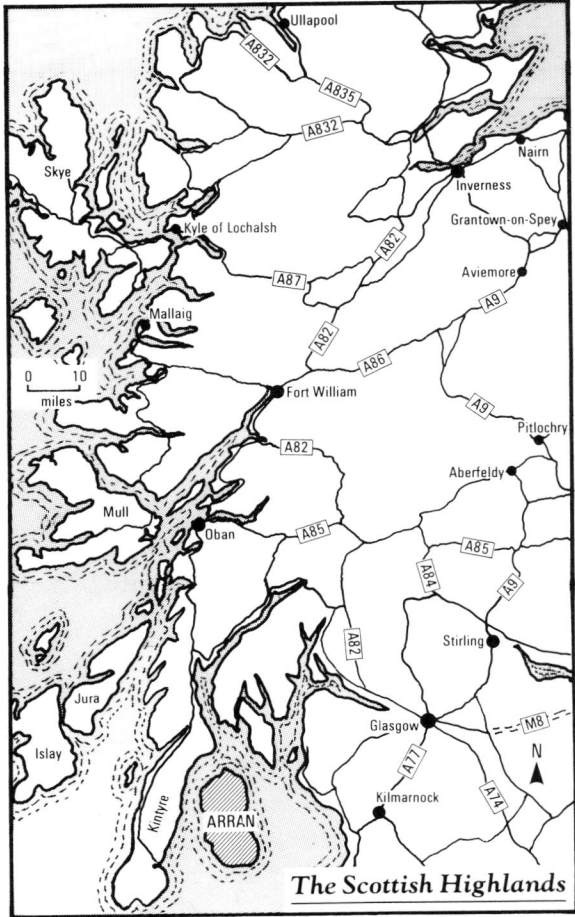

The Scottish Highlands

Walkers and hill climbers are well catered for
with interesting things to do. The central mountains
radiate with three sub-dividing legs from the
central peak of Cir Mhor. None are higher than
Goat Fell's 2,866ft, but all are truly inspiring
mountains. Glens and coastal walks complete the
rest of the delight awaiting anyone who takes his
exercise in unsophisticated places.

There are sea angling competitions annually,
check locally for dates of these events. Salmon and
trout fishing are carefully preserved.

Places of Interest

Brodick Castle National Trust for Scotland
property. Magnificent rhododendron and azalea
gardens, alpine plants, water gardens.
Firth of Clyde steamer trips Check locally
for times of sailings. From Brodick and Lochranza.
Lochranza Romantically-situated ruined castle.

Goatfell

Car ferry to Claonaig-on-Kintyre.

Raised beaches   At the end of the last ice age the reduction in the weight of ice pressing on the land allowed parts of Scotland to lift several feet higher. Arran is an excellent example. The old cliffs can readily be seen all round the island, usually about 20 – 50ft above the modern beach.

Brodick, Lamlash, Whiting Bay, Blackwater-foot   Excellent beaches. Boats for hire. Golf course open to visitors.

Corrie, Sannox, Pirmill   Tiny unspoilt 'artists' villages. Pebble beaches, the haunt of sea birds.

WALKS IN THE AREA

Whiting Bay   Glenashdale Burn (filled with bluebells in May, waterfall, etc.)

Lamlash to Brodick via Claughlands Point   Coastal walk.

Glen Cloy   A quiet glen leading from Brodick (Arran's 'capital').

Glen Rosa   Dramatic scenery.

Goat Fell   An easy climb, either from Corrie or Brodick Castle.

Sannox to Lochranza by coastal track   Sea scenery and the famous Fallen Rocks, remnants of a toppled rock pinnacle.

Glen Sannox   Mountain scenery and traces of old barytes mines.

Bennan Head   Most southerly point of Arran. Views of Aisla Craig ('Paddies Milestone').

Lochranza   Base for glens and ridges north of the main summits.

Index of Areas